"Martyr to the Truth"

"Martyr to the Truth"
The Autobiography of Joseph Turmel

Translated by
C. J. T. Talar AND Elizabeth Emery

Edited by
C. J. T. Talar

With an Afterword by
Émile Poulat

☙PICKWICK *Publications* · Eugene, Oregon

"MARTYR TO THE TRUTH"
The Autobiography of Joseph Turmel

Copyright © 2012 C. J. T. Talar. All rights reserved. Except for brief quotations in critical publications or reviews, no part of this book may be reproduced in any manner without prior written permission from the publisher. Write: Permissions, Wipf and Stock Publishers, 199 W. 8th Ave., Suite 3, Eugene, OR 97401.

Pickwick Publications
A Division of Wipf and Stock Publishers
199 W. 8th Ave., Suite 3
Eugene, OR 97401

www.wipfandstock.com

ISBN 13: 978-1-61097-837-8

Cataloging-in-Publication data:

Turmel, Joseph, 1859–1943.

"Martyr to the truth" : the autobiography of Joseph Turmel / Joseph Turmel. Translated by C. J. T. Talar and Elizabeth Emery. Edited by C. J. T. Talar.

xxiv + 222 p. ; 23 cm.—Includes bibliographical references and index(es).

ISBN 13: 978-1-61097-837-8

1. Turmel, Joseph, 1859–1943. I. Title.

BX4705.T85 T85 2012

Manufactured in the USA

To M. Michel Le Normand, colleague and friend. In sincere appreciation for sharing his knowledge of Joseph Turmel and the contexts that formed him.

"Martyr de la vérité, je dois en être l'apôtre."

Joseph Turmel

Contents

Preface | ix
Introduction—C. J. T. Talar | xi

PART ONE: How I Freed Myself of Dogma
  A Translation of Joseph Turmel's *Comment j'ai donné congé aux dogmes*
  Translated by C. J. T. Talar and Elizabeth Emery

  Introduction | 3
  1 At the Angers Faculty of Theology | 5
  2 At the Major Seminary at Rennes | 11
  3 March 18, 1886 | 21
  4 After Liberation | 26
  5 Dismissal | 33
  6 At the School of Late Vocations | 41
  7 At the Chaplaincy of the Little Sisters of the Poor and at the Former Convent of the Carmelites | 49
  8 My Introduction to the *Revue d'Histoire et de Littérature Religieuses* | 62
  9 First Condemnation in 1901 | 65
  10 My Introduction to the *Revue du clergé français* | 75
    Alfred Loisy | 82
    Note on Three Jesuits | 91

PART TWO: How the Roman Church Freed Itself of Me
  A Translation of *Comment l'Église romaine m'a donné congé*
  Translated by C. J. T. Talar

  Introduction | 95
  1 Dupin and Herzog | 97

2 First Denunciation in 1908 | 105
3 Second Denunciation in 1929 | 138
4 The Condemnation | 152
   Conclusion | 174

APPENDIX
  I The *Nouvelles Rennaises* of January 29, 1931. The Death of Cardinal Charost | 191
  II A Letter of Salomon Reinach to the *Mercure de France* | 193
  III Note on My Theological Tracts | 194

Editor's Notes | 197
Bibliography of Works Published Under Pseudonym | 219
Afterword—Émile Poulat | 223
Index | 231

Preface

JOSEPH TURMEL WROTE HIS autobiography, the story of his "deconversion" from Catholicism to Freethought, with the intention of publishing it as a single volume. Circumstances dictated otherwise and it appeared in two parts: *Comment j'ai donné congé aux dogmes* in 1935, and *Comment l'Église romaine m'a donné congé* four years later. The "donné congé" of the titles is a bit difficult to render precisely. "Dismissed" can sound too abrupt. For it is apparent from Turmel's account that he lost his faith only after a protracted and painful struggle. Moreover, his formal separation from the Church through excommunication likewise occurred as a result of events that unfolded over a number of years. In a more colloquial rendering, "rid of" captures something of the force of Turmel's throwing off dogma and, in an ironic sense, it can be applied to the Church's eventual excommunication of him. As Turmel shapes it, however, his narrative is one of liberation—his hard-won liberation of himself, and his "apostleship" of truth in service of liberating others. Hence the choice of "How I Freed Myself From Dogma" and "How the Roman Church Freed Itself From Me." While a number of Catholics lost their faith during what is termed the "modernist crisis" at the outset of the twentieth century, few have been so forthcoming of their struggles to accommodate modern thought to the ancient faith. Turmel occupies an extreme position in Modernism, but in that very extremity illuminates how issues were framed and in turn responded to by orthodox theologians.

Since the autobiography was intended as a single work, it is continuously paginated in the translation. However, Notes and Appendices have been left in their respective volumes. To clearly differentiate Turmel's notes from the editorial notes, the former have been retained as footnotes while the latter appear as numbered endnotes. Letters and certain documents are

Preface

given in italics in the French original and that practice has been retained here. In the second volume where bold is used for emphasis, that has been changed to italics.

We would like to acknowledge the assistance of Christine Thirlway, who carefully read through the entire translation and made many suggestions that materially improved its quality. We are also grateful to the Archives of the Archdiocese of Rennes for information on several priests Turmel mentions in the autobiography. Likewise to our colleague Giacomo Losito for his help in providing background on several others who figure in the narrative. M. Émile Poulat's work has long been both inspiration and resource for the study of Roman Catholic Modernism. His contribution of an Afterword to this volume is greatly appreciated. Not least, the expertise of M. Michel Le Normand of L.P. #35 in Rennes has been of great assistance in clarifying aspects of Turmel's life and its contexts.

Introduction

C. J. T. Talar

> "Martyr de la vérité, je dois en être l'apôtre."
>
> Joseph Turmel

JOSEPH TURMEL (1859–1943) BEGINS his autobiography with his ordination to the subdiaconate—an early indication that he is not going to provide a strict chronological account of his life, commencing with family background and early years. His biographer, Félix Sartiaux, had already provided some indication of that period in *Joseph Turmel: prêtre, historien des dogmes*.[1] Rather, Turmel's volumes may be placed under the category of "thesis (auto)biography"—represented by such classics of the genre as Augustine's *Confessions*, John Henry Newman's *Apologia pro Vita Sua*, Rousseau's *Confessions* and *The Education of Henry Adams*. All are "works that use the author's life to argue a certain point of view."[2] Thus, although Turmel's life centered on his writings, there is relatively little substantive discussion of them or their content, except when those bear upon the polemical exchanges with critics or interactions with members of the ecclesiastical hierarchy. There is also a large chronological gap, following upon the controversies that centered on two of Turmel's pseudonymous writings under the names of Guillaume Herzog and Antoine Dupin[3]—basically coincident with the condemnation of Roman Catholic Modernism in 1907— and a renewal and escalation of those controversies in the latter 1920s. If the drama of Newman's *Apologia* can be said to reside in his early conversion to an evangelical Christianity and midlife conversion to Catholicism, Turmel's deconversion from the Roman Church and how he fashioned his

Introduction

subsequent vocation in relation to that body constitute the dynamic of *Comment j'ai donné congé aux dogmes* and *Comment l'Église romaine m'a donné congé*.[4] And beyond that, much of his claim on our interest.

Briefly, to appreciate something of that claim it will be necessary to situate Turmel in relation to Roman Catholic Modernism.[5] There has not been agreement among scholars on how to position him. As I have argued elsewhere,[6] Turmel may be seen to stand in a closer relation to the modernist movement than has generally been credited. With that in hand, it will be possible to examine a somewhat paradoxical aspect of the autobiography: for someone whose life was largely absorbed in books and lived in a world of ideas, Turmel is very open regarding the emotional toll his struggles with faith and reason exacted from him. The clashes within Roman Catholicism that coincided with "La Belle Epoque" (1890–1914) and were condemned by the Vatican in 1907 under the label of "Modernism" had an emotional impact on those involved—especially on partisans of renewal who saw their initiatives rejected by Rome. The emotional restraint exhibited by many of those who subsequently wrote of their experiences emphasized the intellectual dimension of the crisis, creating a one-sided impression of its effects. As Albert Houtin observed in his own autobiography,

> As I have never dwelt on the emotional side of the crisis I had passed through, nor expressed my great sorrow in any book, I have often been represented as a pure intellectual, happy in being delivered from mythology. The truth is quite different. My emancipation was very painful.[7]

Still, ideas figure more prominently in *Une vie de prêtre* than do emotional responses to events. By contrast, in his autobiography Turmel is less interested in setting forth and defending hard-won intellectual positions as he is in defending a line of conduct lived out over the course of decades.[8] Having lost his faith in 1886, Turmel decided to remain a priest in the Church—which itself required justification. Further, having come into possession of what he regarded as the truth of things through his independent research, he concluded that the Church had systematically worked to deceive him—as it had all those indoctrinated in its seminaries. Therefore he produced under his own name and under a veritable team of pseudonyms writings that sought to undermine the received view of Catholic dogma. When critics sought to penetrate the pseudonymous shield and identified Turmel as their true author, on multiple occasions he flatly denied authorship, both in print and under oath to his bishop—again requiring

Introduction

justification of his conduct. The emotional density of Turmel's account is not only an integral part of his aim of providing moral justification of his conduct; it serves as a reminder that, in the midst of a conflict between orthodoxy and heresy, his is a very human story. The ideological dimensions of the modernist crisis can tend to overshadow its human side. Turmel's narrative of his life can provide something of a balance.

TURMEL AND MODERNISM

> Should we not, in any case, admire the Church? She spotted these first-rate minds: Hébert, Loisy, Houtin, Turmel, to name only them. She has, over time, inspired their ideal. The solitude, the hours of silence and meditation that she organized, the discipline she inspired in them, have strengthened their constant preoccupation with goals higher than their own concerns.[9]

If one takes initiatives at reform of the Church as *a* defining characteristic of Modernism, then it is questionable whether Turmel could really qualify as a Modernist. For he had lost his faith before the loosely connected initiatives that ultimately acquired the name "Modernism" had gathered momentum and, further, worked to subvert Catholicism rather than renew it. Thus there are scholars of Modernism who have discussed Turmel only *in relation to* Modernism rather than as a true Modernist. If one begins, however, not with the anti-Modernist encyclical *Pascendi dominici gregis*[10] and its condemnation and then proceeds to qualify individual figures as "Modernist" or not—but with Modernism as it emerged within Catholicism, then Turmel acquires a different aspect. For others, the practice of pseudonymous publications subversive of dogma, coupled with the maintenance of outwardly correct ecclesiastical conduct, held to be a characteristic tactic of the Modernists,[11] sufficed to install Turmel among their ranks. While with historical hindsight Turmel's position may be distinguished from those of Modernists, at the time of the crisis, if anything, their positions in the minds of anti-Modernists became assimilated to his. Moreover, from Turmel's own perspective, he differed from the Modernists, but not on the basis of fundamental aims as much as the tactics employed in realizing them. In his mind, the goal of destroying dogma was common to all. However, while some Modernists did this through subterfuge, through use of equivocal formulas, he did so more straightforwardly.[12] Turmel thus

Introduction

may begin to appear less as a marginal figure and more as one whose work contributed to the orthodox perception of Modernism in significant ways.

He did so on the terrain of historical theology, especially through his patristic scholarship. The dominant neo-Thomism began from the developed dogma and then proceeded to marshal proof texts in its support, claiming a unanimous consent on the part of the Church Fathers;[13] Turmel interjected countertexts disruptive of that harmony, uncovered partial citations truncated to prove a point, and confronted those with a restored text to establish a counterpoint. If the approach of the reigning orthodoxy can fairly be designated a "supernatural positivism,"[14] Turmel's approach— one shared with some of his Modernist contemporaries—manifests an historical positivism.[15] His distinctive mode of employing that approach facilitated identification of his pseudonymous works with him by orthodox critics, leading to difficulties that form a good deal of the autobiography's narrative.

Orthodox critics found in Turmel an understanding of "development" that included alteration and corruption. An understanding that held the identity of dogma and its interpretation cheaply—to the point where Turmel was seen to create oppositions where they did not exist, to inflate discrepancies into contradictions, and to make differences of perspective into irreconcilable divergences—all this with the intent of undermining the authority of the Fathers.

His neo-Scholastic critics were right in seeing more than a difference over a particular dogma in Turmel's writings, more also than a serious disagreement over methods. At stake was the very understanding of dogma itself. However, these critics were surely incorrect in their confident assertion that the hermeneutical principles they invoked were sufficient to cover the process of historical transmission. In emphasizing the necessity of critical methods to regulate the work of historical reconstruction Turmel saw farther. However, the historian's task was more complex than he envisioned, as others, Loisy, for one, were able to discern but not satisfactorily resolve. The condemnations of Modernism in 1907 would not resolve them either; only suppress open discussion of them for decades. They would reemerge decades after the disputants had passed from the scene.

The exchanges between Turmel and his critics reveal, not merely disagreements over the detailed interpretation of texts, but how those texts may function as data for theological reflection, the methods appropriate for working with those texts, and the problems both data and methods

Introduction

are tasked with solving. At a deeper level, their exchanges reveal profound disagreement over the very nature of history and of theology, and how the two stand in relation to another. At the deepest level reside epistemological assumptions that form a sort of mirror image of one another.[16] Turmel and those who shared his mindset do not exhaust the range of epistemological possibilities within the modernist movement. However, in the very extremes of his position, in both pseudonymous writings and in those presented under his own name, he influenced authorities' perceptions of critical historical scholarship, contributing in his way to the eventual severity of their responding to it in the condemnations of 1907. While on one level Turmel represents a departure from the usual use of patristic scholarship within Christianity, on another he is symptomatic of a broader hermeneutical crisis induced in Roman Catholicism by the intrusion of modern historical consciousness into that tradition. Under the dual pressures of the Kantian legacy in philosophy and the impact of historical criticism on Scripture and religious tradition, the boundaries of interpretation shifted and the classicist synthesis no longer seemed adequate to moderns. A broad-ranging reinterpretation of Catholicism was, in consequence, called for.[17]

THE MORALITY OF APOSTASY

> Our emotions are an integral part of our moral character, and so evaluations of persons in the light of their emotions are among the most fundamental moral evaluations of people that can be made. In fact, any moral assessment of a person which failed to consider that person's emotional life is likely to be seriously inadequate and potentially misleading.
>
> Justin Oakley[18]

Over the past several decades, the study of emotions has re-emerged as an area of serious interest—to the point that "the development of emotions research has been called a 'revolution' in scholarship."[19] Linguists, neuroscientists, sociologists and psychologists, philosophers and historians have contributed to a deeper understanding of emotions in ways that have challenged the field of religious studies.

An area that reflects the impact of renewed interest is that of ethics.[20] Work by philosophers such as Justin Oakley and Robert Solomon[21] has emphasized the cognitive dimension of emotions (while not neglecting affective and volitional aspects) as a way of integrating emotions into moral judgments. Emotions not only motivate behavior, they focus attention, organize memory, and aid in interpreting social situations. While emotions can inhibit rationality, they also play a positive role. "Our emotions *situate* us in the world, and thus provide not the motive for rationality, much less its opposition, but rather its very framework."[22] Emotions are engagements with the world and are thus not simply self-enclosed feelings. Insofar as they constitute evaluations of the world they bear an external relation to their intentional objects and an internal relation to the way those objects are constituted in consciousness.[23] Emotions then are ways of seeing, interpretive perceptions that can read a situation correctly or incorrectly; they embody beliefs about the situation and its salience; lastly, these intentional perceptions and beliefs engage values, "mapping events onto the subject's own sense of personal importance or value."[24] Viewed in this light, emotions are cognitive-evaluative, as well as affective. An appreciation of the complexity of emotions enables a corresponding appreciation of their centrality to ethics. This is so "not just because there are evaluations and appraisals already built into our emotions, and not just because our emotional behavior tends to have ethically significant consequences, but because we are continuously evaluating and appraising our own emotional responses." And whether we affirm or deny them, that affirmation or denial is not only about the emotion. "It is the emotion as a reflection of one's *self*. It shows or betrays who one is."[25]

From this perspective, the emotional responses that surface in the course of Turmel's account provide an important hermeneutical key for understanding not only his conduct but his sense of self that underlay that behavior.

A sense of moral indignation at being deceived by the Church permeates the pages of the autobiography, as does a sense of moral righteousness over the choices regarding strategies to counter it. The emotions so prominently displayed in those pages do more than motivate a line of conduct. Clearly, they play an important role in shaping his perception of situations and of people, in forming his beliefs about them, and his evaluations of his own behavior as well as that of others. In turn, his emotional displays do represent his sense of self. In short, in Turmel's emotional life we find resources for understanding his moral decisions and moral justifications.

As a prelude to appreciating choices Turmel made and how he legitimated those, it is necessary to gain some initial sense of the clerical education of the time and ways in which he found it intentionally deceiving. During the last quarter of the nineteenth century, French Catholicism, which had suffered under the long-term effects of the French Revolution, underwent an intellectual renewal. The effects of that would not be felt in provincial seminaries until the final decade of the century, and even then selectively. Turmel was educated with the traditional manuals which carefully controlled the information presented to their readers. Research was not encouraged and seminary education consisted essentially of a two-year memory course in philosophy and a three-year memory course in theology—little calculated to stimulate curiosity beyond the textbook. Even during seminary days Turmel exhibited a lively intellectual curiosity as well as a voracious appetite for independent reading. His assignment after ordination to teach in the theologate in his diocese enabled him to indulge both. His initial contacts with critical biblical scholarship, much of it from Protestants or exegetes independent of any religious tradition, challenged, then undermined many of the traditional positions he had been taught. To understand the effect of historical critical scholarship on him, it is necessary to understand something of the Scholastic mentality in which he was formed.

Christophe Théobald has characterized that mentality under the rubric of "dogmatism." This constitutes a system of Christian truths guaranteed by an infallible authority. In consequence, historical facts function as sign and proof of supernatural dogma which subsists in the flux of history essentially untouched by its particularities. Emphasizing the speculative side of dogma requires no historical skills or training on the part of the theologian for the adequate performance of his task. The elaboration of a dogmatic system proceeds according to its internal logic, not according to the vagaries of historical circumstance. As Théobald justly concludes, "Because one could believe it possible to attribute the same value to dogma, to legend, and to the historical fact, that of an historically verifiable reality, the attempt to reconcile orthodoxy and history inevitably leads to the suppression of history."[26] As Houtin found when he challenged the legend surrounding the figure of Saint René, said to have been miraculously raised from the dead seven years after his demise, a line was quickly drawn from disbelief in the miracle involving Saint René to disbelief in biblical miracles more generally. In a conversation with his bishop Houtin was told: "If you cannot admit the resurrection of St. René, you cannot believe in that of the young man of Sarepta nor of Lazarus. If you do not admit tradition in the case of St. René, why should you admit it in the matter of auricular confession?"[27] "Rationalism" shares the same epistemological commitment to historically verifiable reality. Only in its case, a positivist orientation to history eliminates legend and historicizes dogma as a human product, not a supernatural revealed truth. If not historically verifiable, then legend and dogma cannot, in any sense, be true. The title of the English translation of Turmel's two volume *Catéchisme pour adultes—Religious Inventions and Frauds*—captures the basic thrust of his critique.[28] In both camps the reality or non-reality of dogma are held to be scientifically verifiable. For the dogmatist dogma en bloc conforms to the historical facts and one accepts it; for the rationalist it cannot be sustained by historical fact and thus dogma is rejected.[29]

As a result of his independent research, Turmel uncovered an increasing number of facts that he perceived to be at variance with the reigning theology. For a time he—painfully—lived with a growing tension between faith and facts, between the truths he had been taught and the truths he had acquired. Turmel's account of the shattering impact his encounters with critical exegesis had upon his faith provides valuable testimony to the effects of that scholarship and enables appreciation of the anxieties it aroused among orthodox Churchmen.[30] In 1886 his faith could no longer withstand the repeated shocks he experienced as a result of his research. The reconstruction of Christianity set out by the biblical scholarship of the day won out over the version of Christianity he had received in his early religious and later theological formation. This posed a major dilemma: should he publicly own up to his unbelief and leave the priesthood?

To do so would be to shatter his life, to devastate his parents, to deeply wound the priest who had been to him an adoptive father; moreover, it would be tantamount to a public admission of guilt, of accepting responsibility for his loss of faith, for falling away from the truth. In his mind, his "crime" was to have broken through the illusion, to have refuted the lies which had ensnared him. To have admitted guilt on the Church's terms would have been to let the Church win. Hence,

> In a burst of indignation I cried out: 'Because I have discovered the trap in which the Church ensnares the faithful and particularly aspirants to the priesthood, I should be obliged to condemn myself and my family to dreadful sufferings? No, that will not be. Promises made at knifepoint grant no rights to the cutthroat who exacts them. They impose no obligation on the victim who signs them. They are null. The Church that systematically hid the truth

from me, that fed me lies, acted like a relentless cutthroat toward its victim. Methods differ; dishonesty is the same. The Church has no rights over me. I certainly do not have to accept the verdict it would pronounce if it knew my state because this verdict would be merely a shameful travesty of justice.'[31]

The concern for justice renders this incident more than an emotional outburst of anger. One may properly speak of moral indignation. That emotion continues to shape Turmel's perceptions of the essential nature of the Church, of his obligations toward it as compared to his obligations to the truth of things, of his reconfiguration of his vocation as one of "martyr to the truth" and its dedicated "apostle," committed to subverting the continuing deception on the Church's part and to using whatever tactics would serve that goal.

In 1892 a lapse in discretion by Turmel partly revealed his loss of faith in Catholic dogma. His difficulties in giving intellectual assent to dogma were attributed to a sort of mental breakdown caused by overwork. Turmel acquiesced to a diagnosis he knew to be false and was consigned to a marginal position in the clergy, eventually leaving him with a great deal of discretionary time to research and write. Initially he worked to assemble "the clearest, most decisive proofs of the hollowness of Christian dogmas" with the idea of one day publishing them after leaving it.[32] In 1897, however, he gained entry into the pages of the *Revue d'histoire et de littérature religieuses* which enabled him to fulfill his aspiration to being an apostle of the truth while still within the Church. As he progressed from debunking doctrine to taking on defined dogma, Turmel thought it prudent to publish under pseudonym. A study of the dogma of the Trinity that appeared under the name of Antoine Dupin and another of Marian dogmas under that of Guillaume Herzog unleashed a storm of protest and signaled the demise of the *Revue*. Since Turmel wrote with a distinctive style, orthodox defenders of dogma sought to amass a body of evidence indicating him as the veritable author.

The controversy escalated to the point of causing difficulty for Turmel's archbishop, who sought to regulate the matter by having the accused declare under oath that he was not the author of the offending articles. Turmel justifies his deception of his archbishop by declaring that, in reality, it was the Roman Church which he set out to deceive, and justifies his deception in terms reminiscent of the passage quoted earlier. He notes the "virtuous indignation" of the "Pharisees" toward him, but states that he would take that seriously when they have studied and struggled with the problems raised by the authorship of biblical books or the history of dogma, and have presented the results of their investigations to the Holy Office.[33]

When, around this same period, Turmel's principal writings published under his own name were placed on the Index, he publicly submitted. Thereafter his name disappeared from publications, to be replaced by a whole team of pseudonyms who continued his work of revenge upon the Roman Church. In 1929 the campaign against him was renewed, and this time a "smoking gun" was discovered, establishing without a trace of doubt his identity with "Herzog." Under the impression that he would be left in peace if he made a clean breast of it, Turmel admitted not only to the writings published under Herzog and Dupin, but also to those under fourteen other pseudonyms that had appeared since. In November of 1930 he was excommunicated by the Church and eventually affiliated with Freethinkers.

At the close of his narrative, Turmel refers to "the feigned indignation of the apologists, who have sensationally denounced what they called my lying" in order to direct attention to their own deceit in keeping the truth hidden from all questioners. Rather than a matter of his own failure in his duty as accused, it is a case of his judges first failing "in the most important of their professional duties," and thus "their immoral conduct deprived them of all right to the truth."[34]

In deceiving the authorities Turmel has preserved his ability to reveal the truth he has uncovered through his scholarly labors:

> Rehabilitation being an illusion, my only possible hope and my sole ambition was to enlighten souls of good will . . . . This program of life was my sole plank of salvation: I clung to it. In the absence of the justice that the hierarchy would never consent to render me, it satisfied the desire for revenge . . . that unceasingly seethed in me, and also the thirst for the apostolate embodied in the motto: Martyr to the truth I will be its apostle.[35]

An air of moral indignation over injustice suffuses the pages of the autobiography; a desire for revenge against the institution that has deceived, marginalized[36] and insulted him is reiterated; these are "strong emotions" that Turmel confesses to feeling, and which have their counterparts in those who oppose him. How do they enable us to understand his decisions and their justification, indeed the very sense of self that emerges from the narrative?

Anger is an indication that the boundaries of the self have been transgressed in some way. It is a response to a perceived challenge to one's self worth. When the transgression is linked to a belief in a perceived injustice, one may speak of moral anger or, as a strong emotion, moral indignation.[37] When one acts upon such moral judgments, one form that action may take is enacting a desire for revenge.

While anger may surface in the strong form of moral indignation as a situational emotion, it may also persist over time as a "background emotion," as an ongoing response to persistent injustice. As such, anger may persist in the fabric of one's life, playing a crucial role in the explanation of one's actions, but may not always be consciously felt.[38] Even when it does not result in actions, anger can serve a purpose, in that, as the offended, even humiliated party, one can emerge as nevertheless superior, even righteous. As Robert Solomon remarks, "It is a powerful psychological position. It is emotional politics at its most profound and subtle, whether or not effective in the world."[39] From Turmel's narrative, it is apparent that, prior to finding outlets for his critical findings, he was sustained by a sense of righteousness and integrity. It is equally apparent that the ability to bring those findings into the public forum, especially under his own name even if he had to be content with rather oblique statements of his conclusions, gave him great satisfaction. As he notes with regard to the decision to publish his initial articles in the *Revue d'histoire et de littérature religieuses* identifying him as their author, rather than under a pseudonym:

> A victim of the school of lies, I hastened to wage war on its agents, to rub their noses in texts, to return some of the blows they had dealt me.... I wished to harass the Christian faith, to strike at it obliquely. But I also wanted it to know the source of the blows. My revenge would have been incomplete if the clergy of Rennes, who suspected the cause of my misfortunes because of repeated indiscretions, imagined that I was crushed forever.[40]

Solomon's comments on anger afford additional insight. He views every emotion as containing both objective and subjective intentions, the former oriented toward changing the world, the latter toward transforming one's view of his world. Anger, then, comprises both a subjective indictment and a desire, however indirect or ineffective, to punish.[41] As such it may well reflect, not a single judgment, but "a network of interlocking judgments concerning one's status and relationship with the offending party,

Introduction

the gravity and mitigating circumstances of the offense and the urgency of revenge."[42]

An additional consideration is the effect of the quest for revenge upon the would-be avenger. It can consume the avenger's life, as it appears to have done in Turmel's case. In the midst of that quest for a restoration of moral balance the avenger may be driven to resort to morally objectionable actions. One may well subscribe to Montaigne's dictum that sometimes "a man must do wrong in detail if he wishes to do right on the whole." But then he may risk paying a moral price for being "wrong in detail" in the loss of his morally good character.[43] In the course of his narrative Turmel is compelled repeatedly to defend his moral character by emphasizing his goal of doing "right on the whole," thus justifying tactics that came under moral indictment from his critics.

While a sense of righteous anger suffuses Turmel's account, emerging at times in intense outbursts of moral indignation, other strong emotions also figure. He reveals the intense suffering he experienced at several junctures and in several forms, in his early attempts to reconcile the teaching he had received and the results uncovered by his research, in his dismissal from the seminary faculty and marginal status among the diocesan clergy, in the suffering he caused his mentor—the priest whom he characterizes as a second father to him. Moreover, emotions are not isolated instances of feeling. Emotions are interrelated. For example, shame can be seen to have an affinity with anger, in that anger may be a consequence of shame. Both emotions may be mutually reinforcing to the extent that one may view them as a single affect, as "helpless anger" or, in more intense form, as "humiliated fury."[44] Turmel's descriptions of emotional episodes following his dismissal from the seminary and being assigned a lowly position teaching seminarians who had a late vocation lend credence to the connection between shame and anger, as well as the effects of their combination. The focus on anger and indignation in this account is meant to be indicative of the fruitfulness of extending the range of analysis to enhance our understanding the moral significance of other emotions as well.

Even after his excommunication, Turmel continued to wear the soutane, retained the title of Abbé, and continued to say Mass on Sundays[45]—anomalous conduct for a freethinker. There are indications in the autobiography that it is written to establish his rationalist credentials with Libre pensée.[46] The wealth of references to historical and theological literature indicates a certain Catholic interest as well. Turmel had to justify himself in the face of charges of lying, deceitful practice in remaining a priest, sacrilege in continuing to say Mass—all of which could be ascribed to venal motives. His counter to such charges was to invoke his apostleship of truth, supported by the extensive research he had done with both primary and secondary sources. In this sense his apostleship served as a legitimation for his conduct; but he did not expect either hierarchy or the ordinary faithful to be convinced by it. There is another audience, that of enlightened laity, that he does expect may benefit from his life story and the truths he has perceived. He expresses hope that they will wake up to the true nature of dogma as human construct and to the true nature of the Church in its deceptive practice.

However, even if his witness failed to convince either Catholic hierarchy of his moral rectitude or Catholic faithful of the truth of his claims, that witness is not necessarily in vain. In *The Moral Demands of Memory* Jeffrey Blustein reminds us that bearing witness gains moral value "stemming from the sense that one is a good or better person for having witnessed, though in vain."[47] In addition to consequentialist reasons for bearing witness, there is its potential symbolic value. "Bearing witness has moral value because it reveals or expresses our allegiance to the good and the right, our repudiation of the bad and the wrong."[48] And it gives voice to the silent, to those who have been traumatized by injustice or intimidated into silence. Turmel links his quest for truth and his commitment to disseminating it to his personal integrity. He portrays it as the right thing to do; he can do no other. And, at a number of points, he makes reference to those who have paid a price for daring to speak similar truths, or for those who share his truth but dare not speak it.

PART ONE

How I Freed Myself of Dogma

A Translation of Joseph Turmel's
Comment j'ai donné congé aux dogmes

Translated by C. J. T. Talar and Elizabeth Emery

Introduction

ON DECEMBER 18, 1880, five days after having reached canonical age,* I received subdiaconate for which the required age is twenty-one. Fifty years later (November 1930) the Roman Church resoundingly denounced me the world over as a heretic to be avoided by the faithful. Twenty-one years is the morning of life; seventy-one its evening. What underlies the violent contrast between the evening of my life and its morning? It is this I am about to relate.

---

 * I was born on December 13, 1859, at Rennes, 142 rue Saint-Malo (today 136). In 1868, my parents, shopkeepers, took up residence at 21 rue de Penhoët (then called rue de la Poulaillerie). In October of 1870, after several weeks of Latin, Abbé Gendron, curate at Saint-Aubin, sent me to Saint-Martin as a day student. At Easter he placed me in the first form [en sixième].

1

At the Angers Faculty of Theology

THE DAY AFTER MY ordination, M. Guillois,[49] the superior of the major seminary, summoned me and said, "My son, the archbishop has decided to send you to the Catholic faculties at Angers to complete your theological studies. I have been instructed to tell you of this decision. M. Gendron[50] has been told and expects you this evening. You will make your preparations to leave at his house. I have no doubt that you will do your best to justify the trust we are placing in you." Then picking up three volumes from the table, he added, "Père Hurter[51] has just published a theology textbook which has received the highest praise. Here it is. Take it as a mark of my affection." Saying this, he handed me the three volumes. I thanked him and assured him of my ardent desire to do well. I then left the seminary where, twenty months later, I would return as professor.

M. Gendron was the priest who, on August 6, 1870, had started me in Latin. He loved me as a father. On two occasions his care had saved my life. Curate of the parish of Saint-Aubin when he met me, he had held the post of chaplain to the Rennes asylum since the end of October 1875. Each year I spent my holidays with him. He had me stay as usual while I waited to leave for Angers which I did on December 28th.

When I arrived in Angers, the Faculty of Theology, inaugurated in November 1879, was beginning its second year. Its professors were of uneven caliber, and of several of them the less said the better. But I am grateful to Père Billot,[52] who taught me dogma in 1881, and to Père Paultier,[53] who succeeded him in 1882. Later I was able to ascertain that their learning came entirely from Suarez[54] and (in Billot's case) from Pétau.[55] Having immersed myself in the study of Billuart[56] while at the seminary at Rennes,

5

Part One: How I Freed Myself of Dogma

even when I was their pupil I often had a sense of "déjà vu." But in the end they expanded my knowledge of Scholasticism; they gave me what I had come for; they were equal to their task.

At the beginning of my second year at the Rennes seminary I had been given the job of librarian. This meant that I kept the key to the seminarian library and thus had access to a considerable number of books. I made liberal use of the privilege; and personal research soon became a kind of passion which drove the professors' courses utterly into the background. I brought the same state of mind to Angers. The courses there, even those on dogma in which I did learn something, did not engage my attention. Only personal study appealed to me.

I gathered books left and right. First of all Mgr Freppel's ten volumes on the early Fathers of the Church.[57] These books revealed as it were uncharted territory. Territory where everything amazed me: everything, including certain arguments which tended to demonstrate the authenticity of the Areopagite's writings.[58] Mgr Freppel seemed to me a prodigy of erudition, almost superhuman. And I resolved to imitate, at least from afar, the admirable example he set before me. Needless to say, I analyzed the scholarly bishop of Angers' ten volumes at length.

A book that made a deep impression on me without eliciting the same enthusiasm was Père Zigliara's *La Lumière Intellectuelle*.[59] Does the human mind work out its ideas itself or does it receive them ready-made from God? Of these two explanations of the origin of ideas, the former had been taught at seminary and the arguments brought forth in its favor by Saint Thomas, who got them from Aristotle, seemed plausible. But the latter view, which I had subsequently met in Descartes, Bossuet,[60] Fénelon,[61] and other modern philosophers, was quite seductive; and I had returned to it at various times with intermittent conviction. Père Zigliara's book put an end to my hesitations. When I had read this thorough study, I saw clearly that our ideas come from earth and not from heaven. Since then I have always resisted the seductions of ontologism[62] and innéism. More precisely, since 1887 I have subscribed to Spencer's innéism which has nothing in common with Cartesian innéism.[63]

At Angers, the majority of my fellow students knew Hebrew. I did not. It seemed to me essential to rectify this deficiency. I succeeded in obtaining Glaire's *Chrestomathie*,[64] which contains detailed grammatical analyses of Hebrew texts. With this invaluable guide, my introduction to Hebrew no longer posed an insurmountable obstacle. After several weeks, Gesenius's *Lexicon*[65] was adequate to interpret the Hebrew texts of the Bible.

Along with Hebrew I studied German, some snatches of which I had acquired at school. I happened upon Count de Stolberg's *Geschichte der Religion Jesu Christi* (*History of the Religion of Jesus Christ*).[66] I took the first volume of this very orthodox work and began reading. This book accustomed me to deciphering German; but beyond that it taught me nothing, for the edifying stories it told had long been familiar to me. I thus set out to look for a German book whose subject matter might be instructive. At this point, M. Litter,[67] an Alsatian priest who was professor of Sacred Scripture, was explaining Isaiah to us. I asked him whether he would find me a German commentary on the prophet. He gave me Gesenius. Had he taken it from his very modest personal library? I think that he had borrowed it from the Catholic Faculties library. And, as his biblical learning was recently acquired, I am inclined to believe that he had not read it. Whatever the case, I was more than happy with the three volumes he proffered. Thanks to them I was going to study German and exegesis simultaneously, which was what I wanted, thus killing two birds with one stone. I was even going to kill three. For Gesenius, whose *Lexicon Hebraicum* I was using, had of necessity set down the fruits of his mastery of Hebrew learning in his study on Isaiah. So I was also going to further my familiarity with Hebrew. I was overjoyed.

I did not foresee the terrible ordeal awaiting me. All the commentators I had read in seminary considered the Bible a book dictated from heaven and, accordingly, sacred. Gesenius's writing did not deny but ignored the celestial origin of the Bible; and this book, presented as a product of the human mind, lost all sacred character. Two extremely serious consequences followed this fundamental contrast. Firstly, if it emanated from God himself, the Bible would be divine in all its parts; and heaven, which had given this august book to humans, would surely have ensured the exact transmission of its texts. But if, on the contrary, the Bible was a human product, it could not have escaped the interpolations and glosses suffered by all ancient books. Secondly, if the Bible had God for its author, it was bound to announce the coming of Christ, his passion, death, and glorious resurrection. But, all the messianic prophecies that theologians thought they saw in Isaiah and in the other Old Testament books rested on imaginative errors, that is to say, on nothing.

This was the way Gesenius understood it. He pointed out, here and there, in the actual text of Isaiah, glosses that, according to him, had been

Part One: How I Freed Myself of Dogma

inserted by readers and did not derive from the prophet. In addition, he stoutly rejected the messianic oracles. More specifically, he declared that the supposed prophecy of the Virgin Mother (7:14) was the result of a blunder. According to him, Isaiah had in no way announced to Ahaz the virginal conception of Jesus; he had confined himself to saying this: "Your enemies will be crushed before the child conceived today by a young woman will have reached the years of discretion."

The commentaries I had handled had never indicated a single case of a gloss in the biblical texts. Moreover, did not the Council of Trent exclude all possibility of gloss or interpolation in the passage of Session IV where it stipulated that Christians hold as sacred and canonical "with all their parts" ("cum omnibus suis partibus") the books of the bible as they are in the Vulgate? As for the prophecy of the Virgin, it is not only the Fathers who proclaim it with one voice. Saint Matthew himself guarantees it when, after having told of the virginal conception of Jesus, he adds (1:22): "All this took place to fulfil what the Lord had announced through the prophet: Behold, the Virgin will conceive and bear a son, and he will be given the name Emmanuel."

Thus, the first of Gesenius's assertions ran counter to the Council of Trent; the second was condemned by Saint Matthew's gospel; the whole of tradition raised vehement protests against both. But, on the other hand, how can one fail to acknowledge clumsy glosses in texts, obviously interrupting the flow of ideas (for example 7:8b; 9:12)? And how can one believe that the prophet, seeing Ahaz alarmed by the coalition of Syrians and Ephraimites, reassured him by announcing a marvel that would occur seven hundred and thirty years later? After reading Gesenius I seemed to see for the first time the real state of affairs masked until then by a curtain of artifice. But, at the same time I understood the reproaches, even the threats, which the Fathers, the Council of Trent, and Jesus, the object of my love, were heaping upon me.

Distraught by this unanticipated conflict between reason and faith, I appealed to my professor of Sacred Scripture. He replied that the Council of Trent did not prohibit belief in the presence of minor glosses in the Bible and that I interpreted its decree too rigorously. As for the prophecy of the Virgin, he floundered about as he ordinarily did in class. Perhaps his uneasy explanations sought to express what I read shortly thereafter in Bossuet (*Explication de la prophétie d'Isaïe*[68]): "The majority of the prophecies do not appear to be connected with the rest of the discourse into which they are inserted;" the Holy Spirit "knows quite well how to dispense with all the rules of common discourse;" and, in sum, Isaiah, while reassuring Ahaz, could have been transported by the Holy Spirit to the time of the Savior. Alarmed by the prospect of heresy and enthralled by Bossuet's melodious prose, I adopted the conclusion that the illustrious bishop formulated in these terms: "If everything in it were clear, we would believe that we were on familiar ground and in possession of the full light of truth without recognizing the need to be guided. . . . Let us then proceed in the Scriptures with all humility and trepidation."

May of 1882 drew toward its end. I left for Rennes to receive ordination to the priesthood on June 3rd, six months before the canonical age, by virtue of a special indult. During the five or six weeks that followed my return to Angers, I took up Gesenius again. But, for reasons which currently escape me (was the vocabulary too refined? the sentence structure too complicated? Or, more likely, the commentaries in which the flow of thought is constantly interrupted are more difficult to follow than an argument whose spirit is clarified by the context as a whole?) I made progress more slowly with him than with Stolberg. When I left Angers for good, I had probably read no more than a hundred pages of the commentary. It may be too that I had not forced myself to follow a strict order and had passed over certain chapters I judged less important in order to study subsequent ones. In any case, I said goodbye to Gesenius before suspecting the problem of Second Isaiah. And the difficulties that I had succeeded in overcoming were as nothing alongside those I did not know.

Thus my faith emerged victorious from the agonies it had undergone in 1882. But the price of victory was two serious wounds of which I must say a word here. The first stemmed from the origin of unbelief. Before reading Gesenius I was absolutely convinced that the denial of dogmas was the consequence of either passions of the heart, pride, or hatred of the supernatural. This conviction had been impressed upon me by theologians and apologists who unanimously took unbelievers to task over their obstinacy in rejecting, despite the most manifest proofs, the existence of prophecies. And yet, in the conflict regarding the prophecy of the Virgin, I did not for an instant doubt the possibility of prophecy; not for an instant did it occur to me that God could not reveal the future to men; not for an instant did I succumb to the temptations of pride, still less to the temptations of the flesh (my piety was intense, even exalted); not for an instant did I experience a prejudice against the supernatural. The problem confronting me was a

Part One: How I Freed Myself of Dogma

question of fact presented in this form: "In 7:14 did Isaiah really announce that, 730 years later, Jesus would be born of a virgin?" On the basis of my own experience in 1882 I thus observed that unbelief could have its source in the serious study of texts; that theologians slander unbelievers, distorting their innermost feelings, the better to assure their triumph over unbelief; and that mistrust of their assertions was legitimate. First wound to my faith.

My second wound concerned the value of theological exegesis. When I saw the enormous gap that separated Gesenius from theologians on the subject of the oracle of Isaiah 7.14, I tried to understand how it had occurred. It was easy to see that it was the product of two opposed exegetical methods: one that, to explain a text, begins by isolating it from its environment; the other, on the contrary, that illuminates the text using the entirety of its context. The first method is characteristic of the theologians; the second had been adopted by Gesenius. Each had done its work. I have said how the dread of heresy buttressed by Bossuet's authority had gotten me back in step with tradition with respect to the prophecy of the Virgin. Let me add here that this drastic act of submission did not succeed in rehabilitating theological exegesis in my mind. From the day I observed the crushing blow that Gesenius dealt it, I retained for it a disdain all the more irreversible for being partly unconscious. The theologians' arguments continued to hold my attention; but I stopped taking their exegesis of biblical texts seriously. Second wound inflicted on my faith. Not on its integrity, but on its ingenuousness. I still subscribed ardently to all dogmas but now had diminished respect for their official interpreters, a respect that was not completely without aversion. In Gesenius I had read about the misfortunes of the German priest Isenbiel [sic], thrown into prison for having denied the messianic character of the oracle of Isaiah 7:14.[69] My sympathy went out to Isenbiel and I was angry with the theologians I deemed responsible for his misfortune. In reality this cruel measure was the work of Rome. But the thought of incriminating the papacy did not even occur to me. If it had, I would have rejected it as blasphemy.

Toward mid-July 1882, I left Angers, never to return. I occasionally recall the grand boulevard that, from January 1882 daily led me, each afternoon, to the chapel of Notre-Dame-sous-terre. On the way there I said vespers; at the chapel I recited compline; on the way back I read lists of German phrases recorded in a small notebook. By one-thirty I was back at the residence for the rest of the day.

2

At the Major Seminary at Rennes

BEFORE MARCH 18, 1886

I WAS APPOINTED PROFESSOR at the Rennes major seminary on August 14, 1882; my duties began at the start of the school year in October. My teaching responsibilities included Theodicy, Revelation, the Church, and Fundamental Moral Theology. On these various subjects I knew only what was in the manuals. My first year was spent in painstaking research in the seminary library. I went exploring without guidebook or compass. Among the books upon which I chanced I should mention here the *Entretiens sur la démonstration catholique* by Père Dechamps, the future cardinal.[70] This "demonstration" based exclusively on philosophy and without any reference to the texts made a deep impression on me and became the starting point for thoughts I had never before entertained.

    I had known since childhood that God is our Father by grace. For the first time I understood that he was already so by the creation, though to an inferior degree. And this led to seemingly inescapable conclusions. In our culture a father never leaves his child to his own devices. He lavishes on him his care, his counsel; he shows him the path to follow, the dangers to avoid: he is ever watchful. God could do no less for man. Nor could he lose interest in his children. He was bound to help them. The Revelation that brings us aid is the complement and, in a way, the continuation of creation. Since man received his existence from God, he was also bound to receive a Revelation from his creator. And since, of all existing religions, only Christianity presents itself as the heir to Judaism, it follows that the Christian religion is divine in the same way as is its elder, the Mosaic religion. It also follows that the Genesis narratives deserve complete confidence and that God spoke to men from the very beginning.

Given these conclusions, the prophecies and gospel miracles lose nothing of their importance. But their specific role is to confirm the postulates of reason. The texts inform us about what God did; our divine origin tells us what God was bound to do. The two proofs are in agreement. But, before immersing ourselves in the painstaking and intricate study of texts, we have the certainty that heaven has bent toward earth. The existence of Revelation is like the corollary of the existence of God and we cannot doubt Revelation without doubting God himself.* I ended my first year of teaching with the consolation of having put my faith on a tranquil foundation.

During the vacation of 1883 I reopened my Hebrew books, neglected during the academic year, and set about translating the psalms. My goal was to deepen my knowledge of Hebrew. On one page of my notebook I wrote the translation (bound, of around two hundred pages) and on the facing page, my notes, primarily philological in nature, but which also left some space for chronology. I had Abbé Lesêtre's *Les psaumes* to guide me. Lesêtre, later pastor of Saint-Étienne-du-Mont, was one of the oracles of the French clergy.[71] His book, just published, was of the strictest orthodoxy. It was full of information about Hebrew which I carefully took in. I followed it with complete and total docility.

This long, slow and exacting work consumed the morning. After reciting vespers and compline, that is, from two o'clock on, afternoons were devoted to rapid reading divided between biblical questions and theological problems. I studied the *Bible* put out by Lethielleux,[72] a large collection whose publication was then nearing its completion; then I went on to works directed against rationalists and Protestants.

In every case I found the conclusions decisive. Once, however, I was abruptly overcome by a feeling of defiance. I read the commentary on the letter of Saint Jude. Naturally the author upheld sound doctrine. He carefully distanced from the apostle's text the errors that independent exegetes pointed out in it. Unfortunately, instead of imitating most apologists who shamelessly trample over objections, he set them forth with a measure of honesty. They were dreadful. The apostle Saint Jude was roundly accused,

---

* Here I reproduce solely the workings of my thought prompted by the reading of the book. I do believe this was Père Dechamps's thesis but I have not opened the *Entretiens* since 1883.

At the Major Seminary at Rennes

first, of attributing to fallen angels a sin of unchastity; second, of relying on the authority of the Book of Enoch and the Assumption of Moses, apocryphal books with no value. And yet, while the clearer the objections, the more convoluted were the replies. By dint of good will I managed to believe them. However, for the second time, I noted that attacks against Christianity were not always inspired by prejudice or by rank ignorance, but that there were also specious objections.

All the more reason to work on resolving them, but also on acquiring a more exact notion of them. This was at the end of 1883. I had just turned 24 and was engaged in my second year of teaching. Inspired by an ardent love for Mother Church, I wished to defend her against the endless attacks to which she was exposed. However, to be a competent defender, I had to know the adversaries' writings first-hand and not through the sketchy extracts apologists were fond of citing. I thus asked permission to read works on the Index. My request, passed on by my superior to the archbishop who forwarded it to Rome, appeared to be justified. To whom should such permission be given, if not to professors of theology? And, two months later, Rome granted the authorization I so much needed.

My reading at once expanded into new ground. In this second zone I first encountered the *Discours du vicaire savoyard*. All the apologists had provided me with extracts but now for the first time I became directly acquainted with it. Certainly, this contact did nothing to strengthen my faith. The story of the Horatii and the Curiatii had taught me that piecemeal offensives cannot equal the power of massed attacks.[73] The disjointed and carved up *Discours* that I had known for five or six years contained nothing alarming. It merited more attention when the mutilations and amputations to which it had been subjected had disappeared, when I could see it in its true aspect. In any case the shock was disastrous for the proof which Père Dechamps's book had suggested. The Revelation that our soul postulates, that God owes it to himself to give us, is a favor accorded to each one of us individually and of which no one can be deprived. It has nothing in common with the primitive revelation spoken of in the Bible, yet which was unknown to the entire human race, save for a few families; nothing in common with the Mosaic revelation, limited to two or three districts of Syria; nothing in common with Christian revelation which three-quarters of humanity has never known. God did not live up to the postulates of the human soul; he did not do what his providence would seem to require. There is a mysterious antinomy between what ought to be and what has

PART ONE: How I Freed Myself of Dogma

always existed. Treating the existence of Revelation as a corollary to God's existence was no more than a dream. And seemingly ineluctable conclusions were nothing but mirages.

I thus rejected Père Dechamps's "demonstration" as an illusion, although a year earlier it had elicited my enthusiasm, and I fell back on the traditional proof, grounded in prophecies and miracles. It was Reuss[74] who would dislodge me from this final refuge.

During the first semester of 1884 I managed to examine most of the "Lethielleux *Bible*" that was the last word in Catholic exegesis. Armed with all the weapons forged by the Bible's defenders, I could face the enemy. At this time the enemy in the biblical domain was, in France, Professor Reuss of Strasbourg, who had just published his French translation of the Bible. I decided to read Reuss. And as I had spent considerable time in translating the psalms from Hebrew, I began by comparing my work with the Strasbourg professor's.

The comparison yielded unanticipated results. Docile disciple of Lesêtre that I was, I placed the most recent psalms in the years just after the return from captivity (536 BC). Reuss, by contrast, pointed out here and there in the psalter clear allusions to the persecution of Antiochus (168 BC). My blind submission to Lesêtre's authority had undoubtedly blinded me to these allusions. But from the moment I encountered them in Reuss, it was impossible not to see them or to dispute them; the weight of evidence was decisive. Take, for instance, the passage in Psalm 43 of the Vulgate where, after describing the misfortunes of his people, the psalmist adds:

> It is *for you* that we are slain all the day long;
> We have not *renounced your covenant*.
> It is *for you* that we are slain all the day long;
> That we are treated as cattle.

Before Antiochus's persecution in 168, the Jews were punished by Yahweh for their infidelity. It was only in 168 that, for the first time, they were persecuted because of their adherence to the Mosaic religion. Thus Psalm 43 could only have been written by one of the victims of Antiochus's persecution.

Lesêtre had also seen the allusions to the persecution of Antiochus that I had clearly seen in Psalm 43 and in several others which need not be mentioned here; for they had been pointed out by critics whom he cited, whose work he knew. He had seen them. But, terrified by the body of Catholic exegetes who would cry scandal, if not heresy and terrified by the Holy

Office which might condemn him, he had not dared express his private opinion but had dissembled. From this experience I drew the following conclusions: (1) As in Galileo's time, the Church today remains obstinately attached to groundless traditions, and imposes them on Catholic exegetes; or, when it does not impose them, it promotes them and looks unfavorably on new opinions. (2) In order to elude the Holy Office which lies in wait for them, or simply to avoid compromising their future, priest-apologists deny what they know full well to be the truth. On dangerous questions they speak contrary to their thought; they do not deserve to be trusted. (3) Rationalist exegetes are not infallible and their assertions should be accepted only after serious scrutiny. But at least their independence makes them sincere; one knows what they think which is not the case with apologists.

This is the state which I had got to by the end of the 1884 vacation. The Church seemed bent on smothering the truth and Catholic exegetes forced to be charlatans. My faith was still alive; for the question of Maccabean psalms did not engage dogma directly; but an inner worm had begun to gnaw on it. In this state of mind I began my third year of professorship.

Having completed the translation of the psalms, I moved on to the historical books, and set about translating them from Hebrew with the help of Reuss. But, as in the past, I supplemented this basic work, whose progress was necessarily slow, with reading. First I attempted to sort out the well-known prophecy of the seventy weeks in the Book of Daniel (9:22–27) that I had to teach my students. Enlightened by Reuss, I had no difficulty in seeing that this oracle referred to the murder of the priest Onias III, killed around 170 by Antiochus, and that only by recourse to a series of crass misreadings could it refer to the death of Christ.

What becomes of the other messianic prophecies if the most important, the most striking of all rests on a misunderstanding? But the surprises were not over. Daniel, who presents himself as a companion of Jews captive in Babylon, who claims to write in 538, before the end of the captivity, is in reality the contemporary of Antiochus Epiphanes, writing around 168. Under the pretense of prophesying, he describes events of his own time that he knows in detail. He also occasionally ventures into the period surrounding 538 in which he is supposed to be writing; but then gets confused and mixes everything up. In short, he does not know the history surrounding 538; however nothing relating to 168 is overlooked. Daniel is a forger; such is the absolutely irrefutable conclusion to which the study of the Daniel prophecies leads. And this conclusion, based on the clearest texts, receives

PART ONE: How I Freed Myself of Dogma

decisive support from tradition; for around 180 the author of Ecclesiasticus, noting the glories of Israel, is silent about Daniel's name which he does not know.

And while my reading cast me in the hornet's nest of Daniel, my translation work set me grappling with the historical books of the Bible. There, as in Daniel, pitfalls and ambushes everywhere. I translated the story of Samuel and found that this holy man had offered sacrifices at Ramah, at Mizpeh, at Gilgal, without heeding the law of Deuteronomy that directed him to sacrifice at Kirjath-jearim where the ark was located and not elsewhere. I translated the story of David, and learned that this great king also broke the law of Deuteronomy in offering sacrifice far from the ark in the area of Araunah the Jebusite. Later I heard the prophet Elijah lament over the destruction of the altars of Yahweh (1 Kgs 19:10 and 14) little suspecting that these altars, dispersed throughout the land of Israel, were condemned by Deuteronomy and, from the viewpoint of the Deuteronomic legislation, their destruction was a good thing. I saw the prophet Elisha (1 Kgs 19:21) offer a sacrifice that was contrary to the same legislation since it was not done at the temple of Jerusalem. And since none of these pious individuals would have broken or been ignorant of the fundamental laws of the Mosaic religion, I was forced to conclude that Deuteronomy, which presents itself as the work of Moses, and is consequently supposed to date from around 1500 BC, did not yet exist in the ninth century. Here, as with Daniel, tradition confirmed the textual evidence; for it told me (2 Kgs 22:8) that Deuteronomy had been "found" in the temple of Jerusalem under Josiah's reign in 622. "Found," that is to say fabricated, in 622 by a forger who, to authenticate his work, placed it under the patronage of Moses.

Daniel—work of a forger! Deuteronomy—work of another forger! This list was soon lengthened. I read the prophets as always in tandem with Reuss, and I caught on their lips a language irreconcilable with the legislation of "Leviticus." To take but one example, Jeremiah does not hesitate to place these words in the mouth of Yahweh (7:22):

> For I spoke not to your fathers, and I commanded them not,
> in the day that I brought them out of the land of Egypt,
> concerning the matter of burnt offerings and sacrifices.

In about 620 Jeremiah is not aware that God has laid down regulations regarding sacrifices during the desert sojourn of the Hebrews. His ignorance is fatal for Leviticus which abounds in regulations on the subject of sacrifice promulgated at that time by God! In Jeremiah's day, Leviticus did not yet exist. And, since it claims to go back to Moses it can only be the work of a forger. For analogous reasons, this conclusion applies to the book of Numbers.

Genesis and Exodus provided me with another curiosity: that of contradictory repetitions. Narratives that repeat what has already been written, using it a second time, are numerous in these two books (and also, for that matter, in the First Book of Kings in the Vulgate—First Book of Samuel in the Hebrew). By way of example, the story of the flood contains two accounts of the motives for this catastrophe, two preliminary instructions to Noah from God, two mentions of the entry into the ark, two descriptions of the deluge, two promises made by God never again to flood the earth. In the same way, in the first chapters of Exodus the plagues of Egypt are reported twice. However, wherever they appear, these repetitions have a particular vocabulary and they are never completely in agreement; there are always divergences between them. In the flood narrative, one of the accounts gives God the name Yahweh, the other calls him Elohim. The Yahwist account sends seven pairs of each species of clean animal into the ark and one pair of unclean animals. In contrast, when Elohim begins to speak, he takes no notice of the distinction between clean and unclean animals; in the narrative attributed to him, the ark contains only a single pair of each species. Finally, in the Yahwist account, the water falls for forty days and, fourteen days after it stops, Noah leaves the ark. In the Elohist narrative, by contrast, the waters remain high for two hundred and fifty days. The same phenomenon occurs in the telling of the plagues of Egypt where God grants the monopoly on miracles sometimes to Moses's staff, sometimes to Aaron's. There also the two accounts disagree. The conclusion that I drew from these repeated differences was that Genesis and Exodus, to say nothing of other books which are full of contradictions, had little or perhaps no historical value.

For most of 1885 I confined myself to the study of the Old Testament. However, a day came when, without interrupting my translation work, I resolved to explore the history of the gospels. My plan was to make a complete and thorough study later on; for the moment, I limited myself to what is termed the infancy gospel (first chapters of Matthew and Luke) and the end of the world prophecy. In the infancy narratives Catholic exegetes, without ignoring the apparent divergences in the Matthean and Lucan accounts, strove to reconcile these discrepancies and proposed conciliatory attempts that were themselves remarkably divergent. Reuss enabled me to grasp the absolute opposition that exists between Matthew's text, in which the parents of Jesus flee to Egypt immediately after the visit of the magi, and Luke's text, where the holy family peacefully returns to Nazareth forty days after the birth of the divine child. Of course he added that faith in Christ was not at the mercy of a problem with chronology; but I had to acknowledge that at least one of the gospel accounts of the Infancy, either Matthew's or Luke's, was little more than a story and that the apologists' defenses were pure illusions. As for the end of the world prophecy, Reuss assured me that Jesus had not erred in any way, but he did demonstrate beyond question that the first three evangelists, falsifying Christ's thought, placed his visible and material return immediately after the destruction of Jerusalem. Which amounts to saying that the gospel story begins with a story and ends with a myth.

Each of these findings was enough to kill my faith immediately, without the least appeal. In fact, over many months, despite the blows they showered upon it, their total force did not succeed in destroying it. Various expedients worked together to achieve this result.

One consisted in isolating dogmas as such from exegetical questions, setting up between the two the "chaos magnum" spoken of by Abraham in the gospel, that is to say an impassable chasm. In order to deepen and broaden this chasm I decided, from the beginning of 1885, to meditate using Hurter's theology course. The book remained permanently open on my mantlepiece. Each morning I read several lines which I digested while walking in my room. When the work of assimilation was complete, I went on to the following lines. So the process continued until the end of the prescribed half hour. During this time I tried to make the Fathers' agreement on dogma come alive. I imagined the Fathers' unanimous chorus of which my masters of theology at Angers had so often spoken: "conclamant Patres." And to the shifting sands of exegesis I opposed the solid rock of Christian dogmas.

Parallel to the meditation on dogmas I resolved to employ diversion. But of what kind? Walking, which I tried first proved ineffective. My thoughts, my preoccupations accompanied me. After several walks (not more than three) I understood that only work, absorbing work, could provide the distraction I needed; so I started to study Sanskrit. After several months' work, I succeeded in deciphering a few texts.

Third remedy: I did what those who suffer do. I felt my burden, once I had shared it, would be greatly lightened with two or three to carry it.

My confessor was the priest who had introduced me to Latin and who had taken charge of my education; he tenderly loved me and was like a foster father. At confessing, in principle I needed only to tell him my sins so I could have kept my state of soul hidden, which was not a sin. However the rights of a father seemed more extensive than the rights of a confessor. So I shared with M. Gendron the difficulties that distressed my soul. Among my seminary colleagues M. Ceillier,[75] the professor of philosophy, combined a superior intellect with outstanding virtues. I had a respect for him that bordered on veneration. I used to seek out his company. Often during recreation the two of us would converse; and our exchanges, never mundane, bore exclusively upon the problems of philosophy and physics that were familiar to him. To him too I bared my soul; I told him the effect my study of Reuss had had on me.

These were the three remedies I sought against the pain that gnawed at me. Now I must tell you how they worked. First of all what I took away from these confidences. At the tribunal of penance it is not unusual to hear pious souls accuse themselves of doubting the faith. The confessor is well aware that these doubts have not been followed by any consent. He prescribes trampling them underfoot, pouring scorn on them, not to look at them as obstacles to communion. The product of good sense, this treatment reassures the penitent and things go no further. M. Gendron and M. Ceillier gave me the same response; they assimilated my state of mind to that of the pious faithful. Both were excusable; they hadn't the least idea of the problems that appalled me. I had been wrong to present them with a situation beyond their understanding. But, once I recognized my error, I profited from the lesson. I withdrew into myself and ceased confiding any further.

Friendship was powerless to heal me. The remedy of diversion was not any more effective. Isolated, far from scientific milieux, what was I going to do with the scraps of Sanskrit I had acquired? And what good would it serve to be ten times more proficient? I concluded that the study of Sanskrit was a mistake. I gave it up and returned to Hebrew.

However Hebrew meant contact with the Bible. And contact with the Bible meant dreadful storms in which dogma was inevitably going to founder if I did not succeed in isolating it from exegesis. Salvation lay in isolating dogma, protecting it from the debilitating influence of exegesis. The other two remedies failed miserably; only this one could preserve my faith. This was the last illusion to which I clung with fierce obstinacy and which was soon to elude my grasp.

Part One: How I Freed Myself of Dogma

If it were only a question of dates, it would have been possible to settle this deep divide between exegesis and dogma. However, the chronological difficulties paled before the facts ranged before me. What worried and distressed, what was beyond bearing, were the deceits, the contradictions, the puerile legends, the myths with which the Old Testament was awash and which even infected the gospels. In the light of these findings what became of the divine inspiration of the Bible? How could one believe that God could inspire forgers with the idea of deceiving us? How could one imagine that he instigated or simply countenanced the written composition of narratives devoid of all reality and contradictory besides? And yet, the inspiration of the Bible, of all its books, all its pages and all its texts is a dogma, one of the fundamental dogmas of Christianity, one of those on which the agreement of the Fathers, the "conclamant Patres" is the most imposing, the most decisive. This dogma was compromised once and for all and with it the "conclamant Patres." One of the assertions that make up Christian dogmatics, the one that is the cornerstone of the building, was reduced to nothing: what would become of the others? The unanimous voice of the Fathers had been used to sanction error on a major point: what was it worth on others? The infancy of Jesus had been transformed by legend: was his resurrection any more believable? To preserve Jesus's honor I had accepted that his prophecy on the end of the world had been distorted, travestied by the evangelists: had his other pronouncements been preserved from a similar fate? Finally, Christian revelation rested on the Mosaic revelation which it claimed to inherit and whose books it had appropriated for itself: how could it endure when its foundation had collapsed? There was no doubt that when the Mosaic revelation, a mixture of fables and deceptions, collapsed it dragged Christianity down with it. And my effort to separate the two was mere fantasy.

3

March 18, 1886

THESE CONCLUSIONS TRIED TO force their way into my soul for a year; and for a year I resisted them. For a year this duel between science, which wanted to impose its verdict upon me, and myself, who rejected it, was day-by-day, nearly moment-by-moment. Throughout this whole period the fighting went on unabated; but nor did the battle ever remain the same. At the outset my reaction against it was instantaneous, stunning. Then, little by little, science's battering became more terrible and my defense weaker. It could not have been otherwise. Every day, in fact, the findings of science were reinforced. Also, every day I caught the apologists red-handed, guilty not only of ignorance but of trickery, and their name alone was enough to invoke in me La Fontaine's[76] words:

> Chameleon people, a people aping their master.

Forty years later, I learned that Mgr Mignot[77] felt the same way and used a more lively term to express it.*

Out of the numerous observations I made, two were particularly painful. One concerned Mgr Freppel. I have already spoken of my enthusiasm for his studies of the early Church Fathers and of the obedience with which I accepted his teaching, including his writings on the authenticity of the Areopagite's books. But one day I read the note in which Tillemont,[78] summarizing the work of Morin[79] and Launoy,[80] shows that the Areopagite was a forger from the end of the fifth century. I realized then that Freppel had set himself up as defender of a thesis whose falsity could not have escaped

---

* He called them buffoons.

PART ONE: How I Freed Myself of Dogma

him, that he had said the opposite of his private opinion solely out of a concern not to compromise his future.

Another equally distressing example of a different type came from a professor of the Rennes Faculty of Letters, Martin, who died around 1884. This phenomenal scholar was also an ardent defender of dogmas; and in one of the notes crammed with texts that filled part of his book on *La Vie future*[81] (note 10 of the second edition) he had defended the authenticity of the Pentateuch against what he called the "paradox of German exegesis." After reading Reuss, I had proof positive that Martin had not the slightest idea of the problem about which he spoke with such assurance. He was most certainly incapable of deception and his sincerity was beyond doubt. But in the end he had given a verdict on a question on which he lacked the requisite knowledge. He had abandoned his habitual integrity precisely on a doctrinal point of major importance. This momentary lapse in scientific method by a scholar whom I deeply admired was painful. It was a pain all the more intense since it had been caused by concerns over faith and, without those, would never have arisen.

Science's increasingly intense attacks also became more persistent. They finally turned into an obsession. What of my defense? It also progressed, but slowly and weakly. Denial, quick at first, was longer in coming and intervened later and later each day. Then it no longer occurred at all and I did not attempt to dislodge the conclusions of science fixed in my mind. This was where I had come to at the beginning of 1886. The conclusions of science occupied my soul like a conquered city; they ruled there without resistance.

But here is where the situation became complicated to the point of incoherence. My exercises of piety lost nothing of their customary punctuality. Each morning, from five thirty to six o'clock, I made my meditation while walking in my room. The recitation of the breviary, spiritual reading, visit to the Blessed Sacrament continued at the same times as in the past. Finally, in the evening, toward nine o'clock, when the seminarians were in bed, I recited my rosary while walking in the cloister. The old habits claimed their due and I did not think of denying them. No act of will interposed; all was done automatically. I deserved no credit for leading a life regular as clockwork since I never went out, except for dining on Sunday evenings with my parents, who lived close to the seminary, and for confession to M. Gendron who, since 1882, had been a member of the chapter. Only the state of my soul made this regularity strange.

March 18, 1886

The gospel teaches that one cannot serve two masters. Taken literally, this oracle is inexact. I experienced this myself, I who for several months thought as a rationalist and acted as a Christian. My mind followed one law; my feeling obeyed another: I served two masters. What is true is that this uncoordinated regime cannot be prolonged indefinitely and that sooner or later offended logic will reclaim its rights. For several months my reason, confined to its intellectual sphere, let habits guide my feelings. However, one day it broke out and decided on no more signs of the cross, or prayers which were for it only ridiculous pretenses.

Suppressing exercises of piety meant eradicating old habits. The latter protested vigorously. They indignantly repeated what the passions had once said to Augustine (*Confessions* 8:11): "How will you be able to live without us?" "putasne sine istis poteris." Deafened by this uproar, reason gave in and provided a stay of execution. But its setback could only be short-lived. The duel between science and faith but lately fought in my soul reappeared, setting reason and habits at odds. It had the same course, the same progress and also the same outcome. Reason stressed its resolve, habits progressively gave up their assertions, their requirements.

They received their coup de grâce on March 18, 1886, a little after one o'clock. I mechanically opened my breviary and made the sign of the cross to begin vespers. It was first vespers of the feast of St. Joseph. The feast brought up the Infancy narratives with their unresolvable contradictions. I abruptly closed my breviary which I had scarcely opened and said in an undertone: "These stories are fables, the Bible is filled with falsehoods, Christian dogmatics is based on nothing; I will no longer recite the breviary." Then, to confirm that these words had not inadvertently escaped and that they expressed an irrevocable decision, I repeated several times in an indignant tone: "Christian dogmatics is based on nothing; it is over; I will no longer recite the breviary."

Several hours later I responded only with a derisive smile to the prompting of habit that called me to matins. However that evening I had a difficult conquest to make. It was nearly nine o'clock. I took my usual walk in the deserted and shadowed cloisters. Suddenly I was surprised to find myself holding the rosary that I had unconsciously drawn out of my pocket. The rosary! From age thirteen I had not let a single day go by without its complete recitation. From then onward it had been my inseparable companion. How could I dismiss it? On the other hand, the "ave marias" it brought to my lips no longer made sense. I was stunned. But habit,

Part One: How I Freed Myself of Dogma

exploiting my embarrassment, seized control and got me walking: I recited some "ave marias." But of course this could not last. After a dozen "ave marias," I halted, out of breath. Then I berated myself for being a coward in having obeyed the tyranny of habit. The shame I felt was salutary. The following evening I had no desire to say the rosary.

It was not on March 18, 1886 that I stopped believing in dogmas; for, over several months faith had no place in my mind. However it was on that day that I realized it was dead and, smelling its putrefaction, expelled the corpse from my soul. On these grounds March 18, 1886 remains the most important date in my life.

Almost half a century has passed since this event that I recount today (October 6, 1931) and which is so significant to me. I have only a few details to add: (1) I would have yielded to a foolish presumption if, at age 25, I had undertaken to expose contradictions and deceptions in the Bible all by myself. Not for an instant nor to any degree whatsoever did I have this ridiculous pretension. My relationship to the Bible was that of an adolescent's to the geometry theorems he seeks to prove. He proves them, that is, he is familiar with the series of deductions which lead to these theorems. He would not have been able to invent steps by himself. The work compiled by several generations of men, from Thales to Euclid, is presented to him ready made. He is asked only to make it his own. This is not beyond his intellectual capacity; and so he is able to prove the theorems of the circumference of the circle or the square of the hypotenuse. No more did I make any personal discovery in the Bible. I simply assimilated the results obtained by Reuss and his predecessors. Before accepting them I always compared them with the assertions of Catholic exegetes. I established that advocates for the Church either sidestepped the objections or misrepresented them, or opposed them with miserable subterfuges. The conclusion that despite myself developed, little by little in my mind, and one day shattered me by its conviction, is that Christian revelation is founded on incoherent stories and falsehoods.

(2) It is possible to struggle against evidence for a time; but soon all resistance becomes impossible: it is necessary to yield. Anyone who cares to repeat my experience will come to the same conclusion. If aspirants to the priesthood received a serious education in seminary, prior to their vows, they would abandon the cassock after a few weeks and return to the world. If the faithful knew a few scraps of truth, they would not long remain under the tutelage of the Roman Church. However, clerics and faithful only have

March 18, 1886

access to books that keep them in the dark. I am mistaken. Even in recent times during which Catholic writers have been under continual surveillance, some apologists, in a sudden burst of honesty, have tried to remove a few falsehoods from their writings. Their ambitions have been modest. They have carefully avoided saying that Deuteronomy, Daniel, the second letter of Saint Peter are the work of forgers. They have limited themselves to lifting a small corner of the veil of truth. Even so this was too much. Several resounding condemnations, one of which concerned a *Manuel biblique*[82] used in nearly all French seminaries, have taught the world that Catholics have to remain submerged in the womb of darkness. In Plato's cave men saw the light only indirectly, but they did see it. In the Roman Church all light must be extinguished.

All light? In the Middle Ages there were wreckers on the coasts who, with cleverly set fires, lured vessels onto reefs where they broke apart, and who then seized the victims. Thus the Roman Church attracts souls and holds them under its yoke. But the fires it uses for this work of propaganda are fueled by lies. It is the archwrecker.

4

After Liberation

Shipboard passengers tormented to the point of exhaustion by the tossing of the ship, recover their health back on firm ground. That was how I felt on the morning of March 19, 1886. The battles in which I had been engaged for over twenty months had filled my soul with an immense sorrow. As soon as I set my foot on the rock of truth it was as if I were flooded with calm and security and forever freed from the tossings of faith.

Forever. I have been told of certain young priests who found their faith returned to them after it had been thrown out. The faith these imprudent men drove away was still alive. Mine, by contrast, was dead; and when one is dead, one is dead forever. From March 18, 1886 onward, I never prayed in private.

The calm and security that never left me were soon joined by another feeling which I must mention here. I considered Christian dogmatics, as a product of the human imagination, of much the same value as Buddhist dogmatics. But Christian dogmas were enshrined in liturgy; and this liturgy had cradled my childhood and sustained my adolescence. During the long months of my crisis ceremonies seemed obsolete, childish or even ridiculous. I was in the Church then. From the day on which, deep down, I knew I had left, my outlook changed. Stained glass windows, looked at from the outside present only formless colors, while seen from inside they are radiant with light. In contrast, looking at ceremonies from the outside brought back childhood memories bathed in poetry. One day when I had gone to say Mass at an orphanage in the city, I was at the altar when children sang a hymn that I myself had sung when I was very young. Moved to the point of tears I had to stop for a few moments. I heard an inner voice

After Liberation

which spoke with a sadness mixed with anger: "Why is all that not true?" Then I understood the tenacity with which the Church seizes children. As the child's teacher she fills him with impressions that will follow him to the end. For the man she becomes the great enchantress. More than once I compared my condition to that of Adam and Eve driven out of paradise for having acquired the knowledge of good and evil: the myth of Eden seemed to have come true in me. These regrets, needless to say, surfaced only intermittently. Recognizing them as products of sentimental psychology, I was never tempted to attribute the least apologetic value to them. I will add that they were swallowed up forever in the great torment of 1892.

Peace in security and regret for lost illusions belong to the realm of emotions. In another area I had, from March 18, 1886, two serious matters to address: in the first place, a life plan; in the second, a program of studies.

First, the life plan. What should I do? Could I remain in the Church? Ought I not to leave?

Had I posed the question to ecclesiastical authorities, their only response would have been to expel me and to make it impossible to continue a ministry that, from their perspective, could only be a horrible sacrilege. If I had let my parents and my mentor, M. Gendron, know of the state of my soul, they would have died of broken hearts. Thus I could not confide in anyone. Asking advice was not an option; and I was reduced to deciding alone the choice that would henceforth determine my life.

The decision did not require much thought; it was not long in coming.

Civil servants know that the smallest breach of duty, legal action aside, will result in an administrative suspension that will shatter their life and bring shame, sorrow or even ruin upon their family. And this formidable prospect ordinarily keeps those who would be tempted to shirk their duty faithful to it. Among the clergy the only real crime in existence is breaking the law of celibacy. When it is made public, it plunges the faithful into deep distress and astonishment. But only rarely does it come to light. Not that breaking the law is infrequent. It is just that such crimes occur in the dark. The faithful are content to shut their eyes and do not want to be made to open them; the authorities, too, do everything possible not to know and not to have to intervene. Liberties are taken with the law of celibacy; but the takers remain in the ranks of the clergy; scandal is avoided: everyone benefits.

All these thoughts went round in my mind; they haunted me, but they also imposed compelling conclusions. To lay aside the cassock that I had

Part One: How I Freed Myself of Dogma

worn for ten years (I had entered seminary in 1876) to return to a civilian life that I had renounced by solemn oaths, would be to shatter my life, and wound my parents and my adoptive father; at the same time it would be denouncing myself publicly as guilty of a breach of duty, a crime.

What was my crime? Here the facts spoke with a bitter eloquence. I have said earlier (p. 24) how the Roman Church, through its aggressive legislation, through the tyrannical condemnations it directs against even the most modest bids for sincerity, keeps truth out of seminaries and crams aspirants to the priesthood full of falsehoods and fables. Its future ministers come to ordination with their minds filled with illusion. Then, taken up with ministry, having neither time nor taste for personal study, they generally tend to stick to the adulterated wares served up to them in seminary: they remain deceived. My crime, the result of intense labor, was to have seen through this deceit and to have refuted the lies which had ensnared me. An inexpiable crime in the view of the Roman Church, which, if she had been aware of it, would certainly have punished me. In laying aside the cassock, in leaving the clergy's ranks, I should have let the Church win; I would have inflicted on myself the punishment that the Church, unaware of the state of my soul, could not.

In a burst of indignation I cried out: "Because I have discovered the trap in which the Church ensnares the faithful and particularly aspirants to the priesthood, I should be obliged to condemn myself and my family to dreadful sufferings? No, that will not be. Promises made at knifepoint grant no rights to the cutthroat who exacts them. They impose no obligation on the victim who signs them. They are null. The Church that systematically hid the truth from me, that fed me lies, acted like a relentless cutthroat toward her victim. Methods differ; the dishonesty is the same. The Church has no rights over me. I certainly do not have to accept the verdict it would pronounce if it knew my state because this verdict would be merely a shameful travesty of justice. I have the right to impose myself on the Church. I will impose myself, I will continue to celebrate the rites to which it has bound me. She can only blame herself for the misfortune that has befallen her in my person. Moreover, other misfortunes of the same kind will inevitably continue to occur, if she does not quickly renounce falsehood and impart honest teaching to her clergy. But she surely knows that her seminaries would empty immediately and that her aspirants to the priesthood would return to the world after a few weeks if the truth were allowed to reach them. With the current regime in seminaries, only priests who have the time and taste for study can enlighten themselves. What is this insignificant loss beside the void that would occur if the teaching given in seminary were based on respect for the truth? The Church derives too much profit from falsehood ever to deprive herself of its services.

Having decided to remain in the Church, I needed to make no change to my life. Nothing was altered, except that study henceforth benefited from the two hours previously taken up with exercises of piety. For ten years I had been passionate about work; as of March 18, 1886, I worked furiously. I was ravenous for knowledge. I hastened to carry the torch of truth into religious and philosophical problems. Over several months I devoured the books of Renan,[83] Albert Réville,[84] Maurice Vernes,[85] Kuenen,[86] Michel Nicolas,[87] Colani,[88] Spencer, Taine (*L'Intelligence*),[89] of Fouillée,[90] Guyau,[91] Ribot,[92] without neglecting Voltaire. When the first effervescence wore off, an automatic classification took place. I grouped my ideas into levels superposed in order of density, I mean to say in order of the importance they had for me. Spencer, Taine, Ribot and Fouillée became my mentors in philosophy. But I did not feel any desire to know more about philosophy and the philosophical reading that I later did does not count. In the history of religion Réville's two volumes, *Les religions des peuples non civilisés*, made a profound impression on me. They seemed be of major importance; later I was gratified to learn that I had not overestimated their value. But my subsequent studies of the religions of Egypt, China, Persia and India, either through Réville or through other authors, put me off; at the end of several years I renounced overtaxing my memory with all this rubbish which only led to unverifiable speculations. I continued my translation of the Hebrew Bible and avidly read Renan's *Histoire du peuple d'Israël* which began to appear in 1887. But in other respects I was interested in Mosaic religion only for the light it shed on the history of Christian dogmas.

The history of Christian dogmas was, from 1886, the predominant object of my studies until they became their exclusive object. In the eyes of believers, all articles of faith come from the apostles, who received them from God; and, from the very beginning, the faithful have believed them. For that matter, this is the way things had to happen, if Christian religion came from heaven; for God himself would have had to place the seal of perfection on his works from the beginning. For believers there is not, cannot be a history of dogmas, unless that term is qualified in a way that distorts its meaning.

Part One: How I Freed Myself of Dogma

But the products of human activity are never perfect in the beginning. They all grow bit by bit; they all are subject to the law of development. Now, I had found pertinent proof that Christian dogmatics owes nothing to God and that it derives uniquely from man. It could not therefore have escaped the general law of development. How was it elaborated? Through what fumblings, what corrections did this great jumble of masonry assume the form it has today? I took on the task of resolving this enigma. It would be a lengthy process. But I had turned twenty-six only three months earlier; I would give whatever it needed. I set off on my explorations. In my initial fervor I had become acquainted with Réville's *Histoire du dogme de la divinité de Jésus-Christ* and with Coquerel's *Premières transformations du christianisme*.[93] These books had installed some markers for my route; I was not wandering entirely at random.

My first lengthy study centered on the "Logos" (the Word). I went back to Philo and read the texts to which Renan, Havet,[94] Vacherot,[95] and especially Jean Réville (*La doctrine du Logos*)[96] had referred. My conclusion was that the theory of the "Logos" derives from Philo and that, to take Havet's expression, Philo is "the first of the Church Fathers." From Philo's "Logos" I proceeded to the "Logos" of Saint Justin, Clement of Alexandria and Origen. Here my guides were Aubé (Saint Justin)[97] and Denis (*De la philosophie de l'Origène*).[98] I established that for all these doctors the "Logos" was inferior to the Father and used by him as agent.

My second study was inspired by Bossuet's *Defensio cleri gallicani* in which he confronts the papacy's claims with history and reduces them to nothing.[99] In his other works, this great bishop is often obliged to make fantastical exegeses of the texts. In the *Defensio* his information is impeccable. What particularly sticks with me from this vast inquiry is that, in the first eight general councils, the episcopate almost always took upon itself to pronounce judgment on pontifical professions of faith. In order to clarify this I immersed myself in the study of the councils. I read, in part, the first volumes of Labbe's collection,[100] taking as guides Tillemont (as far as Chalcedon) and Héfélé.[101] Later, when I became acquainted with Funk's magisteral writings on the convocation, presidency and confirmation of the councils, they taught me nothing essential.[102] The study of the sources had led me to the same result.

It is also Bossuet (*De la communion sous une espèce*) who led me to study the Roman *Ordo* and Mabillon's commentary on this book.[103] At that point I began to learn about the rites of the early Middle Ages, rites that

After Liberation

are for theology what the fossils are for geology; rites that brought back to life concepts long since vanished. I believed that dogmas, except that of the papacy, had accomplished their evolution before the sixth century; the Roman "Ordo" taught me that in the ninth century the real presence had still not made its way into the Roman Church. Ménard's notes on Saint Gregory's sacramentary (that I read next) convinced me that indicative absolution also did not exist at this time.[104] It was as if a new area of the history of dogma had been opened before me. It must surely contain other riches: I promised myself to explore it more thoroughly.

But the Fathers of the first five centuries seemed to deserve priority. Beginning in 1887 I studied Saint Cyprien. Rigault, whose edition I had at hand, made every effort to highlight the good passages; and the suggestions he gave did not fall on deaf ears. Clearly Saint Cyprien considered the bishop of Rome as a colleague and had not the least notion of the papacy. Some time later I read in Bossuet (*Mémoire sur la bibliothèque ecclésiastique de Dupin*) that Rigault was "the least theological of men."[105] By way of protest I wrote in my copy (Besançon edition 7, 192) this note in pencil: "Rigault is a critic of the first order; his notes on Cyprian are the bronze impervious to the venom of theologians."

From Saint Cyprian I went on to the Apostolic Fathers read in the Leipzig edition; then to Saint Justin whom I studied in Otto's text;[106] then to several of the doctors of the fourth century. I would not return to the theology of Middle Ages until 1892. For several months the doctors of the ninth and twelfth centuries were my companions. Several taught that there are four sacraments. Peter Lombard[107] explained that original sin consists of concupiscence and that the Holy Virgin remained tarnished with this stain until the moment she became a mother. Saint Bernard introduced me to his letter to the canons of Lyon in which he declares that belief in the Immaculate Conception is a superstition.[108]

In August of 1892 Saint Augustine's books lay on my table. Two years previously I had consulted them on the subject of penance. This time I wanted to know their thought on the eucharist. I directed myself first to the sermons on first communion, then to the treatises on Saint John. Other works of lesser importance were likewise consulted. All the texts turned the eucharist into a symbol. Not one gave an inkling of the real presence. It was Sunday, August 21st. At the conclusion of vespers I returned to work and drew up the outcome of my inquiry. At five-thirty there occurred an incident following which my pen dropped from my hand. I shall recount it

PART ONE: How I Freed Myself of Dogma

below. But beforehand I must speak of a philosophical advance I have not yet mentioned.

I have said (p. 11) that reading Père Dechamps had led me, in 1883, to consider God, in his role as creator, as a father whose duty is to surround his children with care. Several weeks after my liberation, I returned to this notion, abandoned since 1884. I returned to it spontaneously, automatically. "Yes, I said to myself, a creator God is necessarily the father of the men who owe their existence to him. As such he cannot have remained indifferent to humanity's plight. He must have lavished upon it his moral and material care. In short, Revelation is truly the complement and the prolongation of creation. These two facts are indissolubly linked to one another just as a consequence is to its source. It is impossible to separate them. And, if one failed, it would lead the other into oblivion with it. But Christian revelation is an illusion; it did not exist. Which amounts to saying that no revelation has occurred, since Christian revelation alone is worthy of attention. The human species has been left to itself, to the extravagances of its imagination. Never has a celestial ray of light illuminated its path and guided its way. The creator God's duty was to take care of humanity. In this essential obligation he has failed. And, as he could not possibly fail in this way, the human mind must give up the premise of a nonexistent consequence. Men are not God's children. God is not their father; he did not give them their existence. And the dogma of the creator God is an illusion." Later I studied the problem of evil in its full scope, and my conclusion emerged from this study singularly strengthened.[109] But it was already taking possession of my mind in the weeks that followed my liberation from dogma. From the spring of 1886 I ceased believing in a creator God, in the God of Christianity.

5

Dismissal

THE MINER WHO WORKS one hundred meters below ground extracting coal was no more separate from men than I was, intellectually speaking, from other priests. At meals I had contact with my colleagues, but also with the ecclesiastics of the diocese who came each day wanting to stay at the seminary. Sometimes I envied their blissful ignorance as one might envy the innocence of a child. And then I saw science as a trap into which I had had the misfortune to fall. But one does not waste time regretting a childhood lost forever. I, too, quickly returned to reality. I reminded myself that the Church's lies were the real trap and that study had freed me from them. Then, after this observation, the voice of duty spoke. It said that, freed from error, I ought to wrest the Church's victims from her and devote a part of my life to spreading the truth.

I did not remain deaf to duty's call. At the same time as I worked to acquire the truth, I did my best to be its apostle. The task demanded a great deal of prudence. I needed to avoid shocking people and triggering a reaction from faith. My apostolate began with the narrative of the flood in Genesis. I arranged in two parallel columns the documents which in that book most frequently interlock. I then presented this modest effort to several friends. At the end of a quarter of an hour, all were convinced. All recognized that, under its apparent unity, the flood narrative really contains two narratives. I was careful not to push my demonstration all the way, by showing that these narratives were in disagreement. I limited myself to pointing out their existence. By the same blow Vigouroux's manual was proven guilty of concealing the real problem; it was discredited. And this second result was intentional.

Part One: How I Freed Myself of Dogma

I also read to several friends a dissertation aimed at proving that psalms 43, 73 and 78 of the Vulgate are of Maccabean origin. The demonstration appeared decisive according to theological method. I explained that this was not a question of faith. But I was obliged to refute Vigouroux's manual which placed the closure of the biblical canon at the time of Esdras. And this refutation did little for the prestige of said manual already shaken by the study of the flood.

I also acquainted them with Saint Bernard's letter to the canons of Lyon. Naturally, none of the priests to whom I read it were familiar with it. To clarify the arguments of the holy doctor, I explained that, at his time, original sin was supposed to consist in concupiscence. I took care to add that the actual dogma of original sin was not negated by the prevailing early medieval theory and that the dogma of the Immaculate Conception was not overturned by Saint Bernard's opposition. But my stunned interlocutor was obliged to recognize that the theological manuals left various things unclear.

The priests capable of comprehending these useful pieces of information were fewer than a dozen. Even with them I could not go very far; on the contrary, I soon had to stop. In sum, I had no one in whom to confide. After several hours spent below ground, the miner I mentioned above returns to the surface and enjoys the company of his friends. I was condemned to remain at the bottom of my shaft. Each day I said with the prophet (Isa 55:8): "Non enim cogitationes meae cogitationes vestrae." ["For my thoughts are not your thoughts."] But I had to keep even these words to myself. I was isolated; I suffered a great deal. In 1892, my suffering, which grew even greater, had become intolerable. My boiling thoughts would no longer endure the compression to which they had been subjected for many years. They absolutely had to come out. A day came when the boiler blew. It would not serve any purpose to give a detailed description of the catastrophe and its consequences. I will limit myself to a succinct report without which the rest of my story would be incomprehensible.

In 1887 two seminarians asked me to teach them Hebrew. After consulting the superior and obtaining his authorization, I acceded to their request. From this point onward I always had several Hebrew students under my wing. On August 1st, 1892, I made clearly heterodox remarks to one of them—and one only. Four days later another of my students learned of the August 1st conversation at which he had not been present.[110] He immediately consulted his director, general secretary of the archdiocese who said roughly this: "The superior of the seminary is presently with his family and it would be difficult to speak with him. But in the latter half of August, he will be directing a retreat with sisters at Paramé (near Saint-Malo). It is near your own home. At that time you can go and find him and tell him what you know."

Friday, August 19, M. Ceillier, summoned urgently to Paramé, was informed of everything and told to warn M. Gendron, whom he was not able to meet until Sunday the 21st. That day, toward five-thirty, the door at the far end of the library, whose existence was known only to regular users, opened silently.* It was M. Gendron who, according to habit, entered without knocking. I rose to meet him. Without responding to my greeting, he questioned me in a choked voice: "What are you doing?" I replied that I was in the midst of reading Saint Augustine. He brusquely questioned me: "What have I just heard? They say that you no longer have faith!" Then he summarized the conversation of August 1st. The details he provided allowed no reply. I acknowledged that his information was correct. I added: "It is over." Then I moved away. But he, running after me, cried: "No, it is not over. You will always be my son." Faced with this unexpected display of affection, I stood shock-still, powerless to move a pace or utter a word. He continued: "Tomorrow I will go to Paramé to see the superior. Come to see me tomorrow evening. We will take care of your situation." Then he left.

Each Sunday evening, toward seven o'clock, I dined with my mother who lived three minutes from the seminary. The hour had come: I set off. In seeing my despondency and the difficulty I had in moving, my mother asked me whether I was ill. Instead of reassuring her, I tried to worry her further. She needed to be prepared for acute heartbreak. I barely ate. I left an hour later, doing my best to conceal the agony that tormented me.

Back at the seminary, I went to the library to put away the books lying open on my worktable and standing on the floor about me. Then, overcome with fatigue and emotion, I shut myself up in a seminarian's cell. There, seated in a chair, I passed the night and nearly the whole of Monday. I called on death. But I wanted to die far from my mother and to avoid scandal. My plan was to go abroad and die of hunger in a corner of a field. This scheme did not require abundant resources. I decided to take with me only the hundred francs necessary to cross the frontier and to send my modest savings (in 1882 after my ordination M. Gendron had made me a gift of

---

* Since 1886 I had spent all my vacation time in the library except during ecclesiastical retreats for which I was obliged to leave.

PART ONE: How I Freed Myself of Dogma

several thousand francs) to my brother who would use them to look after my mother.

When evening came I took from the refectory a piece of bread that I ate with a pear and a glass of water. That done, I went with uncertain steps to see M. Gendron, who was back from Paramé. For the last five years he had deposited all his securities with me, which amounted to three thousand francs of annuity, repeatedly telling me that after his death this fortune would be my sole property. I brought him this allowance. He had shed many tears at Paramé and his words were still broken with sobbing. He said to me: "The Superior has put five hundred francs at your disposal; you will be able to access them tomorrow at the Gicquel bank. And then, he has heard you speak several times, with respect, of Fr. de Broglie.[111] He thinks you would do well to consult him. In any case, you should be able to obtain employment outside the diocese in an ecclesiastical collège. You would allege reasons of conscience that prevent you from saying Mass. But make a retreat with the Trappists. I will join you there next week."

My state of collapse rendered me incapable of any reply. I listened in silence to this monologue that was based on absolute incomprehension of my state of mind. I did not interrupt: not even to say that I refused the five hundred francs placed at my disposal. I left without saying anything about my plan.

Tuesday the 23rd I went to my mother's. Surprised by this unusual visit and, moreover, not entirely recovered from the worry that Sunday's encounter had caused her, my mother asked me if I was still ill. I said that the doctor had prescribed immediate, absolute and prolonged rest. I was thus compelled to renounce my professorship and leave the seminary. These words struck terror in my mother's soul and she said in an anguished tone: "What will become of you?" I replied that the diocesan administration would look after me and that I was going to spend some months in the midi. I gathered together all the forces of my soul to hide my distress. But nevertheless I could not conceal from the poor woman that it would be a long time before we should see one another again. I added that my brother would take care of her.

On my return to the seminary, I met M. Ceillier who awaited me. As taciturn, reserved, and even harsh as he had seemed the preceding Saturday and Sunday, he was now affable, benevolent, and considerate. First he said that the previous day he had looked everywhere for me but in vain. Then he offered to buy my library and asked me how he could help. He did not know what service he could do me. At noon, despite my protests, he dragged me to the refectory where I did not want to go and obliged me to dine with him.

Several hours later, I could see that this show of benevolence was an effort aimed at preparing the ground for my conversion. In the midst of a conversation M. Ceillier said to me: "I do not wish to engage in discussion. But I know that evil constitutes for you an objection against the existence of God. Do you not think that the problem of evil is resolved by the mystery of redemption in which we see Our Lord make up for the offense offered to God by sin?" I did not want to oppose any spoken reply to this pious nonsense and I merely gave a sign of denial with a slow shake of the head. M. Ceillier then said in a subdued voice: "I do not insist."

Wednesday, the 24th, I entrusted to M. Ceillier a sealed packet whose content I did not reveal to him and asked him to deliver it to my brother at the earliest opportunity. He promised he would do as I asked.

I had to take the evening train. Immediately after lunch I went to say farewell to M. Gendron. He spoke again of my making a retreat, still completely misunderstanding my state of mind. I let his proposal drop without replying and prepared to leave. Then he broke out sobbing and fell on his knees before me while uttering the following cries and others of a similar sort: "Oh my Joseph! you who were so pious, I beg you, remember your ordination. Think of your first Mass at which you prayed like an angel." I, too, fell to my knees bursting into tears. He took me in his arms, saying: "Give me a comforting word, a word of consolation. I know that you revere M. Ceillier. Do you want to make a confession to him?"

A word of acquiescence replied to this request. When it escaped my mouth was it voluntary? Was it conscious? Forty years later I am inclined to think not. The immense distress of this father on his knees and in tears was infectious; it overcame me and became my own. My acquiescence, when I gave it, was undoubtedly one of those impulsive gestures through which we instinctively bring relief to unfortunates who implore our pity. We ourselves suffer the suffering before us which cuts us to our heart. In promising to go to confession, to go through a rite devoid of any kind of meaning, my thought, to the degree that I had one, was only to appease the sorrow that also deeply grieved me.

The effect was instantaneous. M. Gendron immediately sprang up while saying: "Come, I shall bring you to him." We left. It was around two-thirty.

Part One: How I Freed Myself of Dogma

From the square of Saint-Pierre where we were, to the seminary where we were going, it was a hurried walk of ten minutes. We covered this distance rapidly and in absolute silence. He was as happy as a shipwrecked person who, against all hope, has escaped the yawning abyss and put his foot on firm ground. I was also happy, but nonetheless perplexed. I was going to submit to an examination. What would the outcome be? M. Ceillier had prompted and received the detailed confidences of the young priest shocked by my conversation. Unlike M. Gendron, he was not in complete ignorance of my mental state. He must have understood something of my state of soul. Would he believe my sincerity?

But I was not to dwell long on this problem. M. Gendron went into M. Ceillier alone to inform him of this new development. Five minutes later, he came out and it was my turn to enter. "I wish to go to confession" I said without any preamble. The reply, expressed in an affectionate but reserved tone was: "Willingly, my dear friend." And I knelt on the prie-dieu. Scarcely had my confession begun when M. Ceillier gave me an emotional embrace: "Ah! dear friend," he said to me, "do not lose heart, you are near to Our Savior." I then added: "I wish to submit myself to the Church's authority, to believe what it commands me to believe. But it is impossible to settle my thought on any dogma; I can only rely on the authority of the Church." "This is the essential," replied my confessor, "have confidence, you have faith."

At that moment, with a vehemence that revealed the depth of my soul, I uttered these words: "I would lie if I admitted to having sinned in renouncing faith. I cannot consider myself culpable on this point." But no sooner had this declaration been made than I realized my imprudence. It was irreconcilable with theology, which taught that one cannot lose faith without sinning. I had not reckoned on saying it. It had slipped out. The indulgence that had welcomed my first admissions had induced this frankness. But this time had I not presumed too much of my confessor's liberalism?

To my great surprise M. Ceillier let these words pass without protest. Much later I learned that he considered me a victim of a mental breakdown, of a kind of madness caused by an excess of work and which had made me not responsible. Tactfully, at this time he kept this charitable interpretation to himself, he did not give me the clue to the puzzle. He gently asked me only this: "Since you lost your faith you must have made some pious exercises, recited some prayers?" "Never in private" I said to him. "Not even some signs of the cross?" "None." This unexpected reply left poor M.

Ceillier in disarray. His broadmindedness did not extend to understanding an unbeliever who had renounced all prayer. He remained silent for a short while. Then, taking hold of himself he spoke to me of the goodness of God. Finally he gave me absolution with the order even so to refrain from saying Mass for the three remaining days of the week and to resume my ministry on Sunday, August 28th. In an attempt to reassure him I went immediately to my room to gather all my notebooks (except those which dated from the time I was a seminarian and which, relegated to a cupboard that I never opened, escaped my attention). They formed two groups: one given over to preparing my courses in theology; the other allotted to biblical studies and to the history of dogmas. There were also two notebooks reserved for extracts. The first group was composed of fifteen notebooks each made up of twenty-five sheets of large-format paper. In the second were some thirty notebooks all of which, except one, were bound, each having around two hundred pages. The first group, which represented considerable work on my part, had no value for me. The second, on the contrary, was a treasure in which all my research, either in exegesis or in the history of dogmas, was gathered.

During the four days I spent at the seminary after my confession, M. Ceillier took great care to protect the precious seedling he had just replanted in my soul from the poisonous blast of hell. He thought he would familiarize himself with my notebooks he had in his keeping so as to provide me with a solution for the errors surely contained in them. But the next day, he said with great ingenuity: "I have seen the titles of your notebooks. There are more than twenty that treat Sacred Scripture. I have tried to read one of those devoted to dogmas. But I stopped straightaway because I admit it troubled me. I think it would be best to burn it immediately. Is that not your view?" The slightest hesitation would have meant my loss. I acquiesced in an undertone. Only this obligatory and painful sacrifice lifted me out of my torpor and prompted a presence of mind great enough to ask for the restitution of two of my notebooks, explaining that I had conscientiously volunteered everything, but that the two notebooks in question contained nothing or nearly nothing reprehensible and that they could be useful to me. One, whose table of contents I showed, was only concerned with the Fathers and ought, in consequence, to be inoffensive: he returned it to me without examining it. He skimmed through the other. It contained the thoughts of various authors. Those which were only audacious could pass. However several had an aggressive character. Then M. Ceillier, taking

Part One: How I Freed Myself of Dogma

his scissors, said to me with a slight smile: "I shall leave you the task of cutting them." And, adopting a mask of indifference, I clipped away. This poor mutilated notebook is precious for the memories it evokes. The other contained numerous examples of an archaic theology and notably Saint Augustine's texts on the eucharist. It was this notebook which helped me on the 21st day of August when my life was shattered. It had for me an inestimable price. I was proud of the ruse that I had employed to save it; proud of having succeeded in deceiving, not M. Ceillier, but the great school of error he represented.

David, while among the Philistines, and learning that the king of the country sought to kill him, feigned madness to save his life (1 Sam 21:14). On August 24th, 1892, in order to escape the wrath of the Roman Church which held me in its clutches, in order to save my own life and those of my family, I submitted to the rite of confession, I handed over my notebooks, I feigned madness; I imitated David. It was the Pharisees' choice to close their eyes to the innocent ruse that brought salvation. I congratulated myself and blessed the marvelous chain of unexpected coincidences that made it possible. Among these coincidences, perhaps one of the most surprising was the blindness of M. Ceillier who, after his inquiry to my student of Saturday, August 20th, believed in the sincerity of my conversion. In all likelihood it can be explained like this. A complete stranger to criticism of biblical texts, M. Ceillier understood literally nothing of my objections against the Pentateuch (I had not yet spoken of Daniel to my student) of which he heard only a pallid resumé without having seen the texts and their irresistible force. The Bible, which he had been taught to revere since childhood, had manifestly been dictated by God and only prejudice could obscure its celestial origin. He understood philosophical difficulties: but the latter, as serious as they might be, did not supply any evidence and were always susceptible to solutions. The ordeal had thus opened my eyes and put an end to my frenzy. Moreover, in the course of my confession I had refused to characterize the disappearance of my faith as a sin. Would I have been so frank had I been a dissembler? M. Ceillier, who attributed my protest of innocence to a mental disorder, undoubtedly saw it as proof of my sincerity. And my imprudence probably contributed to saving me.

6

At the School of Late Vocations

NINE TIMES OUT OF ten the unfortunate soul who is struck on the head with a rock or hit by a heavy truck is killed instantly. When, by a miracle, his vital organs are unaffected, he falls unconscious, remains insensible over several days and only slowly recovers the use of his senses. The formidable shock I sustained did not kill me; but it had made me scatterbrained. I was a sort of inert mass. When glimmers of thought intermittently appeared, I saw my mother assured of a tranquil old age, my adoptive father free from the sorrow which would have brought him to an early grave. And this scene gave me a vague feeling of well-being. I then soon relapsed into catalepsy. As for my future, I had not the strength to think about it. Someone would take charge of sorting it out. The judge who held my fate in his hands was the superior of the major seminary, M. Guillois. For the ten years I had been subject to the authority of M. Guillois, I had been only too pleased with his attitude. He had always shown me great benevolence and, in several encounters, went out of his way to be pleasant to me. At the beginning he endeavored, through M Gendron's intervention, to moderate my ardor for work. However, he abandoned these efforts early on and let me have my own way. One day while dining at the seminary, when some ecclesiastics urged me to attend a celebration in spite of my refusal, M. Guillois said to them: "If you imagine you will interest him in anything other than his books, you do not know him."

He believed he knew me. But he had just learned, to his great surprise, that he was mistaken. Over ten years he had never had to reprimand me. But the denunciation of August faced him with a fault that had been concealed in my soul for six years.

Part One: How I Freed Myself of Dogma

And what a fault! One of the most serious a man could commit, the most heinous of all for an ecclesiastic. According to the Church's teaching, a layperson cannot renounce the faith he has professed without incurring a very grave sin. What then of a priest? Now I, a priest, was defiled with this sin, I had renounced the faith of my baptism. While I no longer believed in the rites of Christian religion, I had continued to celebrate them. For many years my conscience had been burdened with the most dreadful sacrileges. And also the most terrible censures. For I had incurred excommunication reserved to the sovereign pontiff. No doubt absolution had been granted me following repentance and confession. But I had received this blessing only by virtue of special powers. As I later learned, M. Guillois replied to M. Gendron and to M. Ceillier who interceded for me: "What do you want? He has incurred excommunication specially reserved to the sovereign pontiff."[112] In truth my fault was appalling.

It was, moreover, inconceivable. As vicar general, a member of the episcopal council, M. Guillois was aware of all the misfortunes involving the clergy, all the scandals great and small that periodically erupted in the parishes. These scandals stemmed entirely from carnal passions or drunkenness. He understood them; he accounted for them. But how to understand the fall into unbelief? Cohabiting priests, pederast priests, alcoholic priests who had crossed his path all remained faithful to their childhood faith. He himself had found reasons only to affirm his faith in the newspaper *Univers*,[113] his sole intellectual nourishment. My case, which he had never met before, appeared as a frightening anomaly. I was for him in the religious order what monsters with two heads or three legs are in the natural order.

M. Gendron and M. Ceillier both tried to sway him. For two or three days M. Ceillier believed that he would achieve victory. According to them, my aberrations derived from a fit of delirium brought on by the unrelenting work to which I had dedicated myself for the last ten years. He willingly accepted this explanation. He believed me a victim of an overinvolvement with books. All three were thus agreed on the cause of my misfortune. All three were horrified by the catastrophe to which excessive labor had led me. But, while my advocates concentrated on the overwork for which they claimed indulgence, the judge focused his attention on the appalling intellectual perversity that, for more than six years, had governed my life and that made a measure of protection imperative. The dialogue went thus:

"Excessive work has struck him with encephalitis and made him not responsible."

At the School of Late Vocations

"Your euphemism means that an excess of work has led him to madness. So be it. But lunatics are always suspect, even when they appear cured; and they cannot, without imprudence, be given employment."

Blinded by affection, M. Gendron and M. Ceillier made hay of the most sacred principles of theology. M. Guillois defended these principles. From the standpoint of orthodoxy alone he was right. Since 1892 I have, thousands of times, cursed the Roman Church that I ordinarily call the beast. But never had I harbored a hateful thought for the executor of her exalted works. I always considered myself lucky to have him to deal with.

And especially to have escaped the Tribunal of my archbishop. If my case had been brought to the episcopal council, I would have been expelled from the diocese. M. Guillois left Cardinal Place[114] and all his colleagues on the council in complete ignorance of my crime. In doing so, moreover, he thought only of his own peace of mind. Informed of my state of soul, the cardinal, who never missed a chance to reprimand his entourage, would have blamed the superior of his seminary and taxed him with negligence. It was thus solely to escape these humiliating reproaches that M. Guillois decided to take care of everything on his own. But I benefited from this tactic which had nothing to do with me: I remained in the diocese. And, if I were cast out of the ranks of the clergy, my two protectors could, at least, entertain the hope of my returning.

In the final days of August, M. Guillois informed the cardinal and his council that a nervous condition contracted through overwork obliged me to resign my professorate and all ministry for an undetermined period. From this day onward I was on the margins of the clergy.

What was to become of me? Five years earlier, M. Gendron had founded "The Work of Late Vocations," which was directed at young men too old to undertake regular studies and which sent them to major seminaries after two years of Latin. Cardinal Place was favorable to this enterprise and he placed at its disposal the major seminary's country house located six kilometers from Rennes. An advertisement was circulated. Young men immediately presented themselves. They came from the diocese of Rennes and from neighboring dioceses. They even came from distant dioceses and from countries outside France. In 1892 the school consisted of forty students, two of whom were Swiss, one an Alsatian, one Belgian, a Negro, a Creole and a Bulgarian. The enterprise thus prospered; but it was largely of a private character. Although Cardinal Place was favorable toward it, the diocese officially ignored it. It did not appear in the diocesan *Ordo*.

Part One: How I Freed Myself of Dogma

On prospectuses it bore the name "Saint Charles" (by way of flattery for Cardinal Place, whose first name was Charles). But M. Guillois feigned to know it only as Hallouvry, the name of the farm annexed to the country house and the name of the house itself on the land register.

In 1892 there were at the "École Saint-Charles" (or, if you wish, at Hallouvry) three professors, one of whom in addition to teaching directed the house in the name of M. Gendron and bore, for the students, the title of superior. One of the other two, recently ordained a priest, had, at his request, obtained a post as curate. To fill this vacancy, M. Gendron had spoken with M. Guillois, who had promised him one of his deacons. The drama of August 21st changed everything. The deacon designated for Hallouvry remained at seminary and I took his place. Lacking any official post, I nevertheless had employment. It was the plank of salvation after the shipwreck.

On the morning of August 29th, 1892, I left the major seminary forever. My library was simultaneously transported to M. Gendron's. I took with me two books, namely my breviary and my Bible. Half an hour later, I entered the school of late vocations. My real circumstances were revealed only after some days. For the moment, I was supposed to have come to the aid of M. Gendron who was going to receive the promised deacon only at the end of September. I thus introduced myself as professor of the major seminary; and it is, I should add, under this title that I had been announced by M. Gendron. The superior welcomed me with a deference in which he never failed from that time onward. Our relations preserved to the end the courtesy they had at the outset. Besides, after the first few days I shut myself up in unsociable isolation. I left as soon as meals were finished. We were together only at table. And, since a student did the reading, we maintained silence.

Death might overtake by surprise. If I died suddenly, the sincerity of my conversion would be believed. Since my confession of August 24th, I was obsessed by this thought; it was a nightmare and appalled me. I had had the courage to let myself be ground down by superstition; I did not have the strength to carry my secret to the grave. Scarcely had I entered my virtual prison where I had to stay for fifteen months, than I prepared to write my profession of faith. At first I intended simply to jot down a few lines to make honorable amends with the truth that filial affection had forced me to deny with my tongue. But before I had even started, recollections tumultuously bubbled from all corners of memory. All imperiously claimed a place and wanted to be mentioned. They were elements of the synthesis that, from my first serious studies, that is, since 1884, had progressively taken shape in my mind. I thought to set up a single stone. And yet here before me were the materials for a complete edifice. They were there, at hand, but in a heap, in disorder, scattered about. It was up to me to classify them, to put them in place, and above all to refine them, to sharpen them; for they were rough.

That required some time. In the meantime, I had a look at the very modest library the school possessed. I noticed several manuals of English presented by an anonymous benefactor. They were of no use to anyone. I took them to my room and applied myself to learning a little English. During this time my mind unconsciously and, in a way mechanically, started to polish up my theological ideas and put them in order. By September 8th I was ready and I sat down to write my profession of faith the composition of which probably required about ten days (space does not allow me to reproduce its thirty or so closely written pages).

Classes lasted two hours. I taught five each week. When my task was finished, I left my room, ostensibly reading my breviary, then disappeared into the park. When I was sure I could not be seen, the breviary was shut and I started bellowing with anger against the Roman Church. After half an hour, I retraced my steps to my room. There I studied English and German with the books that devoted friends passed to me. On Sunday I went out towards nine o'clock, first going to see my mother with whom I ate. I then made my way to M. Gendron's. This good father concealed his sorrow as best he could by talking to me about trivial things. He did not know what to say to me. Fortunately for him, the encounter was short; for, toward three o'clock, M. Ceillier arrived. M. Gendron then left me in the care of my doctor and fled.

A doctor M. Ceillier wished to be and he worked at this role with an admirable devotion. The weekly confession that I made was summed up in these words: "I recite without any difficulty all vocal prayers. I want to believe in all the mysteries; but it is absolutely impossible to put my mind to them. I cannot bear to contemplate any dogma; not even the existence of God. All I can do is submit to the authority of the Church. I am like an invalid who cannot bear daylight and is forced to keep his eyes shut." "My dear friend, faith is above all an act of will; you have the essentials of faith as soon as you want to believe and you accept the Church's authority. Only pray to hasten your cure and to be in a condition to open your eyes to the light." After which we recited

PART ONE: How I Freed Myself of Dogma

together matins and lauds. This done, he returned to the major seminary; while I walked the six kilometers to Hallouvry.

For fifteen months, except for August 1893 (there was no Easter holiday) I gave my ten hours of teaching each week. For fifteen months (even in August I remained alone in the school with the non-French students) I went to Rennes each Sunday and placed myself in the care of M. Ceillier who, with an unfailing patience, endeavored to make me recover my sight. For fifteen months there was no external change.

But this was not the case for my personal frame of mind. Here a profound reawakening occurred at the end of several weeks. As long as I was in the grip of the terrible shock of the final days of August I experienced a kind of lethargy that left me dull of wit. But to the degree that life returned, my thoughts took another direction. The word of the psalmist: "Et peccatum meum contra me est semper" (my sin is always before me) hounded me as a bitter obsession. Degraded, humiliated before the body of diocesan clergy, reduced to fulfilling the task of a seminarian, separated from my books, prevented from pursuing the studies that had been my life for more than fifteen years, I was treated as a criminal. I had, indeed, committed a crime, a crime horrible in the view of the Church, since I had seen the emptiness of its claims. And this insight had been the ineluctable result of a study, originally embarked upon for the defense of dogmas and pursued with integrity, with fervor, with tenacity. I then imagined myself standing in front of all the priests of the diocese and telling them: "Go ahead and study the Bible of which you are ignorant, and you will see if one can avoid my findings. I struggled for nearly two years; most of you would not last fifteen days! You keep your dogmas because you live out of touch with study. I have worked. That is my crime: 'Et pecattum meum contra me est semper.'"

I remained convinced that I had fulfilled a duty in sacrificing myself in order to spare loved ones; and, not for anything in the world would I have wanted to shirk my duty. I would even have accepted my sacrifice stoically had I had a confidant, just one, with whom I could have talked freely. But I could not reveal my state of soul to anyone. I had to conceal it from everyone, even and especially the two priests who took such trouble to console me. This absolute withdrawal into myself became a painful feeling that grew constantly stronger and of which I find the first signs in two notes dated September 26th and 28th.

At the beginning of September 1892 I lacked the courage to take my secret to my grave. Now what tortured me was no longer dying with my secret, but living with it. In the final days of September I was obsessed by the words of Yahweh in Isaiah (63:4): "Dies ultionis in corde meo" (the day of vengeance is in my heart). The idea of revenge took intense hold of my mind and became the supreme motivation of my life. This revenge was, needless to say, purely intellectual in nature. I would let my mother and my adoptive father live out their days in peace. I would wait as long as necessary. However, not yet having attained the age of thirty-three, my turn would inevitably come. At the beginning of the month I was afraid of being overtaken by death. Now I cast this hypothesis aside; I counted only on life. Martyr to the truth, one day I would be its apostle. I would leave the Roman Church; I would wage war on this vile beast that tortured me so horribly. I would assemble the clearest, most decisive proofs of the hollowness of Christian dogmas and publish them. As often happens, I foresaw everything except what did happen. It did not occur to me to remain in the Church and dig myself into a trench in order to combat it. I reckoned on leaving before denouncing its falsehoods. With a naiveté natural to my age and inexperience I was convinced that it would suffice to show priests the truth for them to be won over.

Beginning in October, I set to work and drew up a series of essays. They are still in my drawers today.

Toward the end of February 1893, M. Ceillier asked me to look over the tracts on Religion, Revelation and the Church and to revise them in order to use them for teaching the seminarians in the next academic year. At the same time he placed at my disposal all the books of the seminary library that I might need. The bull with a ring in its nose allows itself to be led. I obeyed. Books were brought to me on Thursdays by the school students who went to find them at the seminary. M. Ceillier also consented, at this time, to return three notebooks I had requested from him. Begun on March 10, the tracts were finished in July. At the beginning of the academic year, the professor of fundamental theology dictated them to his students. They continued to be used, together with the tracts on dogma, until the administration replaced them with Tanquerey's manual.[115] By this time (the beginning of the academic year 1896 or 1897) M. Guillois was bishop of Puy and M. Ceillier directed the Collège Saint-Vincent. Two small tracts on Conscience and Laws that I had drawn up in 1896 were still being dictated to seminarians in the first years of the present century.

All this work did not succeed in occupying me completely. The following note of October 16, 1893 shows my state of soul at this point.

Part One: How I Freed Myself of Dogma

For the last month my torments have attained a degree of intensity hitherto unknown. I now understand the expression "to be drenched in grief." Grief, in its most bitter form, inundates my soul. Sometimes I find on my lips the words of Elijah: Tolle animam meam Domine (Yahweh, take my life). Truly life is a heavy burden for me to bear. Vile superstition can no longer burn people at the stake; but it still knows how to inflict cruel tortures on its victims! If there were at least one kindred spirit to whom I could pour out my soul! But the two priests to whom an indiscretion revealed the depth of my soul are my torturers even though they think they are my comforters. Each Sunday I am condemned to listen unflinchingly to the most useless nonsense and to accuse myself of the terrible crime of having reached the truth. Oh science! You do not hold it against me if I appear to betray you. David had no resource for escaping the Philistines but to counterfeit madness. And the capricious Yahweh let Naaman kneel in the temple of Rimmon. The gospels put words in the mouth of Jesus, inauthentic I may add, against dissembling. You, oh science, you I know are more indulgent; and at the court of history, you will not blush for those who, out of the most respectable motives, have seemed to blush for you. Dreadful superstition keeps watch to surprise me. At the least imprudence it is resolved to cast me upon the streets of Paris to die of hunger. One day I will break my chains. But give me leave to bury my mother before I follow you. Courage! The Hebrew prophet slept for an instant. Then he resumed his walk of forty days to the mountain of Elohim. The strong fall and get back up. Only cowards let themselves be crushed. Suffering must be my life's companion for many a year. Let us accept that . . . .

7

At the Chaplaincy of the Little Sisters of the Poor and at the Former Convent of the Carmelites

Toward November 15, 1893, M. Ceillier sent a letter asking me to let him know at once if I would accept the chaplaincy to the Little Sisters of the Poor that M. Guillois was offering me. I accepted. M. Ceillier's letter was merely a formality. The following December 1st, at the stroke of one o'clock, M. Gendron came to inform me, on M. Guillois' behalf, that my appointment had been made. On Monday, December 4th, at eight o'clock in the morning, I left the Hallouvry school in the farm's horse-drawn wagon. Half an hour later I was in La Philetière (the name of the home for the aged) located in a suburb of Rennes. I find in my notebook a long note dated December 1st which ends with the following: *I must not forget that only the hope of one day being an apostle has sustained me in my distress. I am adopting as motto the words that Second Isaiah places in the mouth of Yahweh*: Ki yôm naqam belibbi, dies enim ultionis in corde meo.

In placing me in a home for the aged M. Guillois thought he had buried the scholar in me and sealed his tomb. As for M. Gendron and M. Ceillier, they saw in this appointment the hand of Providence which, solicitous of my salvation, gave me the cure of souls that might sanctify my own. They little suspected the internal agitation that perturbed me. My hackles rose at the thought that the great school of lies would have the final word and that I would have to renounce present revenge in favor of "dies ultionis in corde meo." The day of my arrival at La Piletière my rule of life was clearly fixed:

Part One: How I Freed Myself of Dogma

1. To fulfill conscientiously, scrupulously the humble ministry of consolation that had been entrusted to me.
2. To prepare myself through study to be the apostle of the truth for which I was a martyr.
3. To make a rule of nearly total isolation.

I rested from study in my ministry; I found consolation from ministry in study. I never took part in the official ceremonies or gatherings of the clergy. I was conscious of living as a sleepwalker shut up in his dream. My dream was to make the truth known. I worked relentlessly.

What did my work involve? The notebooks containing the results of my scriptural research were all, without exception, under lock and key. Simply showing interest in having them would have provoked the gravest disquiet over the sincerity of my conversion. That being the case I had no choice. I had to renounce Hebrew completely and to fall back on the other branch of my studies. Soon after coming to La Piletière I bought ten volumes of Migne's patrology,[116] promising myself to make other purchases when my finances would allow. Furthermore, the Little Sisters drove to the major seminary every day for charity in kind. I frequently sent with them a letter addressed to one of my friends at seminary. The next day they would find a packet of books at the reception desk and bring it in their carriage.

But what would M. Gendron and M. Ceillier say when they learned that, like the dog in Scripture, I had returned to my own vomit? They knew nothing about it. Migne's ten volumes, acquired before the end of 1893, remained for several months hidden deep within a cupboard as if they were dirty novels. Fortunately, it did not take long to realize that my guardian angels made it a principle to avoid coming up to my workroom on the rare occasions when they came to La Piletière, with the obvious intention not to appear inquisitorial. So Migne could emerge from his hiding place. And part of the problem raised by my studies was thus resolved.

But only a part. Here is why. Each Sunday, before going to see my mother, I visited either M. Gendron or M. Ceillier in turn. Quite often M. Gendron was not in. Then I went quickly to where my impounded books languished. I took a few, then left with my companions, some under my arm, others in my pockets. When the Father was in, both of us took great care to restrict ourselves to mundane matters and to avoid questions bearing on religious science. Besides, the interview seldom lasted more than fifteen minutes, at times even less. In sum, my relations with M. Gendron presented no difficulty.

With M. Ceillier it was another matter. Visits with him, as ritualized as a liturgy, comprised two successive acts, namely a confession and a discussion. In confession I do not know who was more ill-at-ease, the penitent or the confessor. The former always brought the same state of soul. He repeated what he had said a hundred times, that he could not bring his mind to bear on any dogma and that all he could do was to submit himself blindly to the Church's authority. The latter reiterated with an unshakable perseverance advice that assumed faith in the penitent. Acknowledgements and exhortations were a performance of hopeless monotony. Nevertheless, one day I heard something new. Assuming a moving tone, my confessor told me that there were priests who were tempted sexually. He added that these unfortunates were in great need of receiving from Our Lord the grace necessary to resist temptation; and he warmly exhorted me to ask this grace from the divine Master. Evidently, the good Father had just learned that one of his penitents had forgotten the promises of subdiaconate and had illicitly satisfied his appetites.

Confession, with the pious nonsense it evoked, was a difficult moment. But the conversation that followed was even more so. Then it was no longer simply a matter of listening to foolishness; I had to submit to an examination and respond to it. Not that M. Ceillier went about his work maliciously nor did he mean to act as inquisitor. He meant to express sympathy. Knowing full well that I spent my afternoons neither playing cards with my confreres, nor pounding the pavement, he inquired about my fortnight's reading. I could not avoid replying and indicating likely readings.

This continual dissembling, imposed on me by force of circumstances, became more and more intolerable. I longed for the day when I could throw off this yoke. It finally came in October 1896. By this time M. Ceillier had been director of the Collège Saint-Vincent for a year. He redoubled his consideration and thoughtfulness toward me. But in his antechamber or on the street where the collège was located, I often chanced upon priests whose very sight was abhorrent to me, given my taste for isolation. Following one of these encounters I reached a decision that had long weighed upon my mind. I wrote a letter to the superior of Saint-Vincent in which, after thanking him for all his kindness toward me, informed him that I was constrained by circumstances to withdraw from his charge. I received a cordial but very reserved written reply. Sometime afterward, M. Gendron said in

PART ONE: How I Freed Myself of Dogma

a troubled tone: "M. Ceillier, with whom I recently dined, asked me about you. And, when I said that he saw you frequently, he replied that you had stopped coming to him. What does this mean?" I explained the reasons for the break; those at least that I could admit. He remained silent. But I sensed that my conversation was a painful enigma for him. As if he feared asking an indiscreet question, he refrained from asking to whom I went to confess.

At the beginning of 1897, I sent my former confessor a card with an expression of my humble gratitude. I expected to receive a card in reply. To my great astonishment, the superior of Saint-Vincent came in person and let himself into my workroom which he had never visited before. Disturbed by this surprising and unexpected visit in the midst of my books scattered about on the table or on the floor, I hid my concern. We talked about, or better I talked about Tillemont, about his prodigious learning. My chief concern was to create a diversion from the studies that then occupied me. At the end of a quarter of an hour, M. Ceillier got up and left without looking especially at my worktable. I saw him out. But just as we were parting I had a sudden outburst in which I expressed with vehemence, almost violence, a number of complaints regarding my lot. Disconcerted by this scene which exposed to view a secret carefully guarded up to that point, M. Ceillier uttered several sorrowful and nearly tearful words whose flow I interrupted by closing the door. Then, emboldened by my fit of honesty, I immediately wrote my former confessor a letter to explain that solitude alone was capable of bringing some balm to my sufferings and to excuse myself for breaking off all relations with him.

I never again saw M. Ceillier after the beginning of 1897. But he still retained my notebooks and I anticipated freeing these hostages as soon as practically possible, that is, when I feared neither dismissal nor M. Gendron's outcries. At the beginning of 1904 the moment appeared opportune. I had just left La Piletière, I no longer held any official position; moreover my relationship with M. Gendron had ended in circumstances related below (p. 57). I had two books taken to M. Ceillier, books that he had lent me earlier and I accompanied them with a note in which I asked for my notebooks. The porter came back with the following missive:

> My dear confrere. Thank you for the books you have returned. As for your notebooks, you may recall that, in accordance with our formal and repeated agreements, you authorized me to do whatever I wished with them, promising—I recall this detail—not to complain if I destroyed them. I retained them for many years; but, having

At the Chaplaincy of the Little Sisters of the Poor

received no claim on your part and seeing illness in the offing, I destroyed them so that they would not be found after my death. I think about you and pray for you every day.

Several months later I obtained additional details. When M. Pautonnier[117] (about whom I shall speak later (p. 63), to whom I recounted my misfortune and who could speak his mind to M. Ceillier, reproached his act of vandalism, he received a reply of which the substance was: "I spent the winter (1900 or 1901) in the south. I burned these notebooks before my departure so they would not be found in my drawers in case of death."

My ending relations with M. Ceillier was one of the chief events of my time at La Piletière and the years that followed, apart from those connected with my publications, which I will discuss later. And here is another.

Before my coming to La Piletière, the religious needs of the home for the aged were provided for by half a dozen priests who travelled throughout France preaching retreats to the Little Sisters of the Poor, coming back in turn to rest at Rennes. They lived in a large, fine house known as the presbytery. This little society suffered the repercussions of M. Lepailleur's disgrace when he was summoned to Rome and shut up in a Trappist monastery for effronteries that had nothing intellectual about them (see Houtin's *Courte histoire du célibat ecclésiastique*, on which I collaborated, p. 233).[118] I was called to replace the Fathers and, on my arrival, was installed in the presbytery. But since this house was to be sold, they began building a chaplaincy near it. One spring Sunday in 1894, as the foundations began to rise, they invited the old people to attend a ceremony to lay the cornerstone. According to custom, medals were placed under this stone and the religious invited me to add to the medals any mementos that I desired. I willingly complied with their invitation. I dropped under the cornerstone a small iron box containing (in Hebrew, as I recall) my motto: "The day of revenge is in my heart" and various other biblical maxims of the same kind. These tokens of my inner turbulence can be found under the threshold.

My *Théologie positive*[119] appeared toward mid-November 1903. Several days later (November 22) I sent the archbishop a letter requesting to be relieved of my post as chaplain for health reasons. I intended to move into the city and to say Mass at home without ever setting foot in a Church. Three days later, M. Gayet[120] came from Saint-Malo to La Piletière and said roughly this: "M. Durusselle[121] the vicar general has informed me that you want to leave your chaplaincy. The Carmelite convent, founded by my uncle M. Adam's mother has, as you know, been abandoned, and the pastor of the parish is responsible for seeing that a Mass is said in the chapel every Sunday. Arrange things with him, and also with the Carmelites' notary. The latter is willing to let you the chaplaincy with its modest garden. As for the pastor, he will certainly be happy to stop sending curates out from the parish Church to say Mass every Sunday."

The affair was settled within twenty-four hours. I left La Piletière on December 7th: the following day I said Mass for the first time in the former chapel of the Carmelites. On Sundays, the chapel was full; during the week the number of those attending sometimes reached twenty. For nearly a year Mass was my sole ministry and I never asked for another. When All Saints Day of 1904 drew near, M. Perrault,[122] the pastor, who liked me a great deal, had the confessional rebuilt (it had fallen down since the departure of the Carmelites) and came in person to the chapel one Sunday morning before Mass to announce to the faithful that from now on I would hear confessions. As long as he lived, that is, until the end of 1907, I heard confessions with the faculties conferred upon me by M. Perrault. And it is also with these faculties that I continued to hear confessions after his death until January 23, 1930. None of the Church Fathers enlightened me—and for very good reason—about how the faculties conferred by a pastor continue after his death. However it may be, I never asked for any, either from M. Perrault's successor or from the archdiocese. In sum, I was officially a priest without assignment, without faculties; and the archdiocese treated me as such, for it paid me an annual allowance of 900 francs and dispensed me from the ecclesiastical retreats to which all the priests granted faculties are obligated (during my stay at La Piletière each year I sent a letter to the authorities declaring that I had made my retreat in a religious house in the area). In reality, I heard confessions, I brought communion to the sick, I gave them extreme unction; and the archdiocese was not unaware of it. My actual situation was in contrast with my legal situation.

At La Piletière, I was half an hour from the city center; at the Carmelites only ten minutes: it was progress. Nearly every week I went to the university library. The municipal library was even easier to access, for, at this time, it opened at eleven o'clock in the morning. I went twice a week immediately after my midday meal. All the same, only the seminary library had certain books. Since my friends of the past were no longer there to get them for me, I decided to consult them in the library myself. My situation was at that time remarkably complex. The orthodox superior, Michel,[123] considered me a heretic (since my disputes with Fr. Fontaine[124] p. 66) and

At the Chaplaincy of the Little Sisters of the Poor

he had forbidden seminarians to buy my *Théologie positive*. On the other hand, this book appeared under the patronage of the Jesuits; besides, two of my treatises on moral theology were still dictated in class. I thus held concurrently the two roles of oracle and miscreant. It was under these circumstances that one Thursday in May of 1904 I went to the seminary. I asked politely to be admitted to the library. The librarian had me enter. But, ten minutes later he returned to tell me, not without embarrassment, that I had to obtain the superior's verbal authorization. I went immediately to request it. Before I could utter a word, M. Michel invited me to be seated. I refused. Then, seeing that he made it a point of honor, I took the seat he offered; I then requested him to authorize me to consult the library's books. In a cold but calm tone, he gave it. I then sprang up like a Jack-in-the-box and left without giving him the time to utter the sentence forming on his lips. I returned to the library which I left two hours later, promising to return. I came back the following Thursday. That day I received the greatest affront I had ever experienced. Because the door of the library was closed and the librarian absent, I went for help to the bursar, Béon,[125] who had been my student eighteen years before; who, from 1892 to 1895, had dictated my course in fundamental theology, and who moreover lived very near the library. I thus knocked at the bursar's office. Béon came to open the door. But, scarcely had he recognized me when, without letting me utter a single word, he slammed the door in my face with a violent gesture. Flabbergasted by such never-before experienced rudeness, I walked slowly away. Michel, the superior, would have willingly opened the library door for me without saying a word had I revealed my trouble to him. But I could not decently ask this service of him. I went to knock on several professors' doors; all were out. Fifteen minutes later, while wandering about the cloisters, I met Béon who was preparing to take the seminarians to the seminary's country house. I approached him hat in hand and asked him to open the library whose books I was authorized to consult. He replied in an arrogant tone, without putting his hand to his hat, that that did not concern him. Then he turned his head and spoke to some of the seminarians. Ten minutes later I finally found the librarian. He opened the library for me and, in order to spare me a replay of this misadventure, promised me that he would henceforth leave his key at the concierge's lodge where it would always be at my disposal. He kept his word. From that day forward, I no longer needed to resort to the boor at the bursar's office. The library key always hung on a nail near the concierge's door. I unhooked it to enter; when I left I returned it to

PART ONE: How I Freed Myself of Dogma

its place. Every Sunday, without fail, I arrived around nine o'clock. Toward eleven I left. That continued until the day when the State, by virtue of the Law of Separation, confiscated the seminary which was its property, that is, at the end of 1906. At that time the diocesan administration transferred the seminary too far away for me to visit easily. Fortunately, at that moment, the university library inherited the contents of the Angers seminary. I lost nothing in the change; quite the contrary.

Nearly thirty years have elapsed since the day Béon shocked me with behavior more worthy of a savage than a civilized man. Today I still do not know what motivated him. We had never had the least difficulty; I had never said a word against him. I see only one way of explaining his conduct. He probably wanted to avenge his close friend Desbois.[126] He was the professor of dogma, who, for ten years, had dictated my course in theology without asking my authorization, and who had honorably delivered the unkindest cut of all after my departure from the seminary, and whom I had put in his place. In any case, Desbois and Béon, these two honorable friends, would later join forces to disgrace me at a fateful moment of my life.

I end this chapter with an account of the fatal conversation in which I revealed the depth of my soul to M. Gendron. For many years I would never have wished, for anything in the world, to disabuse this poor father of his illusion and reveal to him a state of things that could have killed him. All the same, what I tried so hard to avoid happened four years before I left La Piletière, specifically on October 31, 1899. On that day M. Gendron had come to speak about some unimportant affair. As was his custom, he left after several minutes without sitting down; and, as was my custom, I went to see him on his way which, without being completely in the country, was no longer truly the city. It was on this walk that I inadvertently revealed my secret. It slipped out whereas a few years earlier, it never would have done so. It slipped out because I was less on my guard and had relaxed my vigilance. It is this lapse in vigilance that must be explained.

What happened? This: M. Gendron's incomprehension had shifted little by little. I say shifted and not worsened. M. Gendron had never understood anything of my crisis of conscience. His lack of comprehension, already complete in 1892, was thus no greater in 1899. But, in 1892, blinded by affection, he attributed my intellectual aberration to a kind of madness caused by a prolonged excess of work; he saw it as a terrible accident which he wanted to spare any sanction. Then, bit by bit, orthodoxy reasserted itself over affection in his soul. In 1899 he held me culpable. Culpable of a fault

At the Chaplaincy of the Little Sisters of the Poor

that deserved punishment. No doubt the father, who continued to love me, suffered at the sight of my broken life. But the priest deemed my punishment deserved; besides, he saw my appointment to La Piletière as a stroke of Providence that, in putting me in sanctifying contact with other souls, had shown itself solicitous of my salvation. In sum, for a time now he had preached resignation and even tried to kindle in me a feeling for expiation.

That was the sensitive spot. As long as the poor father poured out consolations upon me interspersed with sobbing or confined himself to mundane matters in order to allay his sadness and mine, I was capable of putting up with, of enduring all of it, rather than tearing the veil from his illusions. But his homilies on expiation made my gorge rise. I returned home feeling that one of these days I would not have the strength to master my indignation and that an explosion would occur. It happened the morning of October 31, 1899 on the path leading from La Piletière to the town. In the midst of the conversation M. Gendron said to me: "Remember that you have incurred excommunication reserved to the Sovereign Pontiff." Beside myself, face and fists clenched, I shot back in a feverish voice: "You force me to say that I am innocent. The Roman Church has deceived me. She is the guilty one!"

On hearing this response, in seeing the fury that dominated and transformed me, M. Gendron halted and froze for an instant as if paralyzed. He would not have been any more dumbfounded if a thunderbolt had struck at his feet. In his view I had always remained the child he had met for the first time in the street, early in 1869, and who had said he wanted to be a cherub. I had never shown anything other than the most complete docility. Or, if I had not, at the rare times when I did not follow his advice, I had not gone beyond passive and silent resistance. For the first time I stood up to him. For the first time, I made a show of revolt. It was first of all by this gesture of rebellion that the unhappy father was disconcerted, overwhelmed. As for the words themselves, I soon understood that he had not wanted to believe his ears and that he had taken them for the incoherent expression of a rage that had robbed me of my self-control. Indeed, when he regained possession of himself, after a stunned moment, he calmly asked me in a subdued voice: "What did you say?" "I said that I am innocent, that I have nothing to reproach myself with, that the Roman Church is the real guilty one and that I have silently endured undeserved tortures." This reply each word of which was hammered home struck dread in my master's soul. Nevertheless, even then, he believed that my words stemmed from anger and went further

PART ONE: How I Freed Myself of Dogma

than my thought. Counting on a reassuring response, he said: "But in the end you are Christian, you believe in the mysteries of religion?"

This question, posed in an imploring voice, craved an affirmative response. The irreparable harm still had not occurred; it was up to me to stop it. But, for that, I would have had to hold myself in check; I was incapable of doing so. The eruption of the long-repressed volcano ran its course; it did not obey me, I was just an onlooker. "All that," I said, "was invented little by little in the minds of the Fathers and the theologians." This reply was quite clear. But my master, who clung to his illusions, did not want to understand. As if he required final confirmation, he said to me: "Do you believe in the real presence?" "Saint Augustine," I replied with spirit, "did not believe in it." This time it was no longer possible to have any doubts about my state of soul. But then M. Gendron, under the influence of an immediate reaction, cried out in an imperious, almost incensed tone: "It is the Church, not Saint Augustine, which one must believe." Once more I stood up to him and defiantly replied: "And why, if you please? Saint Augustine, I imagine, was fully aware of his catechism. He knew the dogmas taught at his time better than anyone. And if he was not aware of the real presence, it was because no one was aware of it at that time."

Without replying a single word to these statements, M. Gendron immediately changed the direction of the conversation. In severe terms, in the name of honesty, he adjured me to put an end to the odious sacrileges I was committing daily and to leave the Church at once. Then, incapable, despite his sorrow, of laying aside his habitual irony, he mocked my objections; he ridiculed my pretension of convicting the Church of error and of being right all alone against the entire Catholic world. I replied in substance as follows:

1. "If a religion's value depends on the number of its adherents, preference must be given to Buddhism which counts four hundred million faithful while the Roman Church numbers only two hundred.* The truth is that the two hundred million who profess the Catholic faith would be Buddhists if they were born in China, and that the four hundred million who profess Buddhism would be Roman Catholic if they were born in western Europe or in South America. It is thus infantile to prove the divinity of dogmas of the Roman Church by the number of Catholics.

2. "Objections against Christianity compel recognition because of the clarity of the evidence. They can be ignored; but once one knows them one

---

* This was the number set at this time.

At the Chaplaincy of the Little Sisters of the Poor

cannot but surrender. When one has before one's eyes the textual evidence one cannot refuse to admit, for example, that the books of the Bible, supposedly inspired by God, are full of falsehoods and legends. I add that I would have been incapable of finding on my own these objections whose discovery required extensive research. My role was limited to verifying the results obtained by several generations of honest and conscientious workers. This verification was not beyond my competence. Moreover, it is within the reach of every priest; and I know very well what those who consent to study it will think. As for the verdict of those who judge without knowledge, it seems to me, it has no value.

3. "You speak of honesty. I agree. I joined the ranks of the clergy because I was ignorant of the truth. And I was ignorant of it because the Roman Church systematically hid it from me in the books it placed at my disposal. In order to install me among its clergy, the Roman Church set a trap, she acted against all rules of honesty. And, because I recognized her deceit, does she then have the right to invoke honesty while showing me the door? Does the cutthroat invoke the rules of integrity against his victim? That would be the ridiculous conclusion of your demand in the name of honesty.

"Even so I am ready to leave the clergy. I will leave if the Roman Church promises to attend to my fate, to furnish me with a livelihood consistent with the habits that have become second nature for me. Let the Roman Church enable me to carry on a life of study and I, for my part, will engage to avoid anything that could detract from dogmas in the work I publish, I promise to stick to neutral questions. You protest that this is extravagant. I realize that it is extremely extravagant from a theological point of view. The Roman Church that, still today, teaches that it is lawful to kill heretics, would not hesitate for an instant, were she to know my state of soul, to throw me out into the street and let me die of hunger. That is her justice. Well, for her principles I have the same contempt that she has for my claims. One uses cunning with unreasoning beasts; until now I have resorted to cunning with the Roman Church and I shall continue as long as possible. I will be forced to leave if you denounce me; but left to myself, I will remain in the ranks of the clergy. The Roman Church can blame its own ferocity for the rites its dishonesty has led me to celebrate and that I will continue to perform, which are from its perspective are hideously sacriligious, but which are, in reality, nothing."

PART ONE: How I Freed Myself of Dogma

We had gone to and fro from La Piletière to toll house five or six times. It was nearly eleven o'clock. In a strangled voice, M. Gendron said to me: "I am not responsible for policing the Church; I shall not denounce you." Then he withdrew.

The conversation of October 31, 1899 logically called for a complete break. But I felt that it was not up to me to take the initiative and that my role was to submit. Several days later it was M. Gendron's feast day (November 12th, since his first name was René). I went to wish him well as usual. I also went, on December 31st, to present my new year wishes. The glacial and silent reception I received on these two occasions obliged me to leave immediately. The following fragment of a letter I wrote on November 12, 1900 explains why I believed myself permitted to put an end to such experiences:

> Each year on this date I have come to offer you my respects and well wishes. If I refrain today, it is not because I want to avoid being shown the door as I have been for a year now, it is to comply with your clearly-expressed wishes. One snub more or less means nothing to me who, for so long now, have received so many. But my visits inspire in you a feeling of revulsion that I must respect. I do not therefore wish to inflict my presence upon you.

In 1892 the poor father would inevitably have succumbed to the shock that I had just inflicted upon him in spite of myself. But in 1899, familiarity with the mystery of my conversion had made his work salutary. He endured. Only, when his friends (formerly my own) asked for news of me, he started to cry. And when they sought details, he took refuge in complete silence (I have this information from his servant). It was known then, in the highest ecclesiastical circles of the diocese, that he was suffering, and that I was the mysterious cause. The outpourings of sympathy that were lavished upon him distracted him from his sadness until the day a stomach tumor carried him off after several months of decline (September 4, 1904). Several days before his death, I went to his lodgings. He told them to let me in. When I was close to his bed, I knelt down and made amends for the grief I had caused him. He said to me: "You are what I have loved most in the world." Then he commended himself to my prayers. But, recollecting himself, he added with sadness: "Ah! I forgot that you no longer have faith!"

Cardinal Labouré,[127] the vicars general, and the chapter for which he was dean, attended his funeral. For the first time in a dozen years (with the exception of the burials of my mother and a brother) I took part in an ecclesiastical ceremony outside the chapel where I said Mass. Seated in the front row in the middle of the nave I faced all these decorative personages whose colleague I would have been had I consented to ignore the problems of Daniel and the Pentateuch. When the service was over, a vicar general got ready to climb into the hearse intended to convey the mortal remains of my master to Vitré. But I nimbly slipped in front of him and, donning a surplice that I had until then hidden under my greatcoat, I took a seat in the hearse. He did not insist.

Several weeks later, M. Gendron's niece came to find me and said: "My uncle speaks several times of you in his personal papers which I have just read. He loved you a great deal. Would you like to see to the publication of his sermons? You should know that it was one of his best friends, M. Houeix (pastor of Rochefort-en-Terre, Morbihan), who was the first to tell me that you would be perfect for this task." I accepted. I suppressed some unnecessary arguments that were pointless repetitions. I corrected some lapses in style that the author would certainly have corrected had he reread them. The sermons appeared in the spring of 1906.[128] The niece did what was necessary to assure the book's circulation. But she was not always lucky. Having met a certain Abbé Croulbois[129] in Mayenne, her mother's region, she gave him a copy, requesting him to write a review of it in the Laval *Semaine religieuse*. The latter replied, "I will refrain from recommending a book that drags through the mud the collège ecclésiastique de Château-Gontier where I was a professor." I did not then foresee that the said Croulbois would one day finally end up in Paris and become a notorious snitch (see the *Bulletin de l'Institut catholique de Toulouse*, 1929, p. 217). I also learned shortly thereafter that M. Gendron had left me, through the intermediacy of his niece, a modest life-annuity. The Congregation of the Holy Spirit, which was responsible for administering it, punctually fulfilled its duty until around 1921. Somewhere near that date, foreseeing a storm I had long expected, I succeeded in transforming my annuity into a lump sum paid once and for all. Without this precaution, my annuity would have inevitably been swallowed in the tempest of 1930. It escaped the shipwreck.

8

My Introduction to the *Revue d'Histoire et de Littérature Religieuses*

TOWARD THE AUTUMN OF 1896 I had read most of the Latin Patrology. I had simultaneously familiarized myself with the principal Greek Fathers of the first four centuries. I had also studied several German books of which I will speak shortly. Admittedly this initial survey required confirmation, rectification, expansion. The origins remained enveloped in a fog I tried in vain to pierce. Even for subsequent centuries I did not always see very clearly, and could often put only question marks. In spite of everything, certain facts were definitely established. In the course of my long journeys across the centuries, I constantly kept watch on the evolution of Christian dogmas. I was ready to describe it. In September I set to work.

Where should I begin? Saint Augustine dominated all the Latin doctors by far. He was like the great lamp enlightening the Western Church over the centuries. His writings had thus deservedly attracted my special attention. And, among his writings, I had studied with particular care the long treatises devoted to establishing against Julian the dogma of original sin. Once I was sure of having grasped Augustine's thought on original sin, I applied myself to following it through the Middle Ages; I had witnessed its triumphant march up to the time when, mortally wounded by Anselm and then by Abelard, it was dealt a death blow by Saint Thomas. In short, the history of the dogma of original sin was the one that I knew best. I decided to focus on it.

I wrote this work without knowing when or how it would appear, as, four years earlier in my prison in the School of Late Vocations, I had written my "Profession of Faith." But I had scarcely finished it when its publication

My Introduction to the Revue d'Histoire et de Littérature Religieuses

became certain. I owed this favor to a priest who at that time occupied an important place in my life and of whom it is time to speak.

M. Pautonnier, a priest of the diocese of Rennes, was from around 1882 a professor at the Collège Stanislas. He regarded the study of ecclesiastical sciences as the best means of strengthening the faith and of bringing unbelievers back into the Church. Filled with this illusion, he encouraged young priests to cultivate exegesis, ecclesiastical history and, generally speaking, everything bearing upon religion in one way or another. In September 1894 he came to see me at La Piletière. I was in the midst of studying Pope Saint Leo. I showed him several of this pontiff's texts and gave him my comments on them. It was an entirely fossilized fauna I was showing him. Anyone else would have felt alarmed. M. Pautonnier showed a lively interest in these archaic conceptions whose very existence he had not suspected; but he saw in them all the more reason to resort to study, to separate immutable and divine dogma from the theological rust which too often disfigured it. Without letting him see anything of the true nature of my thought, I informed him of my project of analyzing the whole of patrology and subsequently writing the history of dogmas. This plan pleased him. Only he added that, in order to carry out my enterprise successfully, I ought to supplement textual study with readings of German authors, notably Harnack[130] and Holtzmann.[131] Naturally he had read nothing by these scholars. However Loisy,[132] whom he saw occasionally, set great store by their books. I considered the methods I had used up to now perfectly adequate; I thus welcomed with little enthusiasm the cordial invitation he extended. But he, certain of conquering my indifference by presenting me with a fait accompli, sent me Harnack's *Dogmengeschichte* from Paris a few weeks later.

I read these three compact volumes and I got a great deal out of them. Up to that point I had an unlimited confidence in the direct study of patristic texts. I believed I could limit myself to that method because it had, any number of times, allowed me to see the charlatanism of apologists claiming to follow tradition. It was an error. For a century the Germans had, with their customary tenacity, combed the ancient ecclesiastical literature. Their combined efforts constituted an important capital which had been collected in general studies. It was hugely in my interest to use these syntheses and especially the most recent. Harnack, whose science was overrated, drew his conclusions from left and right without always verifying them. His muddled composition, at least in the first volume, is the result of undigested reading. But his readings are extensive and the footnotes that summarize are, most

Part One: How I Freed Myself of Dogma

of the time, important. I owe to Harnack an initial orientation that Weizsaecker,[133] Holtzmann, Sohm,[134] Pfleiderer,[135] Schürer,[136] etc. would render more precise shortly thereafter.

M. Pautonnier did me a notable favor in obliging me, from 1894, to study German authors. Three years later, he did me another no less important. In spring of 1897 I had him read a chapter of my history of the dogma of original sin on which I had worked for the last eight months. He quickly sought to place it and, a few weeks later, he announced that M. Loisy had agreed to publish my manuscript in his *Revue d'histoire et de littérature religieuses*.[137] However I was asked to condense my work which was too long, particularly to expurgate it by removing certain of Saint Augustine's passages "liable" (said Loisy) "to make a fireman blush." The following September, the vacation brought M. Patonnier back to Rennes and he returned the manuscript he had taken, asking me to make the necessary revisions as soon as possible. But by then my interest in the history of original sin had given way to the history of angels, my work in progress. I read him the initial chapters of this work. He was not at all displeased and lost no time in bringing my second manuscript to Loisy's attention.

Several months later (March 4, 1898) he showed me a letter that Loisy had written him:

> *I have told you how much the history of angels interested me and taught me. On the whole, I believe that M. Turmel's history of dogmas will rival the most scholarly work produced in Germany, that it will furthermore have the advantage of being conceived largely outside any* a priori *system and of being much more clearly expressed. In general M. T. places perhaps a bit too much emphasis on his opinions in so far as they tend to clash with received ideas. A bit more care with regard to language would not stand in the way of their truth. And even a reflection placed here and there to explain how the continuity of tradition subsists through the most surprising differences, would have a better effect on the work's balance—and on the reader's edification—than does the apparent intention of highlighting doctrinal oppositions. I also believe that any mockery with respect to beliefs or persons should be strictly prohibited. Basically M. T. holds present-day theologians in contempt and he is not entirely wrong, but his targets are witnesses to Christian tradition and one might willfully mistake the real object he is aiming at simply in order to transform him into a denigrator of the faith . . .*

9

First Condemnation in 1901

M. Pautonnier considered that dogma, to which he remained faithful, had nothing to fear from my writings, but he understood that theologians would suffer from them and he foresaw that I would become their bête noire. He felt that a pseudonym would be indispensable in sheltering me from their attacks. In his letter of March 13, 1898, I read the following observations dictated by prudence and by faith:

> I believe it would be imprudent to sign your articles... which would almost certainly attract denunciations. You would thus do well to choose a literary name... This measure of caution will not exempt you from necessary precautions to avoid scandalizing the weak. And I know that you will be mindful as well of soothing consciences by showing on occasion that the religious edifice is not compromised by the weakness of theology... There are many who are content with a modest temporary shelter while awaiting the reconstruction of the old building of theology that you will begin demolishing.

Loisy and Lejay[138] disagreed. According to them I had no reason to hide, since, at the worst, my angelology put theologians in a tight corner, but did not impinge upon any dogma. Such was also my way of thinking. The "dies ultionis in corde meo" resonated incessantly in my ears. A victim of the school of lies, I hastened to wage war on its agents, to rub their noses in texts, to return some of the blows they had dealt me through the agency of M. Guillois, who carried out their lofty projects. My prudence extended to not attacking any dogma directly; it stopped there. I wished to harass the Christian faith, to strike at it obliquely. But I also wanted it to know the source of the blows. My revenge would have been incomplete if the clergy

PART ONE: How I Freed Myself of Dogma

of Rennes, who suspected the cause of my misfortunes because of repeated indiscretions, imagined that I was crushed forever.

The angelology, which was too much to swallow even when amputated of its first chapter, began to appear in the August 1898 issue. The articles appeared successively until the end of 1899.[139] The first, which recounted the story of angelic matrimony, amused many lay people. Several young priests read it avidly; others said they were shocked; but theologians told them that this was nothing new and that I had quite simply plagiarized Pétau. These declarations uttered with confidence reassured troubled consciences. The following articles were welcomed with growing sympathy among the young clergy. To give but one example, a Benedictine informed me that the master of novices at Solesmes read my articles to his students, in which the only thing he found blameworthy was their irreverent tone. But I soon heard a change of tune. Early in 1899 M. Gendron severely asked me: "What are you doing? What do you want to accomplish with the writings you publish? If you no longer have faith, stop saying Mass, leave the Church. This is what Père Turpin[140] has just said to me, after being shown an article in the *Revue du monde catholique* in which Père Fontaine denounces you as an insulter of our beliefs. Père Turpin knows your background; he knows why you left the seminary. He was informed by M. Coupel in September 1892. I repeat: 'if you no longer have faith, leave the Church.'"

I replied more or less this: "Because I never play cards, I write during my free moments. But my work bears uniquely on theology and not on the Bible, which I gave up in 1892. The review in which I write was opened to me through the agency of M. Pautonnier. It is directed by priests who hold important posts in the diocese of Paris, who have Cardinal Richard's[141] trust and who would not tolerate the slightest attack on the faith. The quarrel they picked with me is a nasty and petty one and the Jesuit who has gone to war against me simply wants to make himself important by posing as a police officer. M. Gendron calmed down; we spoke of other things. Then I left.

Renan made it a principle not to reply to attacks directed against him. I broke Renan's precept and sent an article to the *Revue du monde catholique*.[142] I was wrong. Père Fontaine crushed me under his disdain, his sarcasm. He explained that I knew nothing of patrology, that I was a total heretic, and, worn out by my persistence in responding to him, he had the *Revue* closed to me. I was reduced to printing at my own expense a reply that I sent to several friends. It was not a model of serenity.

First Condemnation in 1901

However, this bellicose note could not derail the quarrel whose source lay in the belief at the end of the fourth century in the salvation of all Christians. Over the course of 1900, I published in the *Revue d'histoire et de littérature religieuses* three articles on this question.[143] They were found to be decisive and the issue was closed.

Today I no longer have the intense feeling against Père Fontaine that drove me then. No doubt, he knew all the tricks of the trade and used them with an unfaltering panache. But, at heart, his only fault lay in believing that the end justifies the means. If his means left much to be desired, his intentions, at least, were always noble and disinterested. For him, apologetics did not serve as a screen to mask unavowable ambition. He was not a hypocrite who lights a fire in order to gain credit for putting it out, or creates scandal by exposing secrets in order to denounce them and pose as savior. He did not want to land a miter or a mosetta. No, his aim was to protect the faith that was his life. He accused me of a heresy I had not committed. Others suffered the same imputation from him. But all of us against whom he waged war must recognize that we were miscreants who, while avoiding heresy, did our best to steer our readers toward it and that the fearsome Jesuit clearly discerned our game. In sum, Père Fontaine was a true believer and, on this count, he deserves respect.

The three articles appearing in the *Revue d'histoire et de littérature religieuses* were assembled in a booklet entitled *L'eschatologie à la fin du IVe siècle*.[144] The favorable reception it received was, in a way, the clergy's verdict. Several months later, the authorities delivered their own, which bore no resemblance to the former. On June 24, 1901, the archdiocese sent me the following letter:

> *Dear Monsieur Turmel,*
>
> *His Eminence Cardinal Archbishop of Rennes has received from the Cardinal Archbishop of Paris a letter that I have transcribed, included here along with the authentic copy of the attached document.*
>
> Paris, 23 June 1901
>
> *Eminence:*
>
> *I have just received a letter from the Sacred Congregation of the Index concerning a priest of your diocese, Abbé Turmel, who writes in the* Revue d'histoire et de littérature religieuses. *The Sacred Congregation orders that the author be solemnly warned and his work stopped with an interdiction on publishing anything in the future without the approval of ecclesiastical authority.*

PART ONE: How I Freed Myself of Dogma

> I am sending to Your Eminence a copy of the letter I received from Rome requesting that you transmit the decision of the Sacred Congregation of the Index to Abbé Turmel. I think that this ecclesiastic, who is unknown to me, will be eager to submit to Your Eminence's orders with the faith worthy of a Breton.
>
> I shall be grateful to Your Eminence for apprising me of the result of this communication that you will so kindly deliver to Abbé Turmel, and I ask you to accept the respect of my veneration and my religious devotion in Our Lord.
>
> The very humble and obedient servant of Your Eminence,
>
> Fr. Cardinal Richard
Arch. of Paris

> It is thus, as you see, in the name of His Eminence the Cardinal of Paris and of His Eminence the Cardinal of Rennes that I am contacting you. In memory of our former teacher-student relationship, I personally strongly regret the pain you may experience from this blow; but I know your spirit of faith and of wholehearted submission to the Church too well to think for an instant that you would have even a shadow of hesitation in giving us the assurance of a full and complete submission to the decision of the Sacred Congregation of the Index that we expect from you with an acknowledgement of receipt.
>
> F. Durusselle,
Vic. Gen.

When this letter arrived, my mother had been deceased for six years; the strongest link that had held me fast to the Roman Church had thus broken. But I still had M. Gendron close to me; I had my brother, also the old people who venerated me and who would have been mortified by an open rupture. I thus had to repress thoughts of the intense pleasure a letter of farewell addressed to the hierarchy and the clergy would have given me. In sum, the temptation was resisted as quickly as I felt it without the shadow of a hesitation, and I immediately decided to give my submission. Only it seemed to me that the submission gave me a right to insolence. I wrote the vicar general a long letter from which the following are excerpts:

> Some eminent men, among whom I cite the Archbishop of Albi[145] and Mgr Duchesne,[146] have accorded my work great praise and have strongly encouraged me to pursue it. Far from regarding me as an enemy of the faith, they have on the contrary delightedly welcomed me as an auxiliary in the battle they wage against the school of

cretinism so thoroughly chastened today. I note, moreover, that the Congregation of the Index is only partly in opposition to the illustrious scholars whom I just mentioned. The supremely eminent cardinals who last June 7th deigned to take note of me do not accuse me of having committed a heresy, nor even a simple theological error. What disturbs them in my writings is solely their general tendency. And I know from a reliable source that they have been especially offended by my aggressive attitude toward theologians. The horrible tortures to which I have been prey for many years have, I recognize, frequently given rise to disrespectful remarks and violent expression. Also, without regretting anything I have written, not even the note[*] that evoked such strong feeling and in which I denounce, with supporting examples, the methods dear to scholastics, I am disposed henceforth to proceed in the way of moderation which, moreover, I have been following for some time now . . . I bow, as I have said, before the decision of the Congregation of the Index and I am ready to submit my work to whatever examiner His Eminence would care to designate to me.

This letter was sent to the archdiocese on June 25th. Three weeks later (probably due to the cardinal's absence), I received from the archdiocese the following response:

Rennes, 14 July 1901

My dear friend,

His Eminence the Cardinal to whom I communicated your letter was quite satisfied with it. I have, on his behalf, written to the cardinal of Paris to apprise him of the outcome as he requested in the copy of the letter I sent you.

Concerning the articles that you may publish in the future and for which the Congregation asks that you have the Imprimatur of the Ordinary, Monseigneur desires that you send them to me to pass on to him. He requests that you send them soon enough for us to acquaint ourselves with them, which will be quite easy for you. The good cardinal of Paris himself will be very satisfied with the happy outcome of this affair.

Believe . . .

F. Durusselle

---

[*] Note that is found on pages 65-68 of *L'Eschatologie*. [The note in question contained a survey of several methods that, historically, were employed to avoid imputing to the Fathers any suggestion of error: suppression of embarrassing texts, interpolation of texts, and intentional fabrication of false documents, together with examples of each.—Ed.]

Part One: How I Freed Myself of Dogma

In his letter to my archbishop Cardinal Richard said that Rome stipulated that Abbé Joseph Turmel be "solemnly warned" and "his work stopped with an interdiction." He added that I was "unknown" to him. The first of these assertions, far from exaggerating, rather attenuated the language in the letter from Rome which requested a "serious reprimand" "gravi reprehensione," accompanied by a punishment "coerceri," which made the cardinal of Paris himself responsible for the application of these measures "per Eminentiam vestram reverendissimam," and that accused my writings of being audacious, rash, susceptible of scandalizing the weak and of shaking the faith of lay people "propter audaciam et temeritatem qua scripta sunt . . . scandalum saltem pusillorum creare et fidem in laicis proesertim labefactare." By the second assertion the crafty cardinal tried to make it seem that he had not brought a formal complaint against me and that he was completely unfamiliar with the sanctions Rome invoked against me. But why then did the Congregation of the "Index" write to him? Cardinal Labouré, my archbishop, was not taken in by the artifice. He was not naïve. Moreover, he had, at one time, been subjected to the influence of the former bishop of Arras, Mgr Meignan,[147] and pontifical administration inspired in him only very limited respect. He easily recognized the hand of Cardinal Richard in this affair, and this oblique manner of policing the diocese of Rennes mortified him. Unable to toss out Rome's notice, and obligated to forward it to me, he avenged himself by accompanying it with kind words. At that time, the French bishops, protected by the Concordat, were not the marionettes whose strings Rome now pulls. And, to make Cardinal Richard aware of his impropriety, he left it to his vicar general to reply, as proven by the letter sent to me on July 14th: "Yesterday I wrote on his behalf to the cardinal of Paris . . ."

I may add that Cardinal Richard did not delay in throwing off his mask. The following October 7th, he said to M. Hébert[148] (Houtin, *Marcel Hébert*, p. 145).

> Look at the Revue d'histoire et de littérature religieuses . . .
> They claim that this is science . . . dismal science! When one reads these articles, those of M. Turmel, for example, it seems that nothing is left . . . thus (his face, his expression, changes completely, his look becomes hard, almost menacing), thus the Index has authorized me to insist that he no longer write anything without having it reviewed.

There is the admission. This prelate, who told my archbishop he did not know me was carefully reading my work, which, he felt, demolished

Christian dogma completely and infuriated him. It was indeed he who denounced me to the Congregation of the Index. But he would never have had the slightest inclination to read a single line of my writings if his attention had not been drawn to me. This brings me back to Père Fontaine. This bellicose Jesuit sent to each of the ecclesiastical dignitaries of Rennes—beginning with the archbishop—a copy of the abuse he heaped upon me and of the accusations he formulated against my orthodoxy. He could not deprive the archbishop of Paris of this substantial manna. It is to him that I owe the honor of counting the archbishop of Paris among my readers. And my condemnation of 1901 was a consequence of my controversy with Père Fontaine.

RESULTS OF THE CONDEMNATION

The Congregation of the Index's letter disturbed my friends who at once sent me their condolences and also their advice. M. Lejay first set about safeguarding from the clutches of censure two articles that I had sent him without delay, reassuring me of their fate. He wrote (June 27th):

> Your two articles are being typeset. They will appear under the common title: "La doctrine du péché originel dans saint Augustin: 1 avant la controverse pélagienne; 2 pendant la controverse pélagienne."
>
> I shall profit from the delay that has so long overwhelmed us to do a double issue of 192 pages. It is possible to allow you fifty or so pages without raising any eyebrows. If you want, M. de Nolhac will send you an official letter refusing to return your articles and informing you that, the cost of typesetting being paid, they have become the property of the Revue. Afterwards, you will see what you must do.

The two articles on Saint Augustine that I had sent to the *Revue* at the first warning sign appeared in the double issue of October. At Rennes they were so annoyed by a misadventure of which I will soon speak that it did not even occur to them to call me to account. Cardinal Richard, on the other hand, who had received official notification of my submission in July, of course believed I was toeing the line. No difficulty arose.

I had thus succeeded in saving two articles. But what would happen next? The expectations of my friends and I were thrown by a completely unexpected turn of events. Toward the middle of September, in accordance

PART ONE: How I Freed Myself of Dogma

with my promise of submission, I sent a manuscript to the archdiocese. Fifteen days later, a young priest, M. Delépine, who had studied theology at the Roman College with the personal secretary Charost,[149] came to say this: "M. the Vicar General Durusselle to whom you sent a manuscript gave it to M. Charost. Unfortunately, after reading it, M. Charost misplaced it. He is extremely upset over this accident and will come to present his apologies in person. He asked me to tell you of his visit."

Had I kept even a modicum of company with the Rennes clergy I would have known that Abbé Charost's absentmindedness and muddles were a byword. My life as a recluse had left me in complete ignorance on this subject. Also, in learning of the loss of my work, I felt intensely irritated and angry. The next day Abbé Charost appeared at my residence. He sent in his card with my servant. I returned it to him with these words: "I cannot receive this gentleman." He returned to the archbishop's residence whence he wrote as follows:

4 October 1901

Monsieur Abbé,

I did not come to inform you of the disappearance of your manuscript: I assumed that you had been told of it. I came to tell you the bitter regret this incident causes me. I cannot forgive myself for this so very unfortunate mistake. I realize that this work must have cost you a great deal of trouble and research. It displayed a very extensive knowledge extremely pertinent to the subject. It implied an outstanding concern for truth and moderation.

The Cardinal, I feel, was inclined to give the Imprimatur. *But I have no official authority, and the Council, of which I am not a member, judged differently. I came to tell you on behalf of M. Durusselle who asked me to do so, that its opposition does not imply any unfavorable assessment of your work in itself, nor any prohibition against printing it. It means, according to the Vicar General, that the description of the uncertainties and trial and error of Catholic thought in matters of dogma is of a nature to disturb the Christian laity. The Index wanted to remind the Ecclesiastical Tribunal that this is a question of appropriateness and prudence that it cannot let pass.*

I came, secondly, to put myself at your disposal in order to repair, as far as I am able, the completely unintended wrong I have done you. I would have been happy to transcribe, if need be at your dictation, the work that you have in your mind and perhaps virtually in your notes. In truth, you can accept this offer quite simply made without being in my debt, for it really would be doing me a service.

Please . . .

A. Charost

In the official part of this letter, Cardinal Labouré and his secretary Charost, hiding behind a nonexistent council, refused me the "Imprimatur" all the while pretending not to prohibit printing. But what was the point of the so-called liberty they favored me with when Rome prohibited me from publishing anything without my ordinary's approval? I felt like the victim of a horrible joke. However, I feigned not to have understood and several days later sent a manuscript to the *Revue*, reserving the right to dispute my error if difficulties arose.

It was not long before I found out that there was no duplicity where I thought I had seen it, or rather that there was, but not such as I had imagined. I learned from the same Fr. Delépine that Cardinal Labouré, humiliated by the affront inflicted upon him by Paris and Rome in admonishing him to keep an eye on one of his priests, had refused to go along with it. He had said in reference to me: "Since Cardinal Richard has denounced him, let him keep watch over him if he wants; as for myself, I am leaving him in peace." He left me in peace, in fact. My manuscripts took themselves off to the *Revue d'histoire et de littérature religieuses* without passing through the archdiocese and Cardinal Labouré never disturbed me. Cardinal Richard, for his part, no longer had the right to inspect my manuscripts since he had received official notification of my submission. The Paris Ecclesiastical Tribunal could no longer concern itself with me, lest it offend its sister at Rennes; the Rennes Tribunal said to that of Paris: "I leave him to you since you claim he belongs to you." The weapon that Cardinal Richard had taken up against me was turned against him. As for myself, as beneficiary of this little conflict, I was free.

On condition, naturally, that I did not pass certain limits. But which ones? Up until the end of 1901, fighting without a mask I had avoided not only direct attacks against dogma, but certain bold statements likely to scandalize narrow minds. My other method had been to lower the visor and resort to a pseudonym; yet this was in fact the case for only two published articles, one in the *Revue d'histoire et de littérature religieuses* of July 1901 under the name of Denys Lenain, the other in *Justice sociale* of August 13,

Part One: How I Freed Myself of Dogma

1901 under the signature of Goulven Lézurec."[150] From the day when my freedom was solidly established, I extended the limits of my boldness and felt I could, without disguise, dig about in the theologians and the Fathers at my ease while sparing only dogma proper. My venture worked perfectly for several years, in spite of a complication of which I must now speak.

---

* I shall profit from this occasion to establish the true text of the following sentence in the article: "The Providence that permitted a false explanation of the dogma of the Redemption to reign for nearly one thousand years in the Church, allowed, at the same time, the doctrine of satisfaction to undergo a long eclipse from the death of Saint Paul to the appearance of Saint Anselm."

10

My Introduction to the *Revue du clergé français*

ON AUGUST 20, 1900 I received the following letter from M. Bricout,[151] secretary of the *Revue du clergé français*:

> Would you like to write articles for us on each of the four eminent men named by Leo XIII in his Letter to the French Clergy: Pétau, Thomassin, Mabillon, Bossuet? . . . These are delicate matters and our Revue *is not as daring as the* Revue d'histoire et de littérature religieuses; *but it is possible nonetheless to speak with some freedom . . . Naturally you will sign in your own name the four articles requested.*

And, a year later, on August 30, 1901, Denys Lenain, too, received the following letter addressed by the same secretary to the RHLR, who forwarded it to me:

> One of our subscribers is asking me to recommend a book treating the following subject from the Ecclesiastical Congresses: 'Celibacy in the Latin Church and Greek Church.' I enjoyed reading your short note in the Revue *d'histoire et littérature religieuses (last issue, p. 458), which inspired me to approach you . . . There might even be an opportunity to treat this subject in our* Revue du Clergé Français. *One could no doubt say without giving offense something good of this topic if one kept to history, without drawing any conclusions opposed to* current *practice. What do you think?*

Denys Lenain refused the proffered gift. Joseph Turmel accepted and, several months later, I sent M. Bricout articles on Pétau, Mabillon, Thomassin,[152] articles that were to be followed by a longer study on Bossuet. Pétau,

PART ONE: How I Freed Myself of Dogma

which opened the series, was scheduled to appear in August 1901 when, on July 22nd, I received this letter from M. Bricout:

> *You did not inform me of the incident related to the Congregation of the Holy Office's letter. But one of my highly-placed friends, who knew of it, advised me, before publishing your work, to approach Cardinal Richard about you. I did so yesterday. The Cardinal, on the strength of M. Lesêtre's very favorable evaluation of your article on Pétau, does not oppose publication, but he requests that it should be delayed. As you can well appreciate, I can only obey. I hope to obtain authorization to publish your three articles December 1st and 15th and January 1st . . . Best to be patient. Neither you, nor we, nor truth will lose anything: we will profit from it.*

Then several weeks later (October 16th) M. Bricout wrote me again:

> *Cardinal Richard informs me through M. Lesêtre, pastor of Saint-Etienne-du-Mont, that your articles must have the preliminary approval of your Ordinary before we can publish them. There is nothing to say: we must do what is asked of us.*

Every year newspapers describe the passing back-and-forth of the budget between the Palais-Bourbon and the Luxembourg, as if they volley a tennis ball to each other until they agree. If I may compare small things to great, my poor manuscripts were thus tossed about for nearly six weeks. After receiving them from M. Bricout, I sent them to the archdiocese of Rennes. They returned them with a pleasant note giving me complete freedom and I sent them to the secretary of the *Revue du clergé français* informing him of the favorable disposition of my Ordinary. M. Bricout replied that Cardinal Richard required a formal "Imprimatur" and not merely the assurance of favorable dispositions. The Rennes Tribunal, when I communicated this decision, entrenched itself behind the law and put forward as an excuse an article of the "Index" under terms of which only the archdiocese of Paris was qualified to give the "Imprimatur" to writings published in its diocese. Cardinal Richard, informed by M. Bricout of the reply from Rennes, was unyielding, and for a third time I had to return to the attack with my superiors. My letter must have been sharp, for M. Charost wrote to me:

> *I am determined to reply to your second letter of this morning to tell you that, in spite of conduct that could have offended me, nothing would be more distasteful to me than to cause you embarrassment*

My Introduction to the Revue du clergé français

or to hold up the publication of work done with the competence and scientific care that you display.

But they persisted in hiding behind the law, declaring it beyond their power to give me the "Imprimatur." In granting it, one would have strayed beyond one's jurisdiction, would have done what only Cardinal Richard was in a position to do.

Irritated by all this red tape, I wrote to Cardinal Labouré himself to enlighten him about the inextricable predicament I had been in for more than a month and which, despite my willing desire for submission, I could not escape. The cardinal replied through his vicar general:

30 November 1901

My dear friend,

His eminence the cardinal charges me with the following reply to the request you have made regarding your articles on Pères Pétau, Thomassin, Mabillon.

According to the regulations of canon law, if the editor wishes to secure the Imprimatur *affixed to the beginning or the end of your articles in his journal, this* Imprimatur *must have appended the signature of the Ordinary of Paris, who has sole jurisdiction and capacity to give it. The Ordinary of Rennes could only appear there under the rubric* Nihil obstat, *which, while not the usual practice, is not, after all, forbidden. The cardinal of Rennes can do no more.*

Yours, dear friend . . .

F. Durusselle, v.g.

I thus requested, on the off chance, whether they might affix this "Nihil obstat" to each of my manuscripts. They consented with good grace. And my papers once again returned to Paris, equipped with the lightning rod I was testing.

The lightning rod performed marvels. On December 6th M. Bricout wrote to me:

Dear Monsieur,

Cardinal Richard declares himself satisfied. The Ordinary's Imprimatur is not customarily requested for journal articles; it is solely because of your particular situation that he has required for your articles in the Revue *what is normally required only for books: a* Nihil obstat *from your Ordinary. At last it is settled. We shall then begin to publish you on the 15th.*

Part One: How I Freed Myself of Dogma

Pétau did, in fact, appear on December 15, 1901.[153] The three other eminent men of the Church of France had their turn.[154] But this was not all. In 1903 M. Bricout asked me to do the review [chronique] of ecclesiastical history. I accepted. At first there were two per year. Then there were four. Then came Consultations, that is, essays on particular points of ecclesiastical history. I became one of the principal suppliers of the *Revue du clergé français*. My wares did not go down badly with the *Revue*'s clientele; at least according to M. Bricout who wrote to me on February 16, 1906:

> *Our readers appreciate you a great deal; take however many pages you think necessary.*

September 18, 1906:

> *Your last article on Bossuet and contemporary theology was very much appreciated and by excellent connoisseurs. Thank you! Thanks also for your excellent Consultations.*

November 19, 1906:

> *You do so well and your reviews are received so well that I am asked for more of them. Would you be willing to give a review every two months instead of every three months? Your Consultations work wonders.*

January 15, 1907:

> *Your review is of the greatest interest.*

The following February 19th:

> *Your Consultation on Saint Chrysostom and confession has attracted a great deal of attention: Père Bainvel[155] and M. Odelin,[156] Vicar General of Paris, said good things about it to me.*

Nevertheless, M. Bricout sometimes worried in case the Rennes Tribunal might, one day, refuse me the precious talisman of the "Nihil obstat." In his letter of September 26, 1906, he said, with regard to a subject of some delicacy: "Is this not too shocking? Will they give you the 'Nihil obstat'?" I reassured him. He himself soon noted that my superiors were unstintingly liberal. For toward mid-February 1907, I sent him, stamped with the "Nihil obstat" a note on the Inquisition with an openly Voltarian flavor (it appeared on March 1st). Favorably surprised to see that the customs had

My Introduction to the Revue du clergé français

let this forbidden meat slip through, he joyfully wrote to me (February 19, 1907):

> *This good M. Durusselle is admirable. His* Nihil obstat *is extremely useful.*[*]

In the spring of 1907 I resolved to leave the *Revue* in order to devote myself exclusively to longer-term projects that I was being asked to do from various quarters, and I sent in my resignation.

M. Bricout replied:

> *Paris May 30*
>
> "*No, my dear Monsieur Turmel, you cannot do this. It would do you considerable harm because your conduct would be interpreted in a very negative way. You would make me personally very sad... No, it would be a serious failing just now. Our work is a work of the future and you are doing good; with prudence we shall succeed, sooner or later. If you find that a review every two months is too much work, send one every three months as before... Agreed? I am counting on you.*
>
> *Yesterday, in a meeting, MM. Pisani,*[157] *Boudinhon,*[158] *Lesêtre, Hemmer,*[159] *etc., told me how pleased they were with your pages on the Invention of the Holy Cross.*

His insistence disarmed me. I withdrew my resignation: which prompted the following letter:

> *4 June 1907*
>
> *Dear Monsieur Turmel,*
>
> *I thank you most warmly for continuing your regular collaboration with us. I hope this will continue forever. A short review every three months will not overly fatigue and you will be doing good work, salutary work. Times are hard; but with prudence and cleverness one can sort it out... Once again, profound thanks, and take heart.*

However, the concert of praise that accompanied my reviews was not unanimous. Discordant notes sounded here and there. And M. Bricout knew it, for I read in his letter of April 16, 1907:

> *The superior of a major seminary recently wrote that your criticism is 'singularly corrosive.' Beware the Montagnini denunciations!*[160]

---

[*] The examination of my manuscripts fell upon Abbé Charost. He made an oral report to M. Durusselle who then signed the *Nihil obstat*.

Part One: How I Freed Myself of Dogma

> And, in his letter of January 8, 1908:
>
> *Do they not give you any grief at Rennes over your collaboration with the* Revue? *Just between us, several members of the Council of Vigilance[161] here have found your last review 'dangerous for many.' Ah! How careful you need to be! Take heart all the same!*

I must acknowledge that such anxieties were not unfounded. No sooner had I established, on textual grounds, that confession was unknown to Saint Chrysostom, than the same methods led me to realize Saint Augustine's ignorance of the real presence. Here I left Saint Basil to attack the papacy; elsewhere I had Saint Ambrose intervene to reject the fires of hell and the eternal punishment of Christians. In short, all my reviews, except the first in which I had held myself in check, delivered more or less violent blows to Christian dogmas, and the Consultations had the same objective. In sum, I conscientiously devastated dogma in the *Revue d'histoire et de littérature religieuses*, and accomplished the same work with the same application in the *Revue du clergé français* where my manuscripts were never without the Rennes Tribunal's "Nihil obstat."

And it was this "Nihil obstat" that protected me from Cardinal Richard's police. Without this protective shield the Paris council of vigilance would have expelled me at the start from a *Revue* that took pride in its submission to ecclesiastical authority. But what could it say when, at the head of each of my manuscripts, one read the signature of the vicar general of Rennes attesting to my orthodoxy? "Nihil obstat": these two magic words spoke volumes to the archbishop of Paris: "Eminence, legally the articles published in the *Revue du clergé français* come under your authority; you alone have the right to examine them, to judge them. And if we, the Ecclesiastical Tribunal of Rennes, have examined the attached manuscript, it is in response to your repeated order and uniquely to obey you. Well, after examination we declare the foresaid manuscript irreproachable." Faced with this declaration the Paris council of vigilance could only groan: it was impotent. In denouncing my *Revue d'histoire et de littérature religieuses* articles to Rome, Cardinal Richard reckoned on dealing me a mortal blow, but struck himself instead, since these articles were henceforth removed from his jurisdiction. The "Nihil obstat" he had been determined to exact from Rennes for my entrance to the *Revue du clergé français* had caused him the same difficulty. His second weapon, like the first, was turned against him.

Here I will tell you two incidents which occurred during my collaboration with the *Revue du clergé français*.

My Introduction to the Revue du clergé français

The first was caused by an article published by M. Vacandard in the *Revue* of October 15, 1905. In glancing through it I quickly saw that the good abbé had borrowed entire pages from my *Théologie positive*, some reproduced literally, others with small variations and that he had forgotten not only quotation marks, but also to cite me. It was plagiarism in all its beauty. Surprised by this conduct in an author of good reputation in the Catholic world, I protested to M. Bricout who sent my letter to the party in question. Several days later M. Vacandard apologized profusely and offered his contrition. Only he forgot that my complaint was directed primarily to the literal reproduction of my texts which lacked quotation marks indicating their source. In the article "Confession" that he published shortly thereafter in the *Dictionnaire de théologie catholique*, he said at several points that he had used my work, but still forgot to place literal reproduction of my texts in quotation marks.[162]

The second incident was occasioned by a passage in my study on "Bossuet" (*Revue* of July 15, 1906, p. 346) where, speaking of Maccabean psalms, I said that their existence had been recognized by a celebrated Jesuit, the future Cardinal Patrizi.[163] There was, in fact, a Jesuit named Patrizi who had supported the thesis of Maccabean psalms; but this was not the future cardinal, it was his brother. My mistake was pointed out to me by Père Genocchi,[164] professor at the Sapienza, in a very kind letter in which he informed me that this Père Patrizi had at one time had as a student the future Leo XIII. (I am inclined to believe that, without the patronage of this powerful pupil, he never would have been able to publish his thesis on the Maccabean psalms. In any case, for many years no apologist has dared follow him.)

Alfred Loisy

1) As of 1885 Loisy ceased to adhere to the Christian faith. From that time onward he dismissed all dogmas, including that of a personal God. This piece of information is certain, since Loisy himself provides it in *Choses passées* and in *Mémoires*. Despite this decisive personal testimony, M. Leblanc[165] has, in a justificatory memoir (p. 14, 28, 35–47), tried to demonstrate that, up until his excommunication, Loisy retained faith in the sense that he believed in a progressive evolution of the Roman Church. To speak thus is to play with words and introduce an ill-timed pun into a serious discussion. What is universally meant by Christian faith is adherence to dogma. Let us then concede that from this date he no longer had faith.

2) Until 1908, that is for twenty-three years, Loisy remained in the Roman Church, all of whose teaching he had rejected. Except for miniscule exceptions, priests to whom the futility of dogmas has been revealed through study are unable to break their chains. If the Roman Church knew the depths of their souls, after having deceived them with its dishonest methods it would cast them into the street to perish of hunger, being unable, as in times past, to burn them. These disillusioned priests remain in the Church which has bound them to its service only by concealing the truth. It is their right. Loisy followed this example. He sided with Cardinal Meignan, Archbishop Mignot, Duchesne. He cannot be blamed. The responsibility for this situation rests upon the Church itself which resorts to lies to enlist clerics.

3) Loisy made two professions of faith: one on March 7, 1890, in the oath he pronounced after his doctorate in theology; the other on December 7, 1893, in his letter to Leo XIII. In the oath, he declared his adherence to all the Church's dogmas and he committed himself to interpreting the Bible solely in accordance with the Fathers' unanimous consent. In his letter to

the pope, he affirmed "his fidelity to the teachings of the Church and especially to those that are contained in the encyclical *De studiis scripturae sacrae*.[166] From a legal standpoint, these commitments had precisely the value of promises made by a cutthroat's victim at knifepoint: they were invalid. But they warned the author to watch himself in order to avoid cruel reprisals.

4) In 1893, Loisy was dismissed as professor at the Institut catholique. Over the course of the following years, various sanctions were imposed upon him. Finally, in 1902, his book *L'Évangile et l'Église* incurred multiple episcopal condemnations. He protested against these measures that, according to him, were unjustified. His protests exploded most violently when the fate of *L'Évangile et l'Église* was being settled. According to him, it was his enemies (Batiffol[167] and Lagrange[168]) who represented this book as an instrument of warfare intended, in the guise of apologetic, to trouble souls. It was they who made the hierarchy suspicious and brought down condemnation on his writing, condemnation it would otherwise have escaped. It is impossible for us to take his recriminations seriously. His enemies were surely not alone in detecting a hidden purpose in the book, underlying the apparent goal but quite distinct from it. Duchesne, who was not an enemy, wrote to the author (*Mémoires* 2, 157):

> You are so far ahead of us that we still may not be able to understand you. So it must be hoped *for it is your only means of escape.*

And, noting that Cardinal Mathieu[169] had not read the first two chapters, he added:

> It will be just as well if his Eminence does not finish reading it, for it must be said that Hic jacet lepus, [Here is the crux of the problem], and it is a big one.

Besides, we have another account that the author cannot challenge since it is his own. Here is what one reads in *Choses passées*, p. 246:

> *My defense of the Roman Church implied abandoning absolute theses professed by scholastic theology concerning the formal institution of the Church and its sacraments by Christ, the immutability of dogmas and the nature of ecclesiastical authority. Thus I did not limit myself to critiquing M. Harnack, I insinuated,* discretely but really, *an essential reform of biblical exegesis, of all of theology and even of Catholicism in general.*

Part One: How I Freed Myself of Dogma

> ... *One part of my books could find favor with all Catholics; the other part*, despite the precautions *I took with language, and although it presented itself in a way under cover of the former, could give rise to opposition.*

There are certainly strong reservations to be made with respect to this admission (toned down in the *Mémoires* 2, 168ff.), which claims only to call into question Scholastic theology and which, in reality, attacks all the councils. The least one can say is that it is incomplete. Let us take it as it is. The author recognizes that, under the guise of defending the Catholic Church against Harnack, he was proposing to bring about an essential reform of Catholicism, ranging from its profession of faith to the institution of the Church and its sacraments by Christ. What is that, if not a concealed but fierce assault against all Christian beliefs? By his clever tactic Loisy counted on fooling the hierarchy's police and destroying dogmas. People of independent mind will deplore his failure; they will regret that the hierarchy stirred out of its sleep, perhaps shaken up by the denouncers. But they can go no further. Loisy, under the pretext of defending the Roman Church against Harnack wanted to undermine the whole of Christian dogmatics without appearing to do so. Everything he has written since 1893 has had the same purpose. He is wasting his time in trying to put us off the track with regard to his intentions.

5) On March 10, 1904 Loisy was tormented by a qualm of conscience that it is useful to mention. Here is how the *Mémoires* 2, p. 380 recount the event:

> *Do I still believe enough* to call myself Catholic *and is what I believe* Catholic? *I remain in the Church for purposes of moral opportunity, not of faith. It would take little, very little, to make it impossible for me to practice honestly as priest. If this little occurred, I would not be surprised. I even believe that I would not be upset . . . It seems clear enough that, whatever I believe, I do not believe in what the Church teaches and that the Church is not disposed to teach what I believe. Can I with honesty stay in the Church? The Catholic system in its entirety, doctrine and discipline, is contrary to reason and to life. It is not supernatural in origin, it is* sheer madness *in the guise of logic. I shall drag myself to the grave pursued by these misapprehensions.*

If one dismisses all dogmas in 1885, including the dogma of a personal God, one does not wait until 1904 to ask whether one can honestly remain in the Church. This sort of question has to be settled at once. Since

1885 the author had known why he had the right to remain in the Church which had deceitfully trapped him into serving it. He had nonetheless decided to remain in the Church in spite of this. But the damage he suffered finally changed his attitude. Today, he would like to be outside the sanctuary and seeks occasion to leave it. His alleged qualm is only a fiction meant to color his desire. The *Mémoires* were written for the public. The author is playacting here. As for knowing whether one still has Catholic faith at the moment when one is calling Catholic dogmatics sheer madness, this absurd question comes from a colossal lapse of attention. The author, in a fever of anxiety, has not looked critically at what he wrote.

Now let us see what Loisy's feelings were with regard to the Roman Church. On October 15, 1902, on the eve of publishing *L'Évangile et l'Église*, he writes (*Mémoires* 2, 149):

> *The Church is to be* exterminated *as the great enemy of human progress unless it is susceptible to amendment. Inversely, it is to be supported, defended, enlightened by all possible means if it remains the great moral resource of civilization. Those who choose the first see only their own point of view. Yet I believe that the second is true.*

Among those who did not believe an amendment possible is Duchesne (2, 276): "I am less optimistic. We are caught between the necessity and *the impossibility of changing*, and I am afraid we shall not get through it." And again another statement (3, 342): "It is certain that the old game is very sick ... But can we hope for the coming of a new religious system and are we not proceeding rather toward the obliteration of religious feeling?" With Duchesne it is necessary to associate Mgr Meignan who said (1, 229): "I am convinced that our society cannot live without the Church and yet I see that it is in the process of doing without it;" and who, faced with a project for reform, replied (1, 230): "That is difficult, impossible." In 1902 Loisy does not want to be so pessimistic; he still thinks the Church capable of reform. But he does not deny that there are serious reasons against his view; he recognizes that one can believe in the impossibility of an evolution without losing heart. And, imagining this to be so for a moment, he does not hesitate to draw its consequence: "The Church is to be exterminated as the great enemy of human progress." In the meanwhile he disparages the Church's current regime and puts its defenders in their place. On November 16, 1902 he writes (2, 158):

Part One: How I Freed Myself of Dogma

> *It is certain that the Church's current regime is a school of lies and servility ... The imbeciles, the cowards, the liars are sitting pretty and the right thing to do would be to squash them like vermin between finger and thumb ... Catholicism's future must not be left to a troop of fools and liars dragging along behind them a papacy all too politicized and an episcopacy all too ignorant.*

To squash the Church's defenders as vermin because they are fools and liars! In 1902, that is the program of the man who will later boast of hating nothing, of having only love at heart!

In 1902, Loisy still hoped to bring the Church in line with history and science. And his love went to this ideal Church, to this Church of the future whose father he would one day be. Little by little, he perceived that his ideal Church was an illusory dream and that the present Church would keep its tares. He then no longer in any way nuanced the disparagement he was heaping on the Roman Church. On May 10, 1904, he wrote (2, 386):

> *Real Catholicism is not in the least a part of moral progress, of such incomparable value that its defects can be overlooked. It is a formidable obstacle to the intellectual progress and true morality of the contemporary world, which simply wants to go forward.*

In another twenty-five years his thought would be complete. The author of the *Mémoires*, having once again denounced "the tyranny" of Roman Catholicism, adds (1, 179):

> *It must be opposed but not only by argument for it will be vanquished only by societies' reaction against its unbearable yoke and its absurd claims.*

One reads in another place in the same work (3, 338):

> *I never counted on Italy to save our hapless globe from pontifical tyranny. It is the planet's responsibility to save itself and without too much trouble it could do so.*

In any case he knows that nothing can be expected from Catholic scholars. He says (2. 249):

> *The apologists can only blind themselves to the obvious monstrosity of this absolutism. Indeed, Catholicism's leaders will never abandon their absurd claims while Catholic scholars seem to believe in the divinity of this delirium.*

Let us sum up. The tyranny of the Roman Church is "an unbearable yoke;" its "claims" are "absurd;" its absolutism is an "obvious monstrosity;" its leaders give evidence of "delirium;" Catholicism is a formidable obstacle "to intellectual progress and to true morality;" it "is not in the least a part of moral progress;" it must not be "opposed only by argument" seeing that it does not listen to it. What is required is "societies' reaction." The author yearns for this reaction which would clear the world of the Roman Church. He finds that it is a long time coming. He is all the more impatient since it would not be much trouble to carry out the work he wants done.

These observations were indispensable for appreciating the value of two allegations found in the *Mémoires* and of which I have not yet spoken. The first deals with my studies on the history of dogmas. Loisy (3, 561), shies away from the very particular attitude I adopted with regard to the Church by outwardly professing Catholicism's dogmas while fighting them to the death in my publications. He views this as a delicate subject on which, out of charity, he will not insist.

I believe I have shown Loisy that he is not in a position to cast a stone at me. All the same there remains a point to clarify. Where have I fought dogmas to the death while professing them outwardly? First, in the *Revue d'histoire et de littérature religieuses* re-established by Loisy in 1910. Later, beginning in 1925, I continued in the collection "Christianisme" and in the *Revue d'histoire des religions*. But it is in Loisy's *Revue* that from 1910 to 1922 Coulange, Lagarde, Vanbeck, Dulac, Lawson, Gallerand, Michel, Perrin, Delafosse took it in turn to wage war on dogmas, to the death. And how was I introduced to this *Revue*? Did I approach Loisy? Did I beg him to accept my writings? It is Loisy who took the initiative and who asked for my collaboration. Several times he did not hide the fact that he needed long articles and that the *Revue* would not have worked without my collaboration. Loisy would not have been able to salvage his review nor publish his studies in it had I not been there to supply him with copy. Of course my manuscripts would have remained buried in my drawers had the *Revue* not provided an outlet for them; Loisy deserves my gratitude for the enormous favors he did me. Yet, if he judges that I have forfeited honor, I do not see how he can escape criticism for complicity.

Naturally Loisy does not broach this question. On the other hand, he insists on closely associating M. Couchoud[170] and M. Sartiaux[171] with my excommunication. According to him (3, 560) both "contributed ... to the event." And, on page 544, no doubt judging my excommunication a most amusing spectacle, he calls it "a grand theological Punch and Judy show" that I put on with the aid of several collaborators, among whom is "Doctor Couchoud." I am pleased to learn that Rome's decree so delighted him. But I am obliged to tell him that M. Couchoud and M. Sartiaux had nothing to do with it. The glory of this fine work belongs exclusively to three great stars of the French Church named Rivière,[172] Saltet,[173] and Verdin.[174] And it wrongs these illustrious personages to rob them of the smallest particle of that glory. However, working on the principles inspiring Loisy, one could, I acknowledge, assign them a collaborator. Who? Well, to find him one has only to trace the venture of denunciation to its beginnings. It began with a report based on an article by Gallerand. This article would never have appeared if Loisy had not asked me for copy for his journal. From which it follows that from Loisy's grotesque point of view it was he who "contributed" to what he calls "the event."

The second allegation concerns the hatred of the Roman Church of which Houtin and I would be found guilty. In a fit of rage verging on epilepsy (3, 558) Loisy submerges us in virulent insults on this topic, and he heaps up grandiose phrases to explain that all hatred is fanaticism and that all fanaticism is mental derangement. People ignore the raging cries of a drunkard and, when Loisy wrote page 558 of tome 3 he was drunk with anger. I shall not waste time hurling back his insults. I shall not even repeat the statement of Père Lagrange who (3, 542) called him Tartuffe. I merely want to express the common-sense truth that hatred is not in itself evil and that it can be a duty. The Roman Church systematically hides the truth from the clerics whom it enlists in its service; whenever it can, it wrings the neck of those who bring awkward truths to light; it forbids its faithful access to the books in which these truths are taught. This immoral regime which enslaves souls has broken my life. But it has also given it direction. Martyr to the truth, it seemed to me that I had a duty to be its apostle. It is to accomplish the work of apostleship that, for the past fifty years, I have endeavored to bring a small ray of light to a few minds blinded by error. By the same token I fought the Roman Church and became its enemy, since spreading the truth means fighting error. I have nothing but aversion for a power that, for more than fifty years, has tortured me for unmasking its lies. But, in giving expression to this feeling, I lag well behind the author of the *Mémoires*. In any case, a person is not qualified to preach love for the Roman Church when he has struck it sledgehammer blows by the dozen and when he dreamt of squashing its apologists like vermin.

What led Loisy led to a paroxysm of rage that caused him to lose control of his ideas? Everything can be explained by hatred, a violent hatred that possessed him with regard to Albert Houtin. For several years Houtin saw Loisy often. He appreciated his talent. But he also perceived a number of slight shortcomings of which he took note. Renan said (*Souvenirs d'enfance*, p. 347[175]): "If ever a comic author wanted to amuse the public with my foibles, I would ask one thing only, namely to let me collaborate with him." Loisy thinks he has reached perfection without the slightest stain. As long as he did not know about those damning notes about him, he did not stint in his praise for Houtin. From the day he became aware of the crime of lese majesty perpetuated against him, he felt only an aversion bordering on horror for the guilty party.

No doubt the reader will wonder on what grounds I could have become the butt of the aversion showed for Houtin; it is not clear how the one is connected to the other. I will tell you. M. Sartiaux, a railway engineer for the Compagnie du Nord, was associated with Albert Houtin. He published several of his friend's notes about Loisy in a book entitled *Mon expérience, Ma vie laïque*, published under his auspices. This was why Loisy harbored a hatred against him equal, if not greater, than he had for Houtin.

But me? Well, I sinned against Loisy. Without knowing it, true, but I did indeed.

It was in 1926. Albert Houtin had just died. M. Sartiaux, with whom I was not acquainted, informed me that his friend had left a history of ecclesiastical celibacy incomplete. And he asked me to complete it. I accepted. Nearly half of the *Courte histoire du célibat ecclésiastique* was written by me under the name of Dulac. At this time I was completely unaware of the hatred Loisy bore toward Albert Houtin and M. Sartiaux. But my collaboration allied me with his greatest enemies; the irreverence was unpardonable. Loisy let me know this in a letter of November 19, 1930 in which, after having lamented my relations with M. Couchoud and M. Sartiaux, he added:

> *I deplored Dulac's participation in the* Courte histoire du célibat ecclésiastique.

After a few moments of disbelief, I decided to laugh at the rancor and self-conceit so naively displayed in the letter. Some weeks later, the *Mémoires* let me see the virulence with which these two diseases ravaged the soul of their unhappy victim.

Part One: How I Freed Myself of Dogma

I now move on to a different subject. *Histoire des dogmes* (4)[176] points out Loisy's partial agreement with the way I explain the origin of the Pauline epistles. This agreement which I take as an honor leads me to two comments:

1) Loisy appropriates half my system without informing the reader that he borrowed it from me. I am bound to let him know that his conduct is seriously incorrect.

2) After having used half my system, Loisy did not have the right to make out that he rejected it as a whole. But this is what he does in disdainful terms on page 9 of *La Naissance du christianisme*.[177] In the *Mémoires*, where he already borrows from me, the disdain is accompanied by crass insults explained, it is true, by the author's paroxysms of fury.

Note on Three Jesuits

THE JESUIT LEBRETON[178] (*ÉTUDES* 1934, March, p. 627), spoke of the letter of Saint Polycarp (that I translated and commented on), without knowing the first thing about the topic. But he took the opportunity to let fly an impertinent remark. He did what he could, that is to bluff.

The Jesuit Doncoeur,[179] in the midst of his review of a novel (*Études*, 1934, January, p. 97), hurled a crude insult. I restrained myself from wrangling with this foul-mouthed individual.

The Jesuit Cavallera[180] published (*Dictionnaire de théologie catholique* t. 12, 2590) a paean of praise of his colleague Portalié[181] who conducted such a fine campaign of denunciation against me in 1903. He managed to cast a stone at me and to fling another of the same caliber to the archbishop of Rennes, Mgr Dubourg.[182] But he speaks neither of the affront his hero once received from his Paris confreres, nor of the distress provoked by this misadventure in which he was treated as a vile snitch. (See *Bulletin de Toulouse* 1931, p. 245, where these confreres are presented as "the pride of Catholic science").[183] An eccentric historian, Cavallera is also an eminent zealot. The second makes up for the first.

PART TWO

How the Roman Church Freed Itself of Me

A translation of *Comment l'Église romaine m'a donné congé*
Translated by C. J. T. Talar

Introduction

A SHORT WHILE AGO I told how the study of the Bible had ruined my belief in dogma. I added that, persecuted by the Roman Church in those days, I irrevocably decided to be an apostle of the truth for which I became a martyr; and I mentioned the principal writings that I published over the course of 1898–1906. Here I am going to show how the Roman Church, seeing me working at spreading the truth, ended in issuing a decree of excommunication against me. In 1886 I had dismissed dogmas; in 1930 the Roman Church dismissed me. This book, which describes the revenge of dogmas, thus completes the first which told of my revolt against dogmas. Here I assume the reader to be knowledgeable regarding my writings anterior to 1906. Perhaps, however, it is useful to recall that, since 1898, several of my writings appeared in the *Revue d'histoire et de littérature religieuses* founded by Loisy, with Lejay as secretary.*

---

* The story of my life was written at a single stroke in 1931, and it ought to have appeared as a single volume in 1932. Circumstances beyond my control dictated its being cut into two parts which could be published only at different times.

1

Dupin and Herzog[*]

MY COLLABORATION WITH THE *Revue d'histoire et de littérature religieuses* languished. Lejay complained in a friendly way. I sent him some copy. I was not lacking for material. First I picked up, from my old manuscripts, the one on the origins of the Trinity. Then, as the sequel to this study required a complete revision that I did not have time to accomplish, I left the Trinity unfinished and followed it up with a history of the Blessed Virgin that I still found completely satisfactory.

All the writings that I had published in the *Revue* up until that time openly set out to discredit the theologians, to demolish theology. However, with regard to dogmas they limited themselves to oblique and prudently measured blows that the uninitiated could interpret as unintentional lack of precision in language. In all those writings diplomacy was paramount.

---

[*] Since space is lacking for me to expand upon other writings, I limit myself to the following particulars: at several points in my *Papauté*, published in 1908 (p. 247, 276, 280, 300, 303, 304) there occurs the following notice: "This translation appeared for the first time in the *Revue catholique des Églises*." Without this precaution I would have looked like the plagiarist of Dom Leclercq who, in his translation of Héfélé (Tome I, p. 813, 871, 876, 964, 978) published in 1907, paid me the honor of appropriating my translations without informing the reader (to be noted are two additional plagiarisms that in my *Papauté* pp. 257 and 296 I seemed to have taken from Héfélé 1, 819, 916). The same manner of composition reappeared in the article "Mabillon" in the *Revue du clergé français*, May 1902 (compare for example column 009 of the *Dictionnaire* with p. 617 of the *Revue*). Moreover, there are numerous historians whom the Benedictine scholar has silently copied. What he does, in fact, is to work in the same way as the redactor of the Pentateuch fitting together disparate texts from multiple authors. This is what sometimes makes his writing so confusing. Take, for example, the article "Ampoule" in his *Dictionnaire*. In order to understand it at all, it is necessary to read the sources he drew upon. [On Henri Leclercq see note 191]

PART TWO: How the Roman Church Freed Itself of Me

The two studies that I sent at the beginning of 1906 were not in the least diplomatic. The history of the Trinity took apart the great mystery of the Christian religion as one takes apart a mechanism. It laid bare the trial and error that had governed its elaboration. The fundamental dogma of the faith appeared there as a human, very human product, obtained as the result of multiple, complicated revisions that lacked any coherence. However, this very complication shrouded the mystery with an atmosphere of obscurity which only enhanced it. Only with considerable effort could one follow the evolution of the Trinity along its twists and turns. Lacking a serious study one was bound to remain in ignorance and could even consider oneself entitled to deny it.

In the history of the Blessed Virgin nothing of the kind. Here no convolutions, no complication. All was rectilinear and perfectly clear. Mary did not in any way suspect the divine mission of her son Jesus, since she tried one day to stop him, believing him to have "lost his mind;" consequently the alleged message of the angel Gabriel is a fiction. Mary had at least seven children, since the gospels attribute four brothers and some sisters to Jesus; and, consequently, the alleged perpetual virginity of the one who is called the Blessed Virgin is a legend. The Immaculate Conception was rejected by the greatest doctors of the thirteenth century, and her exemption from actual sin was unknown before the twelfth century. No extensive research is required to discover these truths. They are obvious, they cannot not fail to be obvious if one is simply willing to open one's eyes. In short, my two studies on the Trinity and on the Blessed Virgin were both lethal to dogmas; but the second crushed them more surely than the first. To have launched these two offensives under my own name would have been a foolish suicide, since the Church would have struck me down even before receiving my blows. Pseudonymity was required. Each of my works had its own: the history of the Trinity was signed Antoine Dupin; the history of the Blessed Virgin was the offspring of Guillaume Herzog.*[184]

Dupin's work appeared in the course of 1906. The first article upset Péchenard, rector of the Institut catholique,[185] who asked Lejay for an

---

* Dupin's brochure is no longer available; tome II of my *Histoire des dogmes* contains a revised and augmented edition of it. As for the Herzog work, also out of print, it received a second edition, partially abridged, partially corrected in *La Vierge Marie* published by Coulange with Rieder; it also finds a place in tome II of the *History of Dogmas*. I apologize for these remarks that may look like self-advertisement. I make them because of the number of readers who have vainly tried to procure the books about which newspapers and journals assailed our ears in 1929.

explanation. The latter replied that he had never been director of the *Revue* and that the authors never had been accountable to him. Probably the rector had made his complaint solely to cover himself, if need be, with the archdiocese and with Rome. What is certain is that the explanation Lejay gave him seemed cogent and he took it no further.

In the postscript to his letter of December 7, 1906, Lejay tells me that:

> Dupin's first article has generated a correspondence between M. Péchenard and myself that is of no great importance.

This laconic remark is clarified in a letter of August 2, 1908 in which Lejay, then on holiday in Pontailler-sur-Saône, brings to my attention a question that the rector Baudrillart[186] (I shall speak of him later) has asked him; then he adds:

> I reply: I am not up with the Herzog-Dupin question. I have never directed the *Revue d'histoire et de littérature religieuses*. Each collaborator was completely independent of the others as is the case with all scientific reviews. In a letter of July 1906, a record which I can easily put my hand on in Paris, I had the honor of explaining this situation to your predecessor who understood it perfectly. I am not going over this again and again. The insertion of the articles in question has nothing to do with me. Finally, I must point out that the last article of mine to appear in this journal came out in September 1906, as the end of a series begun in January, and that after the publication of the first Dupin article in May-June 1906 I terminated my collaboration as soon as it was possible to do so without creating a fuss (which I did of my own volition) and that Herzog's articles came out in 1907.

Cardinal Richard, who kept himself informed, certainly knew about the Dupin articles. But he did not consider it his duty to intervene. The history of the origins of the Trinity appeared without incident and did not create a disturbance. It was not the same with the first of Herzog's articles, entitled "La conception virginale du Christ." That caused a stir. Scarcely had it appeared when a learned Jesuit, Père Grandmaison,[187] and Cardinal Richard rushed to the defense of the holy ark. Each showed what he could do. Grandmaison tried to refute the irrefutable (*Études*, May 20, 1907). The cardinal promulgated the following ordinance (May 27, 1907):

> We, François Cardinal Richard, Archbishop of Paris, considering that the *Revue d'histoire et de littérature religieuses*, published at Paris, has recently issued, in addition to certain irreverent, bold

Part Two: How the Roman Church Freed Itself of Me

>and dangerous 'Chroniques bibliques,' several articles manifestly contrary to Catholic dogma, namely three articles signed Dupin on the Trinity, and an article signed Herzog on the virginal conception of Christ;
>
>That, in consequence, the collaboration of ecclesiastics with such a compendium would be of a nature to scandalize the faithful and to give it a dangerous authority;
>
>Forbid all ecclesiastics coming under our jurisdiction from collaborating in any way with the aforesaid journal.

Loisy, whose "Chroniques bibliques" were mentioned in the ordinance believed he should intervene to plead his case (*Quelques lettres*, p. 101[188]). He explained that his research, of a scientific order, was not answerable to the cardinal and that the measure taken by the latter against the *Revue* was an intolerable abuse of power. However his eloquent protest was incapable of rebuilding the ruin caused by the pious cardinal whose ordinance immediately received the adherence of most of the bishops. Deprived of its ecclesiastical editors, officially denounced to the entire clergy, the *Revue* was doomed to disappear. But before resigning himself to the inevitable, Lejay managed to furnish the subscribers with the conclusion of Herzog's work. That is what was done. At some point around then he wrote to me in sending the page proofs of the offprint:

>My compliments of the season to you and to your friend [Herzog]. Tell him that we are happy to fall with him in the Thermopyles of Modernism for the defense of civilization against Vatican barbarism.

It was in December of 1907 that the *Revue* ceased publication. Some weeks later several young priests who used to read it whispered among themselves that I was Herzog. And, at the same time, the chaplain of the Lycée, M. Duine, who was in correspondence with Mgr Duchesne, brought a letter from this scholarly prelate directed to me. Here it is:

>There is no mistake. Herzog is you: *Tu es ille vir*. I feel sorry for the archbishop of Rennes, harboring such a serpent at his breast. But I shall not denounce you. Send me your photograph.

The assurance with which Duchesne and several of Rennes' young priests drew, independently of one another, the same conclusions, had a common source. It was not difficult for me to find it. When, at the end of 1906, I had sent in my history of the Blessed Virgin without so much as a glance at it, I had not paid attention to the fact that this work, finished in 1899, had furnished several pages of my *Théologie positive*. The warnings that had just come one after another reminded me of this fact that I had forgotten in a moment of distraction. My manuscript of 1899 had provided copy for my *Théologie positive*. And for the public, whose judgment relied on external appearances, my *Théologie positive* published in 1903 had contributed to Herzog's work published in 1907 under the title *La Sainte-Vierge dans l'histoire*. The two books related closely to each other. A quick comparison was enough to establish this connection; for Duchesne certainly had not worked very hard to get to it; any more than the priests at Rennes. Once established, it was susceptible to two interpretations. One could conclude that Herzog had plagiarized my *Théologie positive*; one could also suspect that Herzog was a pseudonym created by me to serve as a cover. This second explanation, which had won over Duchesne and my fellow diocesans, was no doubt going to attract other support. What made it attractive was that the plagiarist Herzog seemed to have information of his own regarding the theological problems. But the first was not inconceivable. Certainly plagiarists of the scope of Abbé Troncy[189] were rare, who around 1886 defended the divinity of Jesus Christ in a book composed in great part with the assistance of Mgr Ginoulhiac.[190] However marauders who use their neighbor's fortune to increase their own, who right and left grab bits of pages, indeed entire pages, are, even now, not rare. Herzog had made several, rather modest, borrowings from me. But Vacandard (*Congé aux dogmes*) and Dom Leclercq[191] (here p. 97n) had made more extensive use of my work. I had carefully refrained from publicly denouncing the plagiarism of these two writers; why would I have raised my voice against Herzog?

Such is the defense that I reckoned worth making if I was called to appear before ecclesiastical authority. But would this actually happen? The members of the Rennes Council of Vigilance, except for M. Hamard and Abbé Charost, did not even know the name of the *Revue d'histoire et de littérature religieuses*. M. Hamard,[192] who used to read it occasionally, had set it aside completely since 1906. Thus he was incapable of confronting Herzog with my *Théologie positive*. More incapable yet was Abbé Charost who, after his administrative duties, reading newspapers and long daily walks, could do no more than flick through books of current interest, not excluding novels. Moreover, the authorities wanted peace; problems only

PART TWO: How the Roman Church Freed Itself of Me

frightened them. Surely they would never take the initiative for a summons; they would call me in only if I were denounced.

Where would the denunciation come from? At this time, the *Revue du clergé français*, the *Annales de philosophie chrétienne* and certain papers like *Débats* maintained a spirit of liberalism among the cultured portion of the clergy, despite the progress of Roman absolutism. In general the faith was protected, the piety of simple souls respected. Nonetheless the liberty of researchers was also respected. It was not shocking to see them undertake research with no other preoccupation than sincerity; nor any more shocking when they aired their discoveries in specialist reviews as much inaccessible to simple souls as to the mass of the clergy. Apologists were reproached for so often saying the opposite of what they thought. Rome was reproached for wanting to imprison thought in the jail of scholasticism. It was a matter of principle that problems would be resolved neither by fraud nor by the sword, but by free discussion. There was a horror of delation, by which one could get rid of an adversary by feeding him to the Roman ogre. The delator was considered a hideous being, designated by the name "snitch" [casserole] which was a stigma.

I spoke of the cultured clergy. Perhaps I shall be told that this elite was a tiny minority in the Church of France and that the great majority of priests, if they had been able, would have denounced me as a matter of conscience, to avoid hell. No doubt, but these narrow-minded priests had never opened the *Revue*. Or at any rate they had closed it forever from mid-1907 before the appearance of the chapters on the history of the Blessed Virgin in which the apparent plagiarism was found. Thus they were not in any position to confront me with Herzog. Only the cultured priests, numbering scarcely fifty (numerous subscribers had withdrawn by the end of 1906; and then there were lay people; moreover let us not forget that very many of the readers had a special interest and left aside anything outside of it) had read the history of the Blessed Virgin to its conclusion. A good number of them were emancipated from dogmas: this is, at least, what one is led to believe by a statement of Cardinal Richard who, around 1895, said to the Archbishop of Rennes, Labouré, that half of his professors at the Institut catholique had lost their faith (I have this piece of information from a vicar general of Rennes). Those who remained believers were infused with a great liberalism. They did not consider themselves obligated, according to M. Gendron's expression (*Congé aux dogmes*, p. 60) to function as the Church's police. And, not having the excuse of a qualm of conscience, they would have incurred shame in denouncing me to authority that, once the case was submitted, would have been obliged to act.

Convinced that not a single priest in France was capable of committing a shameful act, I quieted the flash of anxiety that Duchesne's letter had caused me. In my reply to the learned historian I said that for good reason, I had no photograph to send him, but I promised to send him in a few weeks a book on the early period of the papacy. Then, discreetly addressing the question of the letters of Pope Liberius,[193] whose authenticity Duchesne had rejected, following Héfélé and other historians, I did not hide the fact that their authenticity appeared to me very probable. Naturally I declared that I had nothing in common with Herzog. I received from the Farnesi Palace a second letter beginning with this gospel text: *Credo Domine, adjuva incredulitatem meam.*[194] That done, Duchesne informed me that he had been going into the question of Liberius, that he had decisively proven the authenticity of the letters of the unfortunate pope, that this work was going to appear shortly in the *Mélanges d'archéologie et d'histoire* and that he would give me an offprint. Three months later I sent the *Papauté* to Rome. From Rome I received the booklet *Libère et Fortunatien*.[195] Let us go back to the first weeks of 1908. On February 16th Bricout sent me the following letter:

> You have undoubtedly read Herzog's article on the *Blessed Virgin in history* that appeared in the *Revue d'histoire et de littérature religieuses* and published by Nourry. Do you think it possible to *explain* and debate (at least assess) this thesis without getting us all burnt and would you like to take this on in your next chronique? If affirmative I will write to Nourry to send you the volume. If you prefer to do a special article on this subject the *Revue* is at your disposal. Tell me what you think of Herzog's work; and, if you are able to accept, the number of pages it requires and the date you will be ready. (Here Instructions relative to the chronique that was about to come out.) Everyone round here is stunned by the Loisy business. And this book of Herzog's! Where will it all end?

My response may be deduced from the following letter, dated February 18th:

> I wrote to Nourry to send you Herzog. Yes, I count on being able to publish these 10 to 12 pages on March 15th. Send them to me toward the end of February with the regulation Nihil obstat. But NB! This will be dissected by all the vigilance councils of France and Navarre. So let it be very 'edifying' and very clear. Let your enemies and ours be furious at seeing you so orthodox.

Part Two: How the Roman Church Freed Itself of Me

On February 28th, a third letter written after reception and reading of the article:

> I have sent your manuscript to the press and plan to publish your article on March 15. However I believe that it will be necessary to make several corrections on the proof. 1. You say virtually nothing about Mary's virginity. Is it that Suarez and Co. speak of it like holiness or the immaculate conception? Is there uncertainty on this point as on the rest? 2. Is the Herzog interpretation of the gospels well founded in relation to Mary's holiness, etc.? In this case what becomes of their truth? I believe that it will be necessary to approach it in the same way as M. Vénard[196] in the chronique that will appear on March 15 regarding Dunand[197] and say: the Herzog interpretation is not critically imperative and we have the Church's authority to tell us that this interpretation is false. 3. I believe that it is not enough to say that *some* texts introduced by Herzog *may be* false or badly interpreted. Based on this explanation his conclusions will indeed appear correct. And what will become of your '*in eodem sensu*'? They will see it as a farce.

I took heed of Bricout's remarks as far as I could. In a note I recommended an article by Père d'Alès[198] that came to my attention only at the last moment, although not without dealing him a sharp blow in passing. And my article appeared: a very orthodox article in which I refrained from examining Herzog's texts out of a lack of the requisite competence, while strongly rejecting his conclusions.[199]

2

First Denunciation in 1908

I JUDGED THAT, AMONG the cultured priests, not a single one would experience the qualms of conscience that would obligate him to denounce me to the authorities. There were two who felt this obligation, both professors at the Institut catholique in Toulouse. One, a secular priest, was named Saltet. The other was the Jesuit Portalié. United, by prior agreement, in this holy enterprise, both displayed an equal willingness, an equal perseverance. The goal was to show me to the door of the Church. However it was foreseen that authority, in whose absence nothing could be done, would show itself to be stubborn; that multiple offensives would be necessary to make it act. Based on this expectation the two associates decided to work in relays and bring forth their critiques one after another in such a way as to prolong the agony.*

SALTET'S CAMPAIGN

Saltet opened fire in two articles in the *Bulletin de littérature ecclésiastique* that were followed by several notes. The first entitled "Un insigne plagiat: La Sainte-Vierge dans l'histoire"[200] heaped insults upon the book's author, Herzog, who was accused of having odiously plariarized my *Théologie positive* and who, by this fact, is treated as a "brazen plagiarist." The second article[201] continues the indictment and extends it to Dupin who is also

---

* Enlightened by the events of 1930, I see today that before embarking on their campaign the two accomplices received the approval and the encouragement of the Holy Office in response to the request of one of them (Portalié no doubt). It is Rome's support that explains the growing conceit with which they proceeded.

PART TWO: How the Roman Church Freed Itself of Me

denounced as the plagiarist of my writings. In reality it is me alone whom Saltet is attacking; it is me that he is denouncing as the true author of the heresies signed by Herzog and Dupin. The intention is clear from beginning to end. At times the denunciation comes through almost in so many words. However this candour is rare. It seems to slip through now and then whereas the real aim is to let readers guess that I am Herzog but not to say so openly. Saltet pretends to take Herzog for an actual person. He covers him with insulting epithets. He even attacks the *Revue* for publishing the plagiarist's prose. An experienced man who knows that the most grotesque assertions impress the naive when they are uttered with enough emphasis, he is not afraid of writing on page 112 of the *Bulletin*: "Simply from the critical point of view 'La Sainte-Vierge dans l'histoire' will be the enduring disgrace of the *Revue d'histoire et de littérature religieuses*. How could the editorial board of this journal . . . have been the victim of Herzog's deception?"* Thus the *Revue* in which Duchesne and Baudrillart had written earlier was discredited: it could no longer have braved public scorn if episcopal authority had not already ended its existence. As for myself, I was spared. With a comic seriousness Saltet exclaims[202] (p. 170), in response to a complaint by M. Bricout: "Whatever may be said, I have not accused M. Turmel. My role as critic is to establish certain facts, to submit them to the reader and to ask for their explanation. It is not I but M. Turmel's advocates who, by their defense, have put him in the position of accused. I leave them with responsibility for this protective action." Then he blustered on about the redoubtable obligations that criticism imposes on those who make it their profession. Why this stratagem? Why this pretense of undertaking exclusively a work of criticism when, in reality, one is playing the role of an accuser?

The answer is found in the French law that prohibits, under any pretext whatsoever, defamation—that is all words and all writings of a nature to injure one's neighbor. In denouncing a heretic, Saltet only wanted to give glory to God; he was driven by only the purest of motives. But the law, indifferent to his intentions, forbade him from defaming me. Caught between his qualms of conscience and the code, he had disgraced Herzog in a way the law could not touch, but which necessarily touched me; he hinted, sure that all would understand; he used a subterfuge that he foresaw would fool no one.

---

* Later I learned that this thrust made at the *Revue* was an act of rancor; Saltet had submitted an article to Lejay who had refused it.

First Denunciation in 1908

No one, in fact, was fooled. Everyone clearly saw that, under the pretext of vituperating against a plagiarist, Saltet was instituting heresy proceedings against me. Duchesne, whose article on Liberius (here p. 103) was being printed when the accusing article reached him, found the means to place, by way of protest, the following note in the proof (*Mélanges d'archéologie et d'histoire*, 1908, p. 51):

> In recent times a process used in questions of authenticity has been notably abused, namely that of printing in parallel columns sentences or expressions in which one imagines one sees conclusive conjunctions. I do not say that this means of proof must be excluded, I say only that it is abused.

This learned prelate was certainly convinced of my identity with Herzog (see p. 100) but a denunciation appeared to him an act of cannibalism. Also, while internally recognizing the strength of the proofs adduced by the *Bulletin*, externally he denied them ("one imagines").

Destined for the public, Duchesne's protest was expressed cautiously. In private judgement was freer, and the verdict was less than flattering for Saltet, whose delicacy of conscience was entirely unappreciated. We have just heard this virtuous apologist cry out, in a burlesque fit of indignation, that Herzog's study would be the enduring disgrace of the *Revue d'histoire et littérature religieuses*. I affirm: no one dreamed of saying that the article of March 1908 had disgraced the *Bulletin*. They were concerned only with the article. When Batiffol became aware of it in Paris where he was in disgrace,[203] he declared that his former subordinate's article was an "unspeakable" act. To his reprobation he joined that of *Études*, that is of the Jesuit Fathers assigned to the editing of this review. From his side, M. Guibert, rector of the École des Carmes,[204] let it be known that the aforesaid article was the object of mocking epigrams among his entourage. No doubt I am going to be asked if these statements are really true. Let the reader be reassured. They were supplied by Saltet himself on two different occasions. The first admission,[205] decisive although laconic, is found in this sentence in the *Bulletin* of 1929, p. 169:

> A minority, among whom were found impressive names of ecclesiastical science and even of religious, more or less openly dared to reprimand the *Bulletin* and two of its editors, Père Portalié and the present author.

Part Two: How the Roman Church Freed Itself of Me

The second admission[206] provides us with the following specifics that appear in the *Bulletin* of 1931, p. 28:

> On March 31, 1908, ten days after my first article, Mgr Batiffol wrote to Père Portalié:
> 'As for M. Saltet's article, they are unanimous in treating as *an unspeakable act*, whatever opinion is set forth on the identity or non-identity of Turmel and Herzog. *Études* would never have published this kind of article. In all likelihood, it will have very serious consequences.'
>
> And on Holy Thursday, the same to the same: 'M. X told me that you were surprised at my feelings over the Turmel-Saltet Affair. They are as follows: 1) "I find the proofs adduced by Saltet overwhelming; which amounts to saying that I am Herzog-Dupin;" 2) I think that the very act of intervening against Turmel is not unreasonably *judged severely here from the moral point of view*, and that your Fathers would never have let one of you engage in a similar controversy in *Études* . . . On May 18, 1908, M. J. Guibert, superior of the seminary of the Paris Institut catholique, wrote, after Turmel's denials: "Twice I have been told that *your former rector mocked* your position. I cannot believe that he used such *hard words toward* you; moreover they were repeated to me by very impassioned people" . . . In July 1908, and although I knew of his impassioned opposition, I did not fail to bring my volume, *La Question Herzog-Dupin*, to his (Mgr Batiffol's) notice. He responded with the words *Saddened thanks* handwritten on his card, which was indeed his style and spoke volumes.'

There were many instances of the mockery to which M. Guibert alluded. Two came to my attention. In one Batiffol said: "It will be necessary to present a casserole in Saltet's honor."[207] In the other he made a play on words, following what is frequently done in the North where the final "t" of Saltet remains silent (it appears that in the Midi it is pronounced Saltète): "What do you expect? His name predestined him to play a dirty trick [saleté]."

Here are the facts.

1. The Paris Jesuits considered Saltet's act shocking.
2. The superior of the École des Carmes, M. Guibert, did not feel any differently, for the *Revue pratique d'apologétique* which he edited tried, several times, to save me, until the day when the prelate Baudrillart,

making use of his superior authority, forced on him an indictment against me (see p. 116).

3. Batiffol bombarded his former subordinate with epithets that were less than flattering. Saltet said that his former rector's animosity disappeared when he was better informed. That is fraudulent. I shall speak later (cf. p. 122) of Batiffol's turnaround. What is certain is that his condemnation of 1908 cannot be attributed to lack of knowledge, since he recognized that the proofs adduced were overwhelming toward me.*

One of the people most irritated by all this uproar was M. Bricout, who made abundant use of my collaboration for the *Revue du clergé français*. On March 22nd he brought the *Bulletin*'s article to my attention and requested that I send a response that he would publish in the *Revue*. Having received nothing from me he reiterated the request. He received the following response that he sent to *La Croix* (May 6):

> I am accountable to my archbishop; and only to him. He and he alone will hear me if he asks. To act otherwise would amount to acknowledging a jurisdiction that I do not recognize; it would be to take seriously a work inspired by hate: I do not wish to, I am not able to.

Then he wrote the following letter (May 5) in which, speaking of the intervention of my archbishop, Mgr Dubourg, he told me:

> The wisest advisors, who are not in any way hostile to you, so strongly advised me to solicit it that I did so in a letter of last Saturday. This morning I received the following letter dated 4 May and signed L. Henry, vic. gen.: 'Monseigneur, indisposed after a bout of flu, has been obliged to interrupt his confirmation rounds. . . . His Excellency has read your letter attentively. When his health is restored, Monseigneur will summon M. Turmel and request all necessary explanations.' It goes without saying that, in my letter, I affirmed that I believed you to be perfectly innocent and that I found you perfectly entitled not to respond to M. Saltet's demands. I reiterated that in your letters you have always declared yourself willing to give any required explanations to your Ordinary . . .

---

* In the *Bulletin* of 1931, p. 245 Saltet made a new admission: "M. Portalié's final days were saddened by the bitterness of a profound disagreement on this subject between him and certain of his confreres who are a credit to Catholic science." ["Le service scientifique de la doctrine d'après S.S. Pie XI et l'Institut catholique," *Bulletin de littérature ecclésiastique* 32 (1931): 228–46.—Ed.]

PART TWO: How the Roman Church Freed Itself of Me

When, on Sunday morning, May 10, 1908, I presented myself at the archbishop's residence where I was summoned, I had never before seen Mgr Dubourg; his very name had scarcely penetrated my hermitage, closed almost completely to reports from outside and I did not know what sort of welcome would be accorded me. On the way, superstition appeared, under the guise of a fury, ready to throttle me to expiate my crime—that of having, under the name of Herzog, unmasked some of its lies. Every day, through the long years, the *Peccatum meum contra me est semper* (*Congé aux dogmes*) droned in my ears. It resonated more strongly as I entered the archbishop's residence. Stronger yet was the agitation which I could never escape even for a day. In spite of myself, were not words of violence going to issue forth?

I do not believe to have ever encountered a gentleness, a kindness, an amiability equal to that which Mgr Dubourg showed me from the moment I appeared before him. "Ah! dear M. Turmel, I shall soon have been here at Rennes for two years and I've never seen you before. Why do you keep so much to yourself so? They tell me you have been unwell? . . ." "Oh! Monseigneur," I replied with energy, "I accuse no one; but I must confess that solitude is my only consolation." After having had me sit down the archbishop said to me: "It is at M. Bricout's request that I have invited you. Here is the letter that he wrote me." And he read me this letter that gave the history of the affair, proclaimed my innocence and reported my declaration: "I am accountable to my archbishop; and only to him. He and he alone will hear me if he asks." Having come to this point the archbishop stopped a moment to express his keen approval and to say to me that indeed I owed no explanations to Saltet, but solely to my Ordinary who had jurisdiction over me.

After the letter was read, Mgr Dubourg, without asking me for a formal oath, said in a paternal tone: "You declare before God, do you not, that you are neither Herzog nor Dupin?" I replied, "Certainly, Monseigneur, I affirm before God that I am neither Herzog nor Dupin." Then in substance I added the following explanations: Herzog and Dupin undoubtedly plagiariazed my work, although Saltet out of bias exaggerated how much. Dupin was even able to see and make use of some of my manuscripts that had not yet been published. But first, Dom Leclercq and M. Vacandard (above p. 101) have borrowed from my writings even more blatantly, borrowings for which I am in a position to furnish immediate proof and of which I have never complained publicly. Second, I am equally in a position to prove at once that my manuscripts have been several times requested, that I have lent them and that they may have circulated.

I had not finished the first of these declarations when Mgr Dubourg stopped me and said while laughing: "But I myself, my dear M. Turmel, have been plagiarized. Can you believe it? Quite recently, one of my colleagues appropriated a pastoral that I had written and published the year previously. It is unbelievable that there are such unscrupulous people everywhere."

For an instant I joined in Mgr Dubourg's triumphant joy, as was only polite. I finished my explanation. Then, having brought with me a letter in which M. Vacandard owned up to his plagiarism and various letters that requested communication of my manuscripts or returned them with thanks, I set to reading these supporting documents. But the archbishop interrupted me, assuring me in warm-hearted terms that this reading was superfluous and that he took me at my word.

I rose to leave. Mgr Dubourg stopped me for a moment to say to me: "Given the emotion that currently prevails in the press, it is indispensable that a note appear in the *Semaine religieuse* to declare that you are neither Herzog nor Dupin. If you are reluctant to draw it up, I will do it myself. However it seems to me preferable that it come from you and that it be addressed to me in the form of a letter." I promised to send the letter as requested. I had brought to the archdiocese the proofs, not indeed of the certainty of the existence of plagiarism committed to my detriment by Herzog and Dupin, but of its possibility. And Mgr Dubourg, before further inquiry had judged these proofs plausible since he had not considered it necessary to acquaint himself with their contents. That being the case, I thought it possible to send the following letter to the archbishop who saw nothing to revise in it and published it in the *Semaine religieuse* of May 16:

> Monseigneur,
>
> To put an end to the press campaign that, for several months, has troubled the religious world, you desired to hear from me on the subject of the writings signed Herzog and Dupin. In the conversation you favored me with last Sunday, May 10th, I began, Monseigneur, by declaring before God that I was neither Herzog not Dupin; then treating the extracts which have been taken either from my books or from my manuscripts, I gave explanations that your Excellency recognized as well-founded.

Part Two: How the Roman Church Freed Itself of Me

> There remains, Monseigneur, the pleasant duty of my expressing to you my very strong gratitude for the paternal benevolence you have shown me.
> Be so good ...

Mgr Dubourg was convinced that, published under his patronage and bolsterd by his authority, my letter would impose silence. He was soon robbed of his illusion, as the following letter of May 22 written by himself proves, that he sent to me by M. Gayet, my former student then colleague at seminary, and then pastor of Saint Germain parish in Rennes:

> My dear Monsieur Turmel,
>
> Things are worsening. Your letter did not appear sufficiently clear. The acknowledgement of extracts taken from your *manuscripts* has upset many people. The sentence where you implicate me and where you declare that I have recognized the well-foundedness of your explanations has been a source of *personal problems* for me, and it would take very little for me to be treated as heterodox. Thus we cannot leave it at that. You must do a second letter, more explicit and more categorical. I ask this in your interest and with good intention. If you were to refuse I myself would be obliged to explain; and it is better if you take action; the best would be for you to do this at once, before the appearance of the Saltet memoir that *La Croix* announced yesterday. I am sending you your friend the pastor of Saint Germain and have taken the liberty of entrusting to him a sort of *basic outline* that you could reproduce with some modifications of style, and this letter written by you could, this evening, be sent by me to *La Croix* which would feature it in its Sunday issue. And we should have peace! For good and all! Your fondly devoted,
>
> Auguste, Arch. de R.

What had happened? Two incidents, one public, the other private.

The public incident was the following note in *La Croix* of May 18, serving as a gloss on my letter that the pious paper had just reproduced:

> So first, M. Turmel declared before God that he was neither Herzog nor Dupin. Let us sincerely rejoice over that.
> Second, he provided his archbishop with explanations regarding the extracts that have been taken either from his books or his manuscripts. This admission is serious; on this point M. Turmel's sacerdotal honor seems to us to require greater clarity. The public

is acquainted with certain facts that it still cannot explain. As M. Saltet stated: 'Light must be shed at any price.'

This note is juicy if, as is very probable, it emanates from "Abbé M. Charles" (Charles Martain) specializing in theological questions and whom *La Croix* thanked in 1912 for matters having little to do with theology (see Houtin, *Ma vie laïque*, p. 21[208]). Not having the text of the paper before me I cannot vouch for anything.

The private incident had its source in the superior of the seminary, Michel; but it stemmed from the aforesaid note in *La Croix*. This quarrelsome superior had read my letter in the Rennes *Semaine religieuse* and had found nothing shocking in it. However, upon learning that the great newspaper of the French clergy had raised suspicions, he rushed to the archdiocese. He spoke rudely to Abbé Charost who, it appeared, was denigrating Saltet's campaign, just as the Jesuits and Sulpicians. He even attacked the archbishop, whose indulgence toward me he reproached. The second of these particulars was furnished forthwith by the bearer of the episcopal letter, M. Gayet, who gave the key to the "personal problems" and the source of the worthy prelate's moaning over nearly being "treated as heterodox." I received the first, shortly thereafter, from M. Henry, honorary vicar general, who added that Abbé Charost had taken his punishment without saying a word.

The "basic outline" of which the episcopal letter spoke had been written by M. Gayet at Mgr Dubourg's dictation. I religiously transcribed this document which was headed "Monseigneur," without making the slightest change. I confined myself to adding the formula of final respect. So that the "basic outline" of a letter was really a letter. Here is the text:

Monseigneur,

You do me the honor of explaining to me that the letter that I wrote to Your Excellency did not appear clear enough and you express the desire that I furnish fuller explanations. I willingly comply with this desire, and, in order to cut short any future misunderstanding, I make the following declarations in writing:

First, I renew my affirmation that I am neither Herzog nor Dupin; that I have acted neither in connivance, nor *a fortiori* in complicity with these individuals whom I do not know.

Second, a word of my first letter having, it seems, led to ambiguity, I declare that, in the explanations submitted to Your Excellency, I had coincidences of a technical and not of a doctrinal order in view.

Part Two: How the Roman Church Freed Itself of Me

> Third, I reject in advance all conclusions or consequences that might be drawn from my writings and that would not conform to orthodoxy.
>
> Fourth, as a Catholic priest, I profess all that the Roman Church professes and reject all that it rejects.
>
> Fifth, affectionate and devoted son of the Virgin Mary, I believe in her Immaculate Conception, her perfect and perpetual virginity, in her divine maternity; in a word, I adhere, with respect to the mother of God, to the integral doctrine of holy Church.
>
> I hope, Monseigneur, that these formal observations will satisfy the most exacting and most difficult spirits.
>
> Please accept, Monseigneur, the respectful homage with which I have the honor of being Your Excellency's very humble and very devoted servant.
>
> J. Turmel

At the end of his letter, Mgr Dubourg said to me: "And we should have peace! For good and all!" He was not aware of Voltaire's remark (*Essai sur les moeurs* chap. 128): "The quarrels among theologians have become the wars of cannibals." Experience was about to enlighten him. Saltet, who had already sunk his teeth into his prey, got ready to tear it to pieces (do not forget that he was secretly encouraged by Rome). When he saw that the archbishop of Rennes wanted to rob him of it, he took a haughty tone and contemptuously put the prelate in his place. In response to the note in the *Semaine religieuse* of May 16 he shot back (*Bulletin* p. 171):[209]

> The judgement to be reached is of interest to several jurisdictions and I have been careful not to forget it, since M. Turmel invokes the jurisdiction of Mgr the Archbishop of Rennes. However, from the scientific point of view this judgement *answers to opinion*. In this regard *the case cannot simply be closed*. Light must be shed at any price.

As he was continuing the game of hide-and-seek and, while pursuing me, pretended to be exclusively concerned with Herzog's plagiarism, the light would supposedly be shed when it was known how the plagiarist had been able to rob me of my property. On this point I had supplied explanations and Mgr Dubourg had taken them as sufficient. To which Saltet replied: "Opinion is the true judge of the matter; it is not within the archbishop's power to rob it of its right and take this on himself." Until this point he had worked alone; as soon as my archbishop intervenes he calls

First Denunciation in 1908

"opinion" to his aid and asks it to check this audacious prelate. What opinion? That of the Catholic world. In the *Bulletin*, p. 180 one reads:

> Faced with such facts the watchword of all Catholics must be: More light, total light. This program always succeeds in the end, everywhere today and especially in the Church.[210]

Thus Saltet calls on all Catholics (at least those of France; but also those of Germany as will soon be seen); he summons them to call for the light and to bar the way to the archbishop of Rennes. In order to stimulate their zeal, he reminds them of all the people who are on the alert and keeping watch on their conduct in order to judge it. He says on p. 171:

> The unbelievers and Protestants will judge the clear-sightedness and resolutness of Catholics by their attitude at the present time.

The Catholic world, it goes without saying, remained indifferent to the entreaties of the denouncer. The journals alone fell in line. But the majority adopted a wait and see attitude. For example, the *Koelnische Volkzeitung* published only on July 30 a specious article in which it dared to say that from "far and near" everyone was asking for a response to Saltet, that my honor was at stake and that my letter did not satisfy "public opinion." At the beginning of July there were still only two journals that took an interest in me, namely the *Revue pratique d'apologétique* of June 1st and *l'Ami du clergé* of June 25th.[211] But the first of these, much to the displeasure of the delator, judged my explanations to my archbishop satisfactory and considered that my letters resolved the matter. Only *l'Ami du clergé* reproduced the *Bulletin*'s language and, after having affirmed that Herzog was a "priest of immense erudition," let it be clearly understood that this priest was me. Of course, in the May 18 issue of which I spoke earlier, *La Croix* had said: "light must be shed at any price." But this observation was anterior to my second letter, anterior to the article in which the *Bulletin* summoned Catholics to impose their will on the archbishop of Rennes.

One takes what one finds when one does not find what one is searching for. Seeing that the Catholic world was not responding to his appeal, Saltet elected the superior of the major seminary of Rennes as confederate. After having firmed up their plans these two great captains made an assault on Mgr Dubourg. Some of the letters that were written at that time are found in Mgr Dubourg's papers and those of the superior of his seminary. It would be desirable for them to be published. For the moment one is

PART TWO: How the Roman Church Freed Itself of Me

reduced to information furnished by Saltet in the *Bulletin* of 1929,²¹² p. 112, regarding the failure of the offensive:

(He announces in a note on p. 111 that he is going to make use of a "long autograph letter of five pages" that was sent to him by the archbishop of Rennes on July 11, 1908 and also "a long letter dated July 10 that he received from the superior of the seminary"):

> Mgr Dubourg considered this first letter of M. Turmel a 'victory' in that, according to him, it put a stop to the identification Turmel-Herzog-Dupin. Around him, all members of the episcopal administration were not as satisfied. At the insistence of M. Michel, superior of the major seminary, Mgr Dubourg decided to ask M. Turmel, through the intermediary of his friend the pastor of Rennes, for a second letter, whose main lines he marked out. This is the document published in *La Croix* of May 24 and that Mgr Dubourg, in his envoi, said he received 'to his great joy.' However, M. Michel wrote on July 10: 'The good archbishop allowed himself to be deceived by M. T. when he consented to be satisfied with M. T.'s second letter. Ah! The wonderful letter!' M. Michel wanted to insist, but without success. He himself wrote: 'Everything has been useless and, for the archbishop, the incident is closed.'

"The incident is closed." It had been closed since my second letter published, at the request of Mgr Dubourg, in *La Croix* of May 24. Like an enraged sea, Catholic literature hurled its waves against me. In the *Revue pratique d'apologétique* of September 1, 1908, p. 801, the prelate Baudrillart²¹³ celebrated Saltet's campaign as "a public health measure," severely condemned Herzog and indicated the joy he would experience when at last this heretic would be identified.* *Études* of February 5, 1909,²¹⁴ to which I had sent a summons through a bailiff, retaliated by citing p. 446 "the great summons" that "the conscience of Catholics" had addressed to me "in vain, ever since the appearance of M. Saltet's book." Several other journals, without mentioning *La Croix*, employed similar language. All this uproar was directed against Mgr Dubourg's decision: "the incident is closed." A second storm was about to break; but Herzog would have no part in that one. The Herzog Affair was to resurrect in twenty-one years. In the interim it lay in

---

* Treated like a wicked villain by Baudrillart, Herzog, if he had not been condemned to remain in obscurity, would have replied to this impudent prelate that the wicked villain is the one who refuses to accept the truth, but tries to strangle it, and not the laborer who endeavors to propagate it.

the tomb to which the archbishop of Rennes had consigned it in sending my second letter to *La Croix*; it was to remain interred without sequel.

I am mistaken: it had two sequels, very slight however, which unfolded, one in Paris, the other in Rennes.

In Paris Lejay was subjected to an accusation that his letter of August 2, 1908 reported in these terms:

> My eminent rector posed the following question to me: 'How, being necessarily informed regarding the Turmel-Herzog-Dupin matter, could you be party to so disloyal a manoeuvre capable of undermining fundamental beliefs? Note well that Abbé Saltet's book has induced a different view regarding the insertion of the Herzog-Dupin articles in the *Revue d'histoire et de littérature religieuses*. In a nutshell he has given substance to the accusation of an alliance or a conspiracy knowingly organized in order to ruin the historical foundation of Christian dogma under the guise of works or authors reputedly Catholic.'

Lejay gave the explanation that I transcribed above (p. 99). Several days later his case was judged by the seven bishop protectors of the Institut catholique. On August 11th, he wrote to me from Dijon:

> Tomorrow the Seven deliberate on my case. Pray to the immaculate Virgin. Perhaps it is the Church's interest that is at stake in my humble person. A proceeding before civil tribunals would be disagreeable for everyone.

In the same letter he returned to the post that he occupied at the *Revue*.

> I was not secretary of the *Revue*. However I served as intermediary between my friends and collaborators I knew such as yourself.

The proceedings turned out well. I don't know if Lejay received any censure; what is certain is that he retained his chair. In maintaining him in his post the "seven" decided that the role of their learned professor at the *Revue d'histoire et de littérature religieuses* was that of a letter box that receives all papers posted to it without any knowledge of them and which is incapable of incurring the least responsibility. The prelate Baudrillart could, had he wished, have obtained a more severe verdict. And it would have been logical for him to do so. In a few weeks, in fact, he was to congratulate Saltet over having performed a "public health measure" (p. 116); and we have just seen how he took as evident Lejay's connivance with Herzog. Thus he ought to have begun by performing a public health measure in

Part Two: How the Roman Church Freed Itself of Me

his own house. But he calculated that, in this circumstance, the advantages of purification would have been much less than the disadvantages. It was from the same motive that, three years later, instead of congratulating Houtin who had just exposed Père Perraud's private life, this worthy apostle of public health violently opposed him. With principles, as with heaven, compromise reigns.

An eminent philologist, very respected in the academic world, towards the end of his life Lejay entered the Académie des Inscriptions et Belles-Lettres. Then he became, with Branley, the glory of the Institut catholique. At one stroke he served to prove the accord between science and faith. On June 13, 1920 he was snatched away by an unexpected death before being able to show his full worth. In the rector's discourse given at the funeral one reads (*Bulletin de l'Institut Catholique de Paris* 1929, p. 172):

> M. Lejay died with the sentiments of faith and piety that fall to priests; he has died having served science and the Church with unflagging and useful labor.

From his side, the President of the Académie said (*loc. cit.*, p. 173):

> I have the duty of recalling how he knew, in a harmonious unity of soul, how to attune the beliefs of the religion whose priest he was and the research of the science that he loved.

The extracts from his letters that have been cited earlier reveal his private thoughts. The following will complete our intelligence. On June 27, 1901, having just heard of my condemnation by the Holy Office, he wrote:

> If you permit me a piece of advice, relax for *a few months and read Voltaire*.

In a letter of the following July 3rd I read:

> These past few days I have talked over the situation with M. Portal[215] who, as you know, is very devoted to us. He is a bit frightened at the thought of the article that is going to appear, being persuaded that they are only waiting for a pretext to strike at you. Nevertheless, I would be more of your mind. You will see what you have to do. Your signature could be suppressed. No one will be taken in; consequently the benefit of the article will remain yours; and it would be very easy then for you to say that it all appeared without your consent. Besides, from now until we have the proofs, we have time to see which way the wind is blowing. You are right not to raise a fuss. Nothing would be more fatal to the spread of

your ideas. We have some chance of influencing minds only while remaining within official Catholicism. A rupture would bring joy to our enemies.

On October 30th of the same year, in reply to a letter in which I told him of a study that I was considering sending him that was not very orthodox, I received the following:

> It is all the same to me whether your articles are revolutionary or conservative. I had thought of a type of article that could annoy the new world of orthodoxy a great deal.

This "type" about which he became more explicit, was the germ of his fine collection, *Textes et documents pour l'étude historique du christianisme*, which still renders great service and which the war unfortunately halted.

Finally, on May 10, 1908 alluding to Saltet's articles, he wrote:

> Certain lay people have spoken to me about this affair with distaste. However the prelates are rubbing their hands. Orthodoxy is in the process of becoming despicable.

At Rennes Abbé Charost characterized Saltet's enterprise by the following euphemism that M. Henry mentioned to me: "This campaign has not been inspired by the desire for peace." By contrast, the superior of the major seminary was roused against me by an indignation that he passed on to some of his professors. One of them in meeting one of my friends who held Saltet in contempt vehemently replied: "It is a duty to denounce heretics." This apostle of orthodoxy had a Roman doctorate, one of those of whom German priests used to say in the past: *doctor romanus asinus germanus*.[216] On the other hand, four years earlier, he had upset my neighborhood by some imprudences, otherwise not very serious. I did my best to excuse him with the wrathful ladies who spoke of nothing less than denouncing him. He, on his part, finding himself with me in the seminary library, unsuspecting of the service I had done him, had shown me, it is true, that I was nothing in comparison with him; but he had deigned to show me a protective sympathy. He did not harbor any ill feelings toward me. He was simply swayed by his superior. The latter made few conquests. Moreover, after several months death put an end to his mounting anger. For a long time I had known that he was powerless to harm me. However his disappearance reminded me of the words of the psalmist: *Laqueus contritus est et nos liberati sumus*; (the net is broken and I have been set free).

Part Two: How the Roman Church Freed Itself of Me

I was set free, but after having deceived my archbishop, say the Pharisees while averting their gaze. I will come back to this problem and to another more serious yet that my work raised. I shall tackle both head on and find a solution to them. For the moment, I limit myself to noting that I deceived, not only my archbishop himself, but the Roman Church, which forced my archbishop despite himself to carry out its lofty works. In spite of himself, for he did what he could to avert the poisoned cup that Saltet presented to him with his denunciation. When the Paris chancery became aware of the March 1908 *Bulletin*, it was appalled and hastened to duck out of it leaving its sister Rennes with the burden of managing the huge scandal that was shaping up. But the Rennes chancery, gripped by the same terror, gave back to its sister Paris the dangerous gift it had received. This information is furnished by Saltet himself in the *Bulletin* of 1931, p. 29, where the following extract from a letter from Batiffol is cited:

> I met a member of the Paris vigilance committee, an elder who spoke to me of Turmel-Herzog with the reserve of a man who is conducting the investigation of the affair *sub secreto*. It appears that Rennes is sending the affair to Paris!!! and Paris to Rennes!!![217]

The chanceries of Paris and Rennes were vying with one another to escape the demands of the Roman legislation that was known and that they feared. Bricout's letter obligated Mgr Dubourg to become enmeshed in this. But then, above all preoccupied with quashing the affair, he accepted my explanations with joy. It would not have taken much for him to have suggested them to me himself. And even if, in order to escape what he called "personal problems," that is to silence the superior of his seminary, he gave me a second letter written by himself to sign, he at once declared the incident closed. In reality it was not with Mgr Dubourg that I was engaged; it was with the Roman Church whose lies I had unmasked and which, to punish me for this crime, wanted to strangle me. I had tricked it as one tricks a cutthroat who wants to kill you, as one tricks the wolf who wants to devour you. Let the Pharisees continue to avert their gaze, I will take their virtuous indignation seriously when they have studied the problem of Daniel or the history of a dogma and have presented the results of their investigations to the Holy Office.

Here I must point out a psychological development that occurred in Duchesne over May 1908 and was revealed by Batiffol in 1922.

Duchesne, who in January of 1908 had seen in Herzog's work only a subject for mocking jokes and who, in April had impugned the denouncer

First Denunciation in 1908

(p. 107), changed his attitude from May 1908 onwards. Then he spoke of Herzog solely in insulting terms and he even praised Saltet in three letters that he wrote him at his time. Likewise Batiffol who, in 1908 had treated the denunciation as "unspeakable," in 1922 ranked it among the claims to glory of the Toulouse Institut catholique (extract from the *Semaine religieuse* of Clermont published in the *Bulletin* 1929, p. 61).[218] Thus at different dates a reversal occurred in the minds of Duchesne and Batiffol. This turnaround has a cause. What is it?

First of all there is a solution that must be resolutely set aside. It is that which would call for a Duchesne and a Batiffol badly informed compared to a Duchesne and a Batiffol better informed; in other words that would say that these two individuals impugned Saltet when they were incompletely informed about Herzog and that they accepted him after more complete information. This must be set aside because it does not stand up to serious examination.

Duchesne had no doubts about the provenance of Herzog's heretical book, when he found it amusing and censured the Toulouse denouncer, since he wrote me in January: "There is no mistake; Herzog is you." On his part, in April of 1908 Batiffol declared the denunciation unspeakable even if proofs were forthcoming to verify it. And, a month later, when these proofs were given to him, he maintained his assessment (p. 108). It is apparent that it is not because they were better informed that Duchesne and Batiffol approved the denunciation after having condemned it. It is for another reason. Which?

Duchesne's change coincided with the reading of my *Papauté*[219] that I sent him at the end of April 1908 (p. 103) and that he declared to be "a malicious book" (letter to Saltet read to me in the course of the judgment of December of 1929). Never imagining that the author had changed his feelings toward me, I myself had asked for the inclusion of these letters that I counted on using for my defense. Herzog's work was amusing and it would be wrong to denounce it, so long as it was not tarnished through contact with my *Papauté*. From the day in which it found itself in company with this "malicious book," it became an impious work from which the orthodox Duchesne veiled his eyes.*

---

* In 1903, speaking of Christ, Duchesne said in a letter: "A brave Galilean convinced that he has a celestial mission" (Loisy, *Mémoires* 2, 277). In 1909 he said of the Roman Church and of the pope: "Ilium, alas! is more and more difficult to live in: the old Priam becomes more grumpy day by day" (Ibid. 3, 221). In 1917 Christian dogmatics inspired him to make the following reflection: "It is certain that the old game is indeed in a sorry

PART TWO: How the Roman Church Freed Itself of Me

And why was my *Papauté* a "malicious book"? Because it did not reproduce with requisite servility the theses dear to the editor of the *Liber Pontificalis*. I acquired this intelligence from a priest who, towards 1910, spent his vacation at Saint-Servan. Duchesne did not forgive me for having, on certain points, strayed from his tutelage. And this is the crime that he made Herzog atone for, he whose *Histoire ancienne de l'Église*[220] has, according to Loisy, shattered all dogmas (*Mémoires* 3, 239).

As for Batiffol, a point of reference was supplied by the information that my friend M. Pautonnier, who lived in Paris, gave me at the end of 1921: "Might you have attacked Batiffol by accident? He accuses you of assaulting dogmas; he is furious with you. Beware of him, for he is capable of anything." This confidence, reiterated many times subsequently, states a fact and conjectures an explanation for it. The fact is Batiffol's wrath against me. The explanation, suspected or glimpsed, is an attack that I may have made on Batiffol. The explanation is correct; it corresponds to reality. I had, in fact, over 1921 published in the *Revue d'histoire et de littérature religieuses*, under the name of Lagarde, a study on the penitential doctrine of Saint Augustine;[221] and, in this article, I had indicated two serious errors on Batiffol's part. The latter read the aforesaid *Revue* assiduously. There he encountered numerous heretical articles signed Coulange, Lagarde, Vanbeck, Dulac, Lawson. And all these writings whose true author did not escape him, had no effect on him. He was inflamed against me and irately accused me of working to ruin dogmas from the day on which, under the signature of Lagarde, I pointed out serious errors on his part.

A further word on Duchesne. Beginning in May of 1908, this man who, in a letter to Loisy (see the note of p. 121) spoke of Christ in perfectly Voltarian terms, thought to render glory to God by spreading round about him the news that I was Herzog, that is, in doing what previously he judged shameful. Toward the end of 1908 Abbé Charost went to Rome to support his candidacy for the episcopate and also to relieve himself of any responsibility in the affair of the unfortunate imprimatur given my *Papauté* (p. 133). After having brilliantly discharged this double task, Charost went to the Farnesi Palace. Duchesne hastened to speak to him of Herzog and to inform him regarding the true ownership of this name. Twenty years later the intelligence would be used. Charost, having become a cardinal,

---

state, and it is not the present circumstances (allusion to the war) that will renew it. But is it really possible to hope for the advent of a new religious system and are we not headed instead toward the obliteration of religious feeling" (Ibid. 3, 442). Here then is the man whom my *Papauté* scandalized.

would tell me what was said to him at the end of 1908. However, at that point, the remarks made at the Farnesi Palace had no repercussions. On his return to Rennes, Abbé Charost, in the course of a dinner at the collège Saint-Vincent, indulged in a fierce attack on Duchesne in front of all the professors. This was of course only on religious grounds. In reality, what motivated him was the pique over having been treated without ceremony by Duchesne whose offhandedness was legendary. Whatever the case, I benefited from his animosity and my relations with Herzog did not attract further investigation. Sometime later Duchesne found himself tracked by the heresy hunters who succeeded in handing him over to the Holy Office. Did denunciation appear at that point a task less noble and less brilliant? What is certain is that he took delight in reading Perrin* whose work was not however perfectly orthodox. I do not believe that the campaign waged in the *Bulletin* of Toulouse in 1929 would have met with his approval.

THE CAMPAIGN OF THE JESUIT PORTALIÉ

The Jesuit Portalié is very likely the author of an anonymous note published by the newspaper *l'Autorité* of March 27, 1908 which, under the pretext of denouncing the plagiarist Herzog, denounced me. The Reverend Father no doubt counted on sowing the wind and reaping the whirlwind. Seeing that no storm was stirred up, he retired from journalism and restricted himself to *Études* where he devoted four long articles to me, beginning on August 5.[222] I say that these articles are devoted to me. Unlike Saltet who affected to confine himself exclusively to the plagiarist Herzog and only attacked me by ricochet, Portalié directly attacks the writings signed with my name; Herzog comes up only occasionally. Then he is thoroughly abused; not however more than Loisy of whom he said (August 5, p. 343) that "never was there seen such overflow of duplicity and such failure to provide documentary authentication;" and a little farther on (p. 356) "by the revelations of his *Lettres* Loisy has dishonored himself to the point that everywhere sympathy has been replaced by contempt."

---

* Studies on certain of Cardinal Billot's theories that appeared in the *Revue* in 1921. Here is what Loisy wrote to me on this subject on November 13, 1921: "Perrin's articles have been noticed in various places. M. Maurice Croiset who read them complimented me on them. I am told that Duchesne was satisfied with them and that he spoke of nothing less than having them read to the pope. And it appears that all the Jesuits have not ignored them."

Part Two: How the Roman Church Freed Itself of Me

We are informed (p. 108) by Batiffol that *Études* was incensed when Saltet published his denunciation. How then did they end up receiving Portalié into their pages? Some high power evidently forced them to capitulate. In any case the fact remains: Portalié denounced me in one hundred twenty pages of *Études*. Let us first be clear about the aim of his denunciation. Later the outcome will emerge.

The objective encompasses two demonstrations, namely: in the first place, in all the writings signed with my name I have worked to ruin the Christian faith; in the second place, the scientific value of my writings is nonexistent.

On the first point the author's fervor is inexhaustible. Speaking of me he writes (August 5, p. 339):

> If you were to go by what he says, up until now the work of theologians, as a body, has been only a deliberate, concerted banditry, which resorted to the most dishonest methods. They claimed to be able to date back to an apostolic revelation dogmas that, according to M. Turmel and his school, have arisen over the course of time. They were sought in the Bible and in the writings of the Fathers and as they were not found there, they were forcibly inserted thanks to forgeries, or by exegetical chicanery ... p. 340. His unique goal, it seems, is to demonstrate the disagreement between the Fathers and the Catholic faith of today ... It may well be that he has not published a single article in the *Annales de philosophie chrétienne*, in the *New York Review*, and even, whatever M. Bricout says and despite the *Imprimatur*, in the *Revue du clergé français*, without each time casting discredit on one of our dogmas and one of our saintly doctors, to the point of maintaining, just a few months ago (no doubt with the approval and admiration of his director) that Saint Augustine did not admit the real presence in the eucharist.

Furthermore, (August 20, p. 514) he says again:

> It is M. Turmel's heavy responsibility to have given the bad faith of theologians the stature of an historical law; he has shown them methodically organizing the sabotage of texts, but an intelligent sabotage that will make those texts say all that is desired.

After these general considerations, Portalié takes the dogmas one by one and shows that I have denied them all. He lingers in particular over the dogmas of the papacy, original sin and eschatology. He says regarding the papacy (August 20, p. 525):

First Denunciation in 1908

> Turmel's most recent book on the papacy is so faithful to his program of denigration of our dogmas that, if Catholics were not alerted in time, it would constitute the most dangerous assault weapon against the primacy of the Roman Pontiff because it is the most hypocritical, since the pamphlet of Janus Doellinger . . . (p. 538). M. Turmel's method remains always the same: he does not openly deny the Catholic faith; but he tries to amass the clouds and the contradictions, then with an air of unconcern: 'Your Catholic opinion is indeed foolish and contrary to history. It is very unfortunate, but I can't help it.'

The dogma of original sin suggests the following observations to Portalié:

> Regarding this dogma's origin, far from connecting it to apostolic revelation, M. Turmel (faithful to his general system of doctrinal evolution), delays it until Saint Augustine. He is the true inventor of original sin . . . It is by a break with the entire Greek and Latin tradition that Augustine, transforming the punishment into a crime, is supposed to have introduced into the Church the theory of a humanity sinful in Adam and to have imposed it on the Church. Thanks to M. Turmel an important law of the history of dogma is supposed to be revealed to us: before Augustine the children of Adam were born punished, after Augustine they were born guilty.

On the question of the last things, here is what is said in *Études* of September 20, p. 760, after the remark that, in certain Catholic circles, hell is no longer preached:

> Now, *Eschatologie à la fin du quatrième siècle* by M. Turmel, is one of the foremost agents of propagation of these ideas. Not indeed that he has proposed the full modernist eschatology, but he has endeavored by every means, not only to imply that the pains of hell concern only feelings and are not external punishments, but to establish in an absolute manner that, for Christians, there is no eternal hell, and that it suffices to persevere in faith in order to assure one's salvation.

The author completely travesties my thought when he imputes the theory of "deliberate, concerted banditry" to me and, what comes to the same thing, when he accuses me of giving "the bad faith of theologians the stature of an historical law." I have encountered apologists fifty years ago who were not sincere, but I always believed that the theologians of the

PART TWO: How the Roman Church Freed Itself of Me

Middle Ages and the Fathers were, with very rare exceptions, entirely in good faith. The forgeries were small in number; the Fathers and the theologians were their victims and not their accomplices. As for belief in hell, it certainly did not displease me to be able to think that I contributed to weakening it. But I owe it to the truth to say that my influence on this point has been non-existent. Thinking to discredit me, the Jesuit Portalié in reality paid me a compliment that I am conscious of not having merited.

Let us now listen to him express the scorn that, examined from the scientific point of view, my writings inspired in him. Speaking of the *Papauté* he says (September 5, p. 615):

> Five hundred pages of the same sort of deformations of texts and events, constitutes the sum of this book of M. Turmel... who with an unmatched boldness has *falsified, deformed, travestied* the most certain facts, the clearest texts and, in particular in this volume, the whole sequence of events of the history of the popes.

On page 612 he announces "the scholarly work" that his confrere M. de la Brière[223] will soon publish on *Saint Cyprien et la Papauté*, following upon M. Turmel. And he uses this opportunity to repeat that "throughout M. Turmel tries to distort the facts and the texts."

On the subject of original sin here is what one reads in the fascicle of September 5, p. 263:

> One volume would not be enough, if one wanted to correct M. Turmel's innumerable errors in his immense monograph on this dogma. This history is to be completely redone, and anyone who entrusts himself to such a guide risks taking the wrong road. There is evidence of great labor and a mass of material. But the absolute failure to understand the subject and the will to make completely false ideas triumph at all points have confused everything... p. 625. Thus it is important to know the value of this law (explained here p. 48) on which it rests. Now, I openly declare, it is one of these historical errors that ought to make any serious critic blush... p. 627. What an ingenious edifice! Yes, as ingenious as a house of cards; you read the texts, there remains only a ridiculous fantasy... p. 628. He is nevertheless trying desperately to maintain his famous law, and is even going to open himself to ridicule for fixing the year in which the idea of the sin-offense appears with Augustine (one of the years 396 or 397)... p. 630. The nature of original sin has not been any less mistreated by M. Turmel. Augustine, according to him the inventor of original sin, teaching plainly

the *heresy* of Luther and Calvin, namely that original sin is simply concupiscence ... a system that, beyond its heretical character, has the misfortune to be perfectly absurd; and yet more, following Augustine a crowd of great masters and saints preserving, explaining, the same formulation over the centuries.

On the belief in the salvation of all Christians, the fascicle of September 20, p. 769 says:

> We maintain that it is not only an error, but a monstrous invention in history ... p. 782. M. Turmel, you think, is going to yield. Ah! you little know his art of healing diseased texts ... Admire the ingenious tour de force: the merciful ideas were adopted by *some*, says Saint Augustine: 'The expression *a quibusdam*, by some, *designates the leaders of a party*' explains M. Turmel ... Ah! if a theologian allowed himself similar fantasy! ... p. 789. I recognize that, in certain passages, Saint Ambrose appears to suppose that the sufferings of Christians will have a limit ... But ought an impartial historian to remain silent, as does M. Turmel, that the bishop of Milan, rather obscure and enigmatic in these passages, elsewhere affirms the Catholic faith very clearly and very often? ... p. 791. The judgment made by M. Turmel regarding Saint Jerome is more unjustified still.

Such are the principal reproaches that Portalié brings against me and that he seasons with numerous insults. Here are several instances.

In *Études* of November 5, 1908 Père de la Brière published the article[224] that Portalié had grandiloquently announced and that must have been undertaken to refute me. He ends his study with this major assertion that he had made several times in the course of his argument (p. 355):

> Saint Cyprien, let us repeat, did not see in the bishop of Rome the real head of the whole Church and the bishop of bishops. He considered the Church as a federation and not as a monarchy. In this regard (the formula that follows is borrowed from me) 'the dogma of the episcopacy more or less completely hid the dogma of the papacy from him.'

And there is how, in the history of the dogma of the papacy, I attempted throughout to distort the facts and the texts.

On the problem of original sin, M. Tixeront[225] writes as follows (*Histoire des dogmes*, 2, 427, speaking of Saint Augustine):

PART TWO: How the Roman Church Freed Itself of Me

> As early or nearly as early as we may go back in his works we find mentioned or supposed, *if not the doctrine of original sin properly speaking*, at least that of the fall, of a damage befalling our nature ... But, *beginning from* 397, Saint Augustine becomes more precise, more complete and more pronounced. The idea that he has in mind and expresses of original sin will be studied further ... p. 472. All things considered however, it appeared to him that in us the sin of origin consists of disordered concupiscence and especially sexual concupiscence ... Saint Augustine principally saw in that the very substance of original sin ... Baptism allows it to subsist *quoad actum*, but effaces what is culpable and evil in concupiscence; it means that it is no longer imputed to sin ... p. 474. Thus concupiscence is a sin with the non-baptized: in the baptized it is so no longer.

In 1909, M. Tixeront expresses Saint Augustine's attitude with regard to original sin exactly as I expressed it in 1901, that is, 8 years before him. He borrows from me my ideas. He even uses my wording. He happens, for example, to group his references in the *arbitrary* order (that is, without a concern for chronology) in which I grouped them myself. I am content to compare the following two groups, while noting that the treatise *ad Bonifacium* also bears the title *Contra duas epistolas pelagianorum*, and that I availed myself of the first designation while Tixeront used the second.

Tixeront 2, 479 note 1	Turmel p. 136 from the offprint 216
For example *Enchiridion* 30;	*Enchiridion* 30;
De perfectione justitiae hominis IV, 9;	*De perfectione justitiae hominis* 9;
epist. 145, 2; *Contra duas epist. pelag.* 1, 4	ep. 145.2; *ad Bonifacium* 1,4

To the references I add short citations of texts that Tixeront omits. I note that the *de perf. justitiae* is from 415 and that letter 145 is from 412, so I am knowingly reversing the chronological order because it is done only here.

I add that Tixeront does not limit himself to using my references. He has profited greatly from my exposition itself. To take but one example his explanation of the proofs utilized by Augustine to demonstrate the existence of original sin on pp. 467–71 is only a summary of mine (pp. 89–109 of the offprint, pp. 406–26 of the *Revue*). From beginning to end one observes the concealed copying, a clever copying, designed to avoid plagiarism, and an idea of which can be gleaned from reading the following observation that both of us make on the subject of the argument adopted by Augustine on *in quo*.[226]

First Denunciation in 1908

Tixeront 2, 468 note	Turmel p. 93 (offprint)
	410 *Revue*
It is known that exegesis does not support Augustine on this point.	Modern exegesis has not ratified the saintly doctor's verdict (a long development omitted by Tixeront follows).

As for the eternity of the pains of hell and the salvation of all Christians, here are several of Tixeront's statements:

> 2, 199. Saint Basil is obliged to note however that the majority of humans (*tous pollous tôn anthrôpôn*), deceived by the demon's tricks, were convinced that the punishments of the other life would have an end. Alas! among these men were found his own brother, Gergory of Nysssa and, to a certain degree, his close friend, Gregory of Nazienzen.

> 2, 335. These opinions (of the merciful) were maintained by very many people (*nonulli imo quamplurimi*); and they were not only widespread in Italy; they had reached Spain; Orosius appears to have shared the opinion of those who regarded all Christians as infallibly saved.

> 2, 335 note 4. In chapter 67 (of the *Enchiridion*) Saint Augustine says that the doctrine of the salvation of all Catholics is believed *a quibusdam*; here it may well be only the leaders of a party.

Coming to Saint Ambrose, M. Tixeront 2, 237 believes that this doctor's thought lacked consistency on the nature of the torments of hell. Then he adds:

> But where it is very consistent is on the respective duration of these punishments. For the demons and the impious, the infidels and the apostates this duration will be eternal . . . For simple sinners it will be different . . . p. 348. So the punishments of condemned sinners will be temporary; they will come to an end.

The same author at 2, 341 says that Saint Jerome abandoned the Origenist doctrine of universal salvation whose partisan he had been at first. Then he adds that having become Origen's adversary, Jerome:

> continued to think that all Christians would be saved in the end and that the torments of simple sinners would not be eternal.

M. Tixeront thus adopts in 1909 the interpretation of the texts over which Portalié had heaped insults upon me in 1908. I add that here, as in

PART TWO: How the Roman Church Freed Itself of Me

the question of original sin, he uses my wording. Here, for example, is the reflection he and I make on Saint Jerome who claimed never to have been an Origenist:

Tixeront 2, 341, line 7 and note 2.	Turmel *Eschatologie* published in 1900 p. 19 line 1
Denials that are occasionally mixed with half-acknowledgements (ep. 84, 3, 6).	Once however he makes a sort of half-acknowledgement (then I cite in its entirety a long text of the letter 84, 3, 6).

Here as well a group of references to Saint Gregory of Nyssa that we introduce:

Tixeront 2, 200 note 1	Turmel p. 8 notes 2, 3, 4, 5, 6
Orat. catachet. 26, 35 cf. 40;	*Catechetica Oratorio* 26, P.G. 45, 69 (Greek text cited).
De animâ et resurr. col. 72, 104, 152, 157; cf. *De Mortuis* col. 524; *Contra Arium et Sabellium* P.G. 45, 1292, 1293	*De animâ et resurrectione.* P.G. 45, 152 (Greek text cited) see ibid. p. 157, 160, 133, 136, 89, 99, 104. *De mortuis* P.G. 56, 524 (Greek text) see ibid. 526, 536, P.G. 44, 1313 (Greek text of the dissertation on 1 Cor. 18. 24). P.G. 45, 1292, 1293 (Greek text of the treatise Against Arius and Sabellius).

And here is how each of us speaks of the impression made in Rome by the book in which Rufinus translated Origen's *De principis* into Latin.

Tixeront p. 334	Turmel p. 20
Many were captivated: priests, monks, especially men of the world ... Women were heard to object that it would be pointless to resurrect with their body.	Priests, monks, laity, everyone at Rome read the book ... They were surprised, filled with wonder, captivated (then I cite in a note the Latin text of letter 84, 6 of Saint Jerome in which the women, taking their breasts and their womb in their hands say 'What good will it do us to resurrect with this body?').

Finally I add the following conjunction of Tixeront with a note from my *Saint Jérôme*[227] published in 1906.

| Tixeront 2, 341 | Turmel, *Saint Jérôme* p. 263 (note 2) |

First Denunciation in 1908

He (Saint Jerome) continued to admit as possible a certain mitigation of the punishments of the demons (in a note reference to *In Isaiam* 24.21).	Nonetheless, the commentary on Isaiah 24.31 p. 288 presents as a plausible hypothesis the mitigation of the punishments of the demons (Latin text follows).

I have just demonstrated how Portalié denounced my heresies and my incompetence. Now we must realize the results of his denunciation. My incompetence appeared peremptorily demonstrated to the readers of *Études*. True, I learned from a priest returned from Paris that, in enlightened circles, the Reverend Father appeared as a mountebank beating the bass drum. But this impression did not penetrate into the mass of clergy who denied my works any scientific value. Such were the outcomes of the accusations of incompetence.

The accusations of heresy had consequences far more serious, first in the archdiocese, then in Rome and finally among the public.

At the archdiocese the result produced by the first article published on August 5th was irritation. They were indignant when they saw Portalié set himself up as dictator of doctrine, hold a tribunal in front of the bishops, and teach a lesson to the episcopacy. And, this arrogance on the part of a member of the Company of Jesus, was recognized as the pride common to the whole body (like Saltet, Portalié was secretly encouraged by Rome). However the second article, that of August 20, changed irritation into anxiety, fear, a fear growing to the point of terror. Here the accusation no longer limited itself to generalities. It entered into the domain of specifics. And, as a beginning, it attacked my *Papauté*. But this book denounced as a "the most dangerous assault weapon" against the primacy of the Roman Pontiff, was equipped with the *imprimatur*; my archbishop stood guarantor of its orthodoxy! And the aggressive Jesuit pointed out with an ill disguised joy this shield that hardly impeded him. He wrote on p. 525:

> Oh! I am not unaware that certain people are going to be surprised. What do you make, then, they will say, of the *imprimatur*, even more, of the double *imprimatur* displayed at the end of the volume?

Afterwards he gave his response. A response whose proof he had sent to the archbishop with a card on which, in haughty terms, he asked Mgr Dubourg if it were acceptable to him. The response extended charity only to the point of not writing in black and white that the archbishop of Rennes and his entourage formed a collection of incompetents; it just let

PART TWO: How the Roman Church Freed Itself of Me

it be understood and concluded that the *imprimatur* "is not intended to restrain the critics."

The archbishop swallowed in silence the affront of the disdainful card (I received this information from M. Gayet) and also the affront of the article published on August 20. The first hurt only the pride of the archbishop and the members of his council of vigilance. The second denounced Mgr Dubourg's negligence to Rome. What happened then? What was the correspondence exchanged between the archdiocese of Rennes and the Holy Office? All that has remained mysterious. What appeared in public was the following note published in the *Semaine religieuse* of September 26, 1908:

> Certain of M. Turmel's doctrinal writings (on Angelology, Eschatology, Original Sin, the Papacy) have begun a debate in Catholic criticism that has repercussions, with the result that these books, until now little known to the public at large, are of a nature to produce at the very least a disturbing impression and an anxiety in certain Christian souls.
>
> The archdiocese is not familiar with the majority of these publications. The *Nihil obstat* granted to one among them solely indicates the absence of condemnable thesis or proposition and is in no way an approval of the book, nor any sort of credit given to its method and to its spirit on which, on the contrary, formal reservations have been raised and corrections imposed.
>
> Nevertheless, Mgr the Archbishop has thought it a duty of his episcopal office vis-à-vis the deposit of doctrine and souls who are in his care to call the attention and judgement of the Holy See to the writings noted above. Not wishing himself to render a ruling in so delicate and so difficult a question, he has solicited the decision of the Holy See, which all await with a respectful and filial docility.

This note said that the archdiocese was unacquainted with all these publications except the book on the papacy. However, since the decree of the Congregation of the Index issued in 1900, it ought not to have been unacquainted. It should have informed itself regarding all of my writings. Why then this lack of interest in my publications? As for my *Papauté*, the archdiocese referred to corrections it had imposed on me. Why had it limited itself to those? Why didn't it impose others? Evidently, Mgr Dubourg did not succeed in exonerating himself of the charge of negligence that the Congregation of the Index had undoubtedly made against him. Another person that my *Papauté* placed in an awkward position was Abbé Charost, responsible for the examination of my book and whose favorable report had very probably been brought to Rome's attention. But Abbé Charost appeared on the roster for promotion. He was destined for a miter. What would become of that? For grave dangers grave remedies. M. Charost traveled to Rome. He was able, without lying, to explain to the most eminent cardinals that Cardinal Labouré had thrown out the decree of 1901 and that, in the affair of my *Papauté*, the real culprit was M. Hamard, to whom the examination of my book had been handed over. What is certain is that his defense appeared plausible, for the miter came out of the affair unharmed.

There remained M. Hamard, whose leniency had caused the trouble. In order to expiate his crime he hunted down the denounced writings and, after having gathered them up, carried them to the archdiocese from which they proceeded to Rome which had summoned them for judgment.

The archdiocese carefully avoided drawing Rome's attention to the two volumes of my *Théologie positive*, to my *Tertullian*[228] and to my *Saint Jérôme*. It restricted itself to Portalié's victims. However Rome, which had taken my measure, decided not to let any of my children escape and to massacre them all. Only it proceeded bit by bit. In the first round figured the *Histoire du dogme de la papauté*, *Histoire du dogme du péché originel*, *Eschatologie à la fin du IVe siècle*. In a nice touch Herzog's book found a place among them. The Congregation of the Index did not say that I was Herzog; it only let attentive readers see that it was not fooled by the pseudonym. This first funeral procession occurred July 5, 1909. The second, on March 9, 1910, included the first volume of my *Théologie positive*, my *Tertullien* and my *Saint Jérôme*. In the very cordial letter that announced this execution, M. Durusselle wrote to me:

> Should I add that I also figure personally in this new trial whose repercussions I have suffered to a degree if, as I have reason to suppose, I signed the *Nihil obstat*.

A third funeral cortege took place on January 2, 1911 for the second volume of my *Théologie positive*.

Without a doubt Rome wanted to wipe out all my writings. Then why did its blows spare my "Chroniques" in the *Revue du clergé français*, my patristic studies published both in the *Annales de philosophie chrétienne* and in the *New York Review* and my *Descente du Christ aux enfers*? Most of the patristic studies seriously undermined dogma; nearly all the "Chroniques" led toward the same goal and often attained it if I am to judge by the following note in *Études* of September 5, 1908, p. 622.

Part Two: How the Roman Church Freed Itself of Me

> We draw attention to the deceitful *reserve* in the last of M. Turmel's sentences. It is pages of this sort that make the historical chronicle of the *Revue du clergé français* a strong force for intellectual upset.

My *Descente du Christ aux enfers*[229] was inspired by the same spirit as the "Chroniques." Certainly all these writings (except the *Descente*) were disseminated in journals and not in book form. However, it is not unheard of for journal or dictionary articles to be honored by the Index. There had probably been an oversight committed either by the Congregation of the Index, or by the providers of its reading fodder.

It is time to speak of the public, at least that portion of it that knew of me and that lived in my circle at Rennes. These simple souls knew nothing of the Saltet-Portalié enterprise up until the day when the *Semaine religieuse* of September 26 discreetly raised a corner of the veil that had hidden it form their gaze. Then they raised a unanimous chorus of protest. For the public at large there are not bad books beyond immoral novels, and the only reprehensible priests are those whose moral lives leave something to be desired. So how could the conduct of a hermit who scarcely left his house except to go to libraries come under suspicion? And how could the heavy in-folios that he was seen loaded down with have served to write bad novels? "Ah!" they said, "if all priests lived like him, there would not be all these scandals that we read so often in the newspapers." In order to give durable form to their protest the ladies requested the pastor of the parish to authorize me to give the benediction of the Blessed Sacrament every Sunday. The pastor (M. Perrault was dead) did not much like me; but he found himself faced with a superior force; he gave me the authorization. On my part I would have given scandal had I refused so spontaneous and eager an initiative. Thus, beginning in autumn of 1908 my ministry was increased by weekly benediction. I recounted the affair to my friend, M. Gayet, who was visiting while this was going on, and added that I intended to give benediction gratuitously, without including a collection. "Take care," he replied out of his experience of being a pastor, "your benediction will be valued by the faithful only if they make their contribution." The collection was taken.

In Proverbs 26:5 there is a profound maxim that had been for a long time inscribed on my list of ejaculatory prayers:

Responde stulto juxta stultitiam suam: Answer a fool according to his folly.

When the first decree of the Index appeared, I took care not to forget the Holy Spirit's precept. Rome requested my submission. It received one that, according to the gospel saying was "good measure, pressed down, heaped up, flowing over," *mensuram bonam et confertam et coagitatam et supereffluentem*. I rarely laughed as much as while writing the following note for the *Semaine religieuse* of July 17, 1909:

> Monsieur le Vicar General,
>
> I hear that three of my writings have been placed on the catalog of the Index. I accept with complete submission the decree that has struck me; I accept it with all the consequences it bears. I am going to order that the one book of the three at issue that is still in print be withdrawn from sale.
>
> Please accept...
>
> J. TURMEL

I knew well that so complete a submission would greatly edify the laity. However I thought that the clergy would detect in it at least a grain of irony. Not at all. Mgr Dubourg wrote me a long and affectionate letter of congratulations. My pastor, whom I never went to see, paid me a very cordial visit and expressed the unreserved joy that my letter had brought him and his clergy. Superfluous to mention the other letters and the other visits with which I was favored. A lady of very respectable age (85) who headed a notable printing firm wished to do better. She sent for me after supper (towards 8 o'clock in the evening) and invited me to get in beside her in the carriage that, every evening, took her on her drive. In the course of the ride she said substantially this: "In the confessional you preach morality to me; here I am going to do so to you. You have made a mistake: it is not a sin. However, now that the Holy Father has pointed out your errors, you must withdraw your book from sale. Here is a thousand franc note. You will send it to the publisher asking him to send you all that was not sold. I sympathize with your ordeal, having myself had a significant one when my husband failed some time ago in an attempt at the deputy-ship; but the salvation of your soul above all else." I could not, as a confessor, disobey such orthodox injunctions from my venerable penitent. The thousand francs were sent to Picard who sent me nine hundred copies of my *Papauté*. Eleven or twelve years later I resold them to the publisher Nourry.

Such was the outcome of the first Indexing. The second once again brought very effusive congratulations from Mgr Dubourg and a very cordial visit from my pastor. But this was nearly all. This time my venerable penitent did not think of my soul's salvation. And the congratulations of my

PART TWO: How the Roman Church Freed Itself of Me

archbishop, still rather lengthy, were written only on a card. The emotion had passed. It resurfaced when the third Indexing appeared. But it then assumed the form of irritation. These executions in small bundles aggravated the public. They said: "There is no end to it. Let them leave M. Turmel in peace. Do we need to know all that?" After the third condemnation, my archbishop sent me his card with two words. My submission, never lacking, in the end lost a great deal of its original solemnity. Still it may be useful to mention the formula that followed the second condemnation (*Semaine religieuse* 1911, January 14).

> Monseigneur,
>
> I published in 1906 a study of historical theology that the Reverend Jesuit Fathers had requested of me, that they had scrupulously examined, that they had approved. Published under their patronage my book received in addition the approval of the Archbishop of Paris. However, it treated delicate matters in which it was easy to go astray. The Holy Office, by decree of January 2nd, has just informed me that errors have been made. Unalterably attached to Holy Mother Church, knowing that it has received the words of eternal life and that it is ever enlightened by the light of the Holy Spirit, I adhere with all my soul to its infallible decision, happy if, by my absolute submission, I am able to console it for the trials that afflict it at this moment.

It pleased M. Charost a great deal who, after having read it, laughingly said to one of his achdiocesan colleagues (communication of M. Henry): "M. Turmel has put the blame on the Reverend Fathers. He has done well. Their arrogance is becoming tiresome."

Before bringing this chapter to a close, I must describe here a visit that M. Gayet paid me in September 1908, after Portalié's initial articles, but before the note in the *Semaine religieuse* that denounced my writings to Rome. With great delicacy and after having recalled the trials to which the great saints had been subject, my former student proposed that I retire to a home established in the diocese of Vannes to take in old priests; he affirmed that this retirement home would certainly be open to me if I wished; he added that I should be very comfortable there. I answered, in substance: "If I left the diocese I would go to Paris; but I have decided to remain here; I have received numerous expressions of sympathy from the faithful of the neighborhood; I shall continue to exercise my ministry in my chapel so long as the archbishop does not prevent it." M. Gayet did not insist. I only noted, on his face, an expression of surprise when I spoke of Paris. After his departure, reflecting on the strange proposition that he had just made to me, it was not difficult to interpret it. My leaving the diocese and going into a retirement home where, far from my books, I should have been reduced to playing cards, would have had two results: first, rid of my presence, the archbishop would have avoided the worry of scandalizing the faithful by denouncing my books in the *Semaine religieuse*; second, I would have been powerless to pursue my work. Evidently M. Gayet had been sent by the archdiocese.

3

Second Denunciation in 1929*

THE DENUNCIATION IN 1929 had extremely serious consequences for me and for the individuals who had recourse to my ministry, since first of all it led Cardinal Charost to pronounce the penalty of suspension and in the end it concluded in the decree of excommunication. I am going to describe the course of events of which I was the victim, Cardinal Charost's conduct and my own. But let us first become acquainted with the denouncers.

---

* The denunciation of 1908—as Saltet himself has acknowledged (p. 24) was condemned by the elite of the clergy. That of 1929, much more odious and more scandalous, ought to have been more vigorously spurned. In spite of the chorus of reprobation that greeted them, the two confederates, Saltet and Rivière, vied in boasting and insolence. They showed off in order to have themselves admired as the saviors of the Church. They succeeded in obtaining support from *La Croix* that has stunned the clergy (see p. 157 the note of the *Semaine religieuse* of Rennes). How can that be explained? One of the associates (likely Rivière) must have from the very outset informed Rome of his discovery. He submitted his plan of campaign and obtained support for it. No doubt *La Croix* received the order to publish the denouncing prose; the respectable journals were informed, one after another, that their support would be agreeable to Rome, Saltet and Rivière were proudly able to raise up their heads, to trumpet their opinions abroad and attack me like third-rate actors (according to them, as will be seen on p. 180, in writing under pseudonyms I was an imposter, spreading falsehoods in scientific writing, etc., etc.; from beginning to end of their campaign cheap drama was their normal element; they swam in it like fishes in water). Rome was behind them; it would not have been good to speak openly what was thought silently. What is surprising is that none of these eminent servants of the Roman Church landed a miter. Here is the probable explanation for this strange fact. In 1911 Saltet (p. 141) profaned the scapular of Mount Carmel: his elevation to the episcopate would have been a slap in the face for the Order of Carmel. In his past Rivière's orhtdoxy had not been beyond reproach. A short while ago he presented a theory of the redemption that the German Jesuit Pesch denounced as a deviation from the traditional teaching. Later he worked harder to align himself with traditional

Second Denunciation in 1929

THE DENOUNCERS

There were five of them. These five great servants of the Church are: Saltet, already named; Rivière, professor at the University of Strasbourg; the priests Croulbois, Boucard and Verdin. I shall speak of Croulbois and Boucard later (p. 143). I will simply say here that, without their intervention, the affair would not have seen the light of day, that they initiated it but remained aloof from the unfolding of events. Saltet and Rivière, in combining their efforts, after a long sensational campaign obtained a judgment that led to my suspension. Verdin was the one who managed my excommunication. In order to obtain this result, two secret letters sufficed, one to Saltet, on December 4, 1929, the other to Pouët,[230] on January 19, 1930. Verdin is the most important of the five. However this genial purveyor to the Holy Office nearly escaped notice. Saltet pompously proclaimed that he was in possession of proof of my identity with Coulange. But he was careful not to name his informer. His name would never have been revealed if M. Sartiaux, enlightened by certain signs during a visit to Pouët, had not discovered it himself. (See his book, *Joseph Turmel, prêtre historien des dogmes*, p. 178). I shall shortly say (p. 160) through what confluence of circumstances Verdin's letters brought about my expulsion from the Church. Here I note only that this powerful collaborator of Cardinal Charost and Pouët, has, in spite of his youth, already made a remarkable career. M. Sartiaux's book provides information on his record of service that has been completed by the newspapers of September 23 and November 26, 1931. For six months Verdin has been a ward of the State prisons.

It is over Saltet and Rivière that we need to linger.

Saltet's Campaign

It unfolded in the *Bulletin* of Toulouse beginning in May of 1929[231] (the March issue that only appeared in May). It ended in dealing with all of

---

teachings. However, to judge by a discreet allusion of Père d'Alès (*Revue apologétique* 1921, November 1, p. 172) [Adhémar d'Alès, "Le sens de la Rédemption," *Revue pratique d'apologétique* 33 (1921): 163–74—Ed.], his effort fell short. I said that the allusion was discreet. But Rivière acknowledged it and it is from him that comes the knowledge that he was its object. Moreover, in *Études* of 1931, d'Alès renewed the attack and explained who was the target of his arrow. Rome makes use of anyone to hand who offers to police orthodoxy. But paying is something else. I do not believe that the colleague of these two gentlemen, Abbé Verdin, was ever rewarded.

my pseudonyms; at the outset its objectives were limited to Herzog and Gallerand.

Herzog is an old acquaintance. The accusation directed against him in 1908 had resulted in a dismissal due to lack of evidence. Why would one come back to him? Because of a new fact presented in these terms, p. 107:

> A card signed J. Turmel and addressed to M. Paul Lejay was added to the Archives of the Archdiocese of Paris. In this card, M. J. Turmel affects to speak in the third person about articles on the *Sainte Vierge dans l'histoire*. He insistently requests M. Lejay to substitute in the *Revue* Herzog's name for Dupin's, which he does not find secret enough. This card is from the beginning of 1907.

This card provided the material proof of my identity with Herzog.

Gallerand was the author of a study on the theology of redemption in Saint Augustine published in 1922 by the *Revue d'histoire et de littérature religieuses*. In 1927 Rivière clearly let it be understood that Gallerand was myself and, on various occasions, his friends transformed these allusions into formal assertions. I denied these allegations and, under Gallerand's name, I sent to Rivière the expression of my profound contempt. Rivière obtained the autographs of my denials and sent them, as well as Gallerand's letter, to Saltet who published facsimiles of everything in the *Bulletin* of Toulouse. Thus they had material proof that I was Gallerand.

As for my identity with Coulange, Delafosse, Perrin, etc., etc., Saltet, after having affirmed it at length, provided a proof that was elegant as well as simple. He informed MM. Loisy, Dussaut and Couchoud of the serious accusations made against me and added in substance: "It is in the journal you direct or in the collection you are in charge of that all these authors have written. If these allegations brought against M. Turmel are false, you cannot, in his interest, excuse yourself from denying them." Naturally the recipients of these fine letters all maintained silence. Immediately, Saltet chanted victory. They had nothing to answer because there was nothing to say, and the proof had been accomplished that the names of Coulange, Delafosse, Dulac, Lagarde, Vanbeck, etc. provided me with screens.

During the campaign of 1908 Saltet affected to catch only Herzog, to concentrate pursuit on this "shameless plagiarist" and also on the *Revue d'histoire et de littérature religieuses* for which, according to him, Herzog would be "the enduring scandal." No one was taken in by this subterfuge; everyone understood, from the first blow, that behind the critic was concealed a heresy hunter who desired my ruin purely and simply. However,

Second Denunciation in 1929

in the end he claimed not to have accused me and to have confined himself to denouncing a plagiarist. In 1929 the affair had taken on a new aspect. This time, the plagiarisms had disappeared. Material proofs of my identity with Herzog and with Gallerand were brought. And since Herzog and Gallerand were total heretics, I myself was convicted of heresy. The denunciation no longer took the trouble to conceal itself behind the so-called rights and responsibilities of criticism. Also one is perplexed when one hears the Holy Office's supplier still invoking criticism and placing himself under its patronage. What can criticism have to do with a proceeding in which facsimiles of writing are associated with divulging a secret card? However, in order to become aware of all the tricks that this polemicist has up his sleeve, it is necessary to read his tirade of 1911 against the Carmelites. In a scandalous undertaking he reduced the scapular of Mount Carmel to nothing. Appalled, the disciples of Saint Elijah countered this sacrilege with a defense (*Études carmélitaines* 1, 1) in which using extremely moderate language they characterized the basis and the form of Saltet's memorial. As for the basis, they reproached the author with (p. 16)

> Ignorance of the sources, the readiness to accept everything without personal verification and a partiality of judgment very far from serene moderation and from the true historian who never harms virtuous people ... p. 23. He rests his article on the untrustworthy, scandalous work of Launoy ... In attacking devotion to the scapular, he diminishes the honor of the holy Mother of God. He will be able to lead the weak: but he will certainly arouse the adverse criticism of the friends of truth ...

Here is what they thought of the form (p. 2):

> He immediately informs us of his critical methods and starts off by dragging through the mud the adversary he wishes to engage ... (p. 3). After having made such scandalous remarks, he continues his insulting comments ... Our task would never end if we wished to reply to the damaging abuse he heaps upon this great memory ... If he has a reputation as a cunning arranger of texts, we can understand why; and, to make use of his own fine language, he cooks his brief and spices up his style in order to stimulate the public's appetite. Such methods of criticism are unworthy of serious men and still more of Churchmen ... (p. 23). His article abounds in invective that outrages the Order of Carmel.

Part Two: How the Roman Church Freed Itself of Me

Saltet began by flinging against his venerable adversaries the axiom: "If you lose your temper, you are wrong." Then he explains that he had not in any way attacked the devotion to the scapular of Mount Carmel but only one of the arguments on which it relies. The initial response was no more than a joke. As for the other it was correct but incomplete. Saltet was, in fact, only attacking one of the scapular's points of support; he simply forgot to add that this support was foundational and that, deprived of this supreme support, devotion to the scapular would fall into oblivion.

When one is strong enough to overturn a popular devotion without laying a finger on it, it must only be child's play to make a denunciation in the name of criticism. Saltet[232] explains to us that denunciation is a duty dictated simultaneously by "scientific considerations" and by "religious considerations" (*Bulletin* 1929, p. 168). By scientific considerations, because "in every genre of historical studies, the first law of criticism is the determination of the author of the document under consideration . . . Without this determination of the author *criticism is not possible*" (same thought p. 176: "in no historical matter . . . is it possible to have a scientific discussion of any degree of seriousness if the true origin of these works . . . has not been determined"). By religious considerations, because (p. 169): "all these pseudonymous works lose a great deal of their harmful force when it becomes known that behind these frantic attempts at demolition . . . is a still active priest who, on two occasions, has deceived his late archbishop with solemn oaths contrary to the truth."

This second rule means that Coulange's books will be less read and less convincing when it is known that I have written them. The meaning of the first is that the scientific value of a book can only be determined when its author is known. And Saltet became indignant (p. 167) over the attitude of a notable religious periodical that, at the time, censured Coulange's book without letting it be known that Coulange was a pseudonym. He exclaims in a tone of voice worthy of Captain Fracasse:[233] "There is something wrong with religious intelligence."

Let us not imagine that the one who spouts this nonsense is taken in by it. He well knows that my books will have a larger and more receptive readership as soon as their true author is known. Nor is he ignorant of the fact that a proof owes its force to its arguments and not to its author. Then why is he not ashamed at having recourse to such foolishness? In order to avoid the greater shame of having to admit publicly his true objective. What he wants is to hand me over to the Holy Office. All his writings are directed

Second Denunciation in 1929

to that. But the educated laity, who admit the necessity of a police force in the Church, reserve the rights of its exercise to the hierarchy. Nothing is more legitimate or more effective from the point of view of orthodoxy than the bishops forbidding the faithful reading dangerous books. Or that when a scandal erupts they discipline the authors of these books. But that scandal is created, out of bias, in order to force their hand and oblige them to take measures that they wished to avoid, the enlightened laity find this sort of undertaking repugnant. Saltet, who wanted to do exactly that is therefore obliged to conceal his real program in order to avoid the reproach of the educated. He dissembles; and in order to dissemble, he renews his tactic of 1908. With a twist. In 1908 he said: "I have not accused M. Turmel; the one I've accused is his shameless plagiarist Herzog." In 1929 he says: "I denounce M. Turmel, it is true, since I am revealing to the public his secret card deposited in the archives of the Archdiocese of Paris, as well as a letter that he wrote under the name of Gallerand. However I do not want, for all that, to hand him over to the Holy Office. My unique goal is to relieve his books of 'a great deal of their harmful force' and also to proceed to a 'determination of the author in the absence of which no criticism is possible.'"

How did Saltet gain knowledge of my card to Lejay? He was informed of its existence and its content in 1922 by the Sulpician Boucard who, at the time when he was named as head of the major seminary at Toulouse, had a conversation with the denouncer in which he said in substance:

> Before coming to Toulouse I was a curate at Saint-Sulpice in Paris. As I was leaving I saw M. Croulbois, a non-beneficed priest [prêtre habitué] of that parish. He showed me a card that had been written to M. Lejay by M. Turmel and which affords proof of the identity of M. Turmel with Herzog. He gave me his permission to acquaint you with this important document that confirms your conclusions of 1908, and he is at your disposal to give you in writing any information that you desire.

No doubt one is curious as to how Croulbois came into possession of my card to Lejay. Here is how. Born in 1855 in the diocese of Laval, in 1880 Croulbois was employed at the ecclesiastical collège of Château-Gontier. This house having closed in 1881 in the wake of a sensational scandal in which three professors were convicted and sentenced[234] and several others compromised (see *Sermons de M. l'abbé Gendron*, p. 444) Croulbois took refuge in Paris and obtained a position in an ecclesiastical collège where he made Lejay's acquaintance. After eight years' absence, he returned, in 1889, to his diocese of origin and remained there twenty-five years during which he published several articles in Lejay's *Revue*.[235] In 1914 he again left his diocese and, at the age of 59, ended up in Paris where he lived within the territory of Saint-Sulpice, but on the fringes of the diocesan clergy. In order to explain this second hegira, Croulbois would have us believe (Letter to Saltet in the *Bulletin* 1931[237]) that he had perhaps incurred the displeasure of his bishop through his association with Lejay. That is a poor joke. A bishop could not dismiss a priest from favor in 1914 for perfectly orthodox articles written in 1904 in a journal in which Baudrillart had just written and that no one yet suspected. Let us simply say that one need not search for the reasons that obliged a senior member of the clergy to remove himself from his own country to end up in poverty on the streets of Paris. Whatever the reason, isolated, deracinated, Croulbois instinctively turned to Lejay who, out of pity, consented to welcome him into his home once a week.

In his letter to Saltet, Croulbois tries to explain how he was able with complete fidelity, after Lejay's death (June 1920), to take my card which he found among the deceased's papers and hold it until 1928 when he deposited it in the archives of the Archdiocese of Paris. His hazy defense breaks down when confronted with the following observations:

a) On his own admission (the foresaid letter) the Archdiocese of Paris ordered him to "hand over anything among Lejay's papers that could concern the history of the Church and the modernist movement." But my card—as events have proven—was of eminent concern to this history. Thus he ought to have handed it over. In persistantly retaining it he violated the orders of his superiors, he acted against the law, he committed an offense that lasted until the day when, at the approach of death (September 1928), he complied.

b) My card, if it bears witness against my orthodoxy, was no less disastrous for that of M. Lejay, with whom I communicated about Herzog's work. Mlle Lejay, the deceased's pious sister, would have hastened to burn it, had she suspected its import. And Croulbois who, to justify his conduct, said he received from this person the authorization to keep my card, simply proves his dishonesty, considering that, in order to obtain this authorization, he misled his friend's heiress, in making her believe that the item in question was of no importance.

c) Lejay, who preferred to run the risk of destitution to revealing the true name of Herzog (Loisy *Mémoires* 3, 150), was firmly convinced that my letters would be burned after his death by the persons charged with going through his papers. It is by a revolting betrayal that Croulbois kept and exploited my card, against the clear intentions of his deceased friend.

Let us return to Saltet. In 1922 he let go, without acting on it, of the proposal that was made to him through Boucard. We shall see how he uses it in December 1928.

Rivière's Campaign

In Rivière there is a denouncer; also a polemicist and an historian. I am going to study them separately.

A. The denouncer. 1. In 1927 on various occasions Rivière let it be understood that I concealed myself under the name of Gallerand, whose work he was supposed to refute in the *Revue des Sciences religieuses*.

2. Annoyed by this delator's methods, I sent him, under Gallerand's name, a letter telling how deeply I scorned him (May 1928). Two months later he secretly denounced me to Cardinal Charost in a letter that he mentions in these terms (*Semaine religieuse de Rennes* 1930, p. 6): "I myself have gone to the trouble of disclosing the affair to his Eminence Cardinal Charost in a letter of July 27, 1928."

3. Under the title of "Une douloureuse affaire ecclésiastique" he published in *La Croix* of July 18, 1929 a summary of the first article written by Saltet in the *Bulletin* of Toulouse. Under the same title he gave *La Croix* of August 8 and November 7 a summary of Saltet's other articles. In the same newspaper there appeared the following November 21 a study that explained and judged Gallerand's work. Finally on December 12 *La Croix*'s readers received new information regarding the "Douloureuse affaire ecclésiastique."

4. At the same time Rivière devoted several pages of his book, *Le Modernisme dans l'Église*, to my pseudonymous writings and concluded: "We still have to ask where the invisible orchestra conductor is to be found, whose magic baton is able tirelessly to conjure up such a series of extras" (reproduced in *La Croix* of December 12 that I am referencing).

5. From various sources I have been informed that he invited—to no avail, however—a professor of the University of Paris to proceed against me.

Part Two: How the Roman Church Freed Itself of Me

6. According to the assertion of the *Bulletin* of Toulouse 1929, p. 218, when Saltet (December 1928) wrote to Croulbois requesting additional details regarding my card which at the time the latter still possessed, he was only fulfilling a promise given "five months" previously to Rivière, who had asked him to take this step "on several occasions." In sum, it is the *Bulletin* of Toulouse that revealed to the public the existence of my card of 1907 to Lejay and which gave a summary of its content received from Croulbois. However, it was on the repeated insistance of Rivière, dating from July 1928, that the summary was, in December, requested of Croulbois who was prompt in giving it. And these solicitations led to obtaining the publication of the foresaid summary. Furthermore, here is the text of the *Bulletin*: "He (Rivière) repeatedly insisted that I *publicly* give my account (regarding the card) beginning by asking for the one M. Croulbois had spontaneously offered" (in 1922)." In 1922, through Boucard as intermediary, M. Croulbois had informed Saltet that he had my card in his keeping and had offered to send a written attestation immediately if it were so desired. Saltet had let the offer drop without following it up; but he had spoken of this affair in conversation with his friends, Rivière among them. The latter, in 1928, insisted that Saltet request from Coulbois the precious written attestation and that this attestation should be published in the *Bulletin*. Thus the initiative for the publication of my card belongs to Rivière. As for the facsimiles of Gallerand's and my writing published in the same *Bulletin* I do not know which of the two associates took the initiative, but logically this role reverts to the one who insistently asked for the publication of my card, that is, to Rivière.

7. During the month of August a priest of the diocese of Albi sent the publisher Rieder a letter addressed to Coulange that was delivered to me. In substance the letter said: "I have read your book *La Messe*[237] that has overturned everything that we were taught in seminary. Would you kindly tell me in what journal you have published, following the same method, studies on Christology of which I've vaguely heard and which I would like to read?" Several days later the same publisher sent a letter from a state school teacher who, interested in sociology, asked where he could obtain an article published by Lawson[238] on the eucharist in Saint Augustine. I did not reply to these two inquirers even though they had paid for the reply. If I had written the letters as asked, facsimiles of my writing would have immediately appeared in the *Bulletin* of Toulouse.

Second Denunciation in 1929

8. I might reasonably have inquired how the clerical journals had been led to act in concert against me. But I did not make any attempt to resolve this question. I have not even read anything of the literature on my person that blossomed at the time outside of *La Croix*, *Études*, the *Revue des sciences religieuses* and the *Bulletin* of Toulouse.

Even confined to the limits within which I was able to follow it, Rivière's activity as a denouncer was considerable.

It was partly occult, partly public.

To the occult action belongs a letter to Cardinal Charost, fragments of which were published in the *Semaine religieuse* of Rennes in 1930, p. 6; the approach made to a professor at the University of Paris, the two letters from the unknown people who attempted to obtain writing samples from Coulange and Lawson. The letter to the cardinal pointed out "coincidences" between Gallerand's letter and mine "that leave no doubt." The author adds: "I do not want a public scandal;" which means that the "public scandal" will happen if the cardinal remains inactive. The proceedings instigated by Saltet are preparing the public scandal that must occur if the cardinal remains silent, and that did occur, in fact, in May of 1929, that is, six months later. In sum, in his secret activity, Rivière has "no doubt" regarding my identity with Gallerand and with Herzog. He requests the cardinal to act ruthlessly against me; he requests Saltet to raise a scandal; he is certain and insistent.

The public action was manifested in the *Revue des sciences religieuses* in 1927,[239] in *La Croix* and in the book on Modernism. However the *Revue des sciences religieuses* limited itself to allusions to the kinship of Gallerand's work with my writings; the book on Modernism contained but a summary of the five articles in *La Croix*. Thus it is to these articles that we must turn.

What first draws our attention is that all are anonymous, except the article of November 7 which, attacking Gallerand's doctrine, had to be signed and bore Rivière's signature. All the others seemed to issue from the editorial office of *La Croix* itself. This makes considerable impression on readers. It inspires their respect and docility in the presence of all the allegations, notably the following (July 18):

> However painful these kinds of affairs may be, they bear too closely upon the honor of the Church for *La Croix* not to consider it a duty to inform its ecclesiastical readers.

Thus it is to save the Church's honor and to discharge a painful but imperious duty that *La Croix* handed over "to ecclesiastics" information

PART TWO: How the Roman Church Freed Itself of Me

that one hundred thousand male and female of the laity took in attentively but also with sorrow (the article of November 21, I know, made more than one pious person cry).

What were the terms in which the so-called administration of *La Croix* reported this "painful ecclesiastical affair"? Oh! It does not overemphasize the importance of Rivière's role. It lingers over him only in the article of July 18 in which it points out his refutation of Gallerand, the letter of insults that this refutation had earned him (what I had condemned was solely the work of delation that accompanied this refutation), the printing of this refutation as a booklet and the name of the publisher from whom this was obtainable. Apart from this clever publicity, Rivière is scarcely named. It is Saltet who, from beginning to end, is in the foreground. It is he who publishes Lejay's card, he who publishes Gallerand's letter. It is not said expressly that the initiative in all that came from Saltet, it is simply allowed to be understood.

As for what concerned me, they first implore me to clear myself of the accusations brought against me, they hope I can justify myself. They write,

> July 18: confronted with this new fact that comes to confirm all the old ones, will M. Turmel decide to provide the explanation that is expected of him? . . . It is to be hoped, not without some anguish, that M. Turmel will not delay in clearing himself.

But soon threats accompany the hope of a justification.

> August 8: either M. Turmel, and this is our fondest wish, will exonerate himself from the accusation made against him, or, let there be no mistake, his silence will be taken as admission.
>
> November 21: if M. Turmel recognized himself as guilty . . . would he act any differently? . . . The charges that are accumulating only add to the necessity for the explanation hoped for by his confreres who are all too justifiably alarmed, to say nothing of his superiors.

On December 12 the threat reached Cardinal Charost. Emphasis was placed:

> on the scope of the assault directed against the Christian faith by the various pseudonyms in question and on the singular deficiency of certain Catholic leaders in this regard.

The reader now grasps the contrast that separates the occult activity from the public activity. In secret a sustained initiative and frenzied anger. In public an effacing of personality under the mask of *La Croix*; an effacing of action behind Saltet; an affected moderation that slides here and there into threats; insistent and reiterated invitations to justify myself; a continual stream of trickery. This trickery extends to the way in which the articles were managed. The first article is written because *La Croix* has the duty of informing a hundred thousand pious souls what two hundred readers had seen in the *Bulletin* of Toulouse, that is, the existence of a card and of secret letters. The second is supposed to complete the first. In reality it contains only repetitions and these repetitions have no other goal than to renew the emotion produced by the first. What is desired is the stirring up of opinion; the rest is pure pretext. The third article restates for the third time what was already published in July and August. However it was necessary to prolong the emotion, to maintain the agitation. The article of December 12 is, for the most part, devoted to a fourth edition of the Herzog and Gallerand affairs; it also returns to my other pseudonyms of which the third artlicle had already spoken. What do these repetitions accomplish? They are extracts from various organs of the religious press. Their objective is to show to the pious female readers of *La Croix* that my writings have struck the entire Catholic world with amazement. Moreover the article begins with this observation:

> Nearly everywhere opinion is beginning to be stirred up in the face of these new revelations by M. Saltet. Here are a few appraisals on this subject collected recently from the religious press.

The majority of these appraisals were borrowed from Rivière's book, that is, from the very author of this article who remains hidden behind the mask of the *La Croix*'s administration.

So much for Rivière the denouncer. Let us now speak of the polemicist. Here are several samples of his style:

Citing Alcuin's commentary on Heb 2:10 he says (*Revue des sciences religieuses* 1931 p. 570, note 6[240]): "This is the *only* text that M. Gallerand cites, who besides does not trouble himself to bring out the thought nor perhaps to notice it since he suppresses the initial exclamation." In reality I cite *three* texts of Alcuin. I cite them one following upon another. The reader who will read my work will see if I have not noticed the import of the commentary on Heb 2:10.

Regarding a passage from Bede who speaks of the innocent lamb sacrificed for us, Rivière says (ibid. p. 570): "In retrieving this text M. Gallerand finds the means to distort it by a mistranslation." According to him, I played false because I translated: "[the lamb] has broken the strength of the lion which had killed him," while the true meaning would be "the lamb has broken the strength of the lion who has killed *us*." In reality my translation reproduced Bede's thought exactly, who said clearly two lines earlier that the lamb was killed. Moreover the texts in which the Fathers say that the devil killed Christ are numerous.

Coming to the doctors of the ninth century, Rivière says (ibid. p. 575) in reference to me: "His documentation is utterly inadequate." At the beginning of this chapter I say that the enumeration of all of the medieval authors would be "as useless as fastidious." Then I add: "Thus there is room for choice and to set aside, especially from the ninth century onward, all those who are not representative of their period and their country." Rivière notes in my work[242] (ibid. 1929, p. 35) a "tyranny of prejudice" to which I would "sacrifice the textual evidence." However several admissions slip out from him here and there. He says (ibid. p. 35): "Again this very prejudice may be justified on some grounds." He also recognizes (ibid. p. 172) that: "the reading of Saint Leo is, at first, disappointing for a mind accustomed to the framework of our theological categories. Not only is there not a single one of his nineteen sermons on the passion that unfolds *ex professo* according to the Pauline schema of the reconciliation between God and the sinner through the sacrifice of Christ, that our doctrine of satisfaction only translates into more precise terms ... But of greater significance is establishing that this theme hardly comes up at all in passing reference and even more rarely still without being amalgamated with that of the demon, his power and his ruin."

Rivière calls me (ibid. 1929 p. 173) a "complete autodidact." When he cannot find fault with my interpretations, he grumbles about my style. He says (ibid. 1929 p. 159): "After having summarized the work in this gibberish that cruelly afflicts the French language but that remains basically exact..." Obliged to recognize that my interpretation is exact, he consoles himself with my jargon.

Regarding Rivière the historian and obliged to be brief, I shall limit myself to these few lines.

In his book on Modernism he presents (on the word of those who have read it: see Loisy, *Mémoires* 3, 543 and 254) the measures taken by Pius X as the legitimation of the Batiffol-Lagrange school. But everyone knows that these two authors were censured by the pope. In the article in the *Dictionnaire de théologie catholique* 10, 2040, he timorously tries to blacken my conduct; however he does not breathe a word of the reprobation which

Second Denunciation in 1929

Saltet's enterprise drew forth, a reprobation that he must have known about. In his first book on the Redemption[242] p. 486 he affirms without flinching that, among all the Fathers, the doctrine of the rights of the demon "remains of secondary importance." On page 406 he has given an interpretation of the most important text of Saint Augustine that completely falsifies its meaning.*

On page 252 he stops at a citation from Augustine's homily on psalm 129:3 just at the point where the citation is going to turn against his thesis (the words he leaves out are: "*de manu captivantis inimici*"). Same phenomenon on p. 236 where a text of Ambrose's *De Virginitate* p. 126 is cited, with the difference that the passage omitted because it was compromising precedes the citation "*eramus oppignerati malo creditori peccatis*" (see my *Histoire des dogmes* 4, 477).

---

* In the *Revue d'histoire et de littérature religieuses* 1922, p. 51 Gallerand pointed out, supported by proofs, this misinterpretation that falsified the entire history of the dogma of the redemption since it bore upon the most important of all of Augustine's texts. However, treating the author tactfully, he did not name him (Gallerand's observation can be seen in my *Histoire des dogmes* 1 367–68 where it is reproduced without any change). Humiliated by this finding to which he had nothng to respond, Rivière took his revenge by denouncing me as the real author of the study signed Gallerand. The rest is known.

4

The Condemnation

1. Cardinal Charost did not respond to the letter of July 27, 1928 in which Rivière exposed me as the author of the articles published under Gallerand's name. The cardinal did nothing to verify the denouncer's allegations: he judged them unimportant and treated them with the contempt they deserved.

2. He was jolted out of his indifference when, at the beginning of May 1929, the *Bulletin* of Toulouse published the article that resuscitated the Herzog affair and compared my writing with that of Gallerand. The archdeacon of Rennes, M. Gayet, came to me in the cardinal's name. In the grip of an emotion that he was not successful in mastering, he showed me the accusatory pages of the *Bulletin* and asked whether I was the author of the writings bearing Gallerand's signature. My negative response instantly brought joy back to his sad countenance. He said to me, smiling: "That suffices: I am going to report your words to His Eminence." He then showed me the page of the *Bulletin* devoted to Herzog. But he added that the cardinal did not wish to stir up this old history dormant for these past twenty years. After which he took his leave, assuring me with a faint smile that I had nothing to fear. The interview had lasted ten minutes.

3. During the summer of 1929, at the same time that the *Bulletin* of Toulouse had expanded its denunciation with the names of Coulange, Delafosse, etc., and that *La Croix* had begun its sensation, Cardinal Charost severely took the two denouncers to task before a prelate among his circle of friends, blaming them for troubling consciences. I have no other details regarding this conversation that came to my knowledge during the second half of 1930.

The Condemnation

4. Later, at a time when Rome must have intervened and that is perhaps not before the final weeks of 1929, Cardinal Charost said to a colleague of his: "Either Turmel or myself will get the sack." This second conversation, like the preceding one, was only reported to me in the second half of the following year.

5. On October 22, 1929, a lady who visited Cardinal Charost two or three times a year, who formerly had the same relationship with Cardinal Dubourg and who came to see me from time to time, said to me in these terms: "Cardinal Charost whom I saw yesterday confided to me a very delicate mission in relation to you that is costing me a great deal to fulfill. He said to me: for the last three months I've received demands to act with regard to M. Turmel. He is accused by two professors of denying the existence of God. I want to save him. I shall do everything possible to prevent his affair from going to the Holy Office: for then I could no longer do anything for him. If there is any foundation to these accusations made against him, let him say so. When one is reprimanded, one shoulders the blame. Tell him to write me. I would prefer that he come to see me. As for the professor in Toulouse, what he has done is appalling."

The next day I sent Cardinal Charost a letter in which, after thanking him for his kindness, I placed myself at his disposal.

6. Cardinal Charost did not reply to this letter. But the following December 2nd, a young secretary brought me on behalf of his master a haughty note that directed me to appear at the Archbishop's residence, the very evening of this day, at five o'clock for an affair of the greatest importance. At the stipulated hour, I was at my judge's door, in a state that, without quite being irritation, bordered on it, resolved on my part not to provoke a scene, but to do nothing to avoid one. At the end of a quarter of an hour, the cardinal had me enter. His welcome was cold, but correct. When I was seated, he said to me in a flat voice, very soft, half stifled and as if intimidated: "I am obligated to warn you that your case is extremely serious, extremely serious. Annoyed by Rivière's denunciations, you have written him a letter under the name of Gallerand. He has obtained a letter signed by you and he has concluded that you are the author of a written work on the redemption published under the name of Gallerand. On my request the items in the case have been handed over to me. I have sent them to a first rate expert near the courts of the Seine. He sent me his report, which concludes that the writings are identical."

PART TWO: How the Roman Church Freed Itself of Me

Here the cardinal prepared himself to enter upon technical explanations based on a movement of the arm that leaves a trace in the writing. And as if to give me an object lesson he moved his arm. But scarcely had he finished his sentence when I cut him short and sharply cried out: "How do you want me to take seriously a report from an expert? The experts have been discredited since the day two or three of them, in a well known trial (allusion to the Dreyfus Affair) attributed to Peter a writing that emanated from Paul."

This vehement retort stopped the cardinal short who immediately put aside the Gallerand affair and passed on to the Herzog affair. He said to me: "You also wrote to M. Lejay a card that is today in the archives of the Archdiocese of Paris and which shows that you are Herzog." To which I replied in substance: "On the admission of the denouncers I speak in this card of Herzog in the third person. They claim that this turn of phrase is a subterfuge. By what right does one draw so serious a conclusion from a few lines jotted down offhandedly on a card? Furthermore, highly placed authorities have recognized that Herzog is a plagiarist but that I am not Herzog. This is the thesis that Père d'Alès himself has just maintained in *Études*.

Here the cardinal, breaking into laughter, stopped me and, leaving aside his flat, hushed voice, replied in a jovial tone: "When I read this article recently, I said to myself: Père d'Alès wants to save M. Turmel out of gratitude for his *Théologie positive*." I replied, "Elsewhere in that same article, Père d'Alès is unjustly severe on me. And his severity itself gives new force to his remarks when he speaks of Herzog. I add that Père d'Alès has not been the only one to take up my defense. M. Bricout has always been supportive."

Interrupting me, the cardinal said in a serious voice: "In M. Bricout you have a very devoted friend. He has spoken of you in excellent terms." I added: "I know that M. Bricout considered Saltet's campaign in 1908 shameful." "Saltet," replied the cardinal, with a triumphant air, "has never seen my writing." I also said that Duchesne was among those who had protested against the accusations of 1908 and, to support my assertion, drawing from pocket the booklet *Libère et Fortunatien* that I had brought with me, I showed to the Cardinal page 51 on which is found the note cited earlier (pp. 107). Invited to read it, I did so . . . However, without paying attention to my reading, the Cardinal replied in his flat and hushed voice: "Mgr Duchesne said to me, to me personally that you were the author of the work signed Herzog and that for him there was no doubt at all." Stunned by this retort that I had not expected, I did not have the necessary presence of mind to recall for my august interlocutor the caustic criticism that he had formerly made of Duchesne before the professors of Saint Vincent (p. 123) and I limited myself to the observation that a note inserted in a scientific journal has a value far superior to a quip that slips out in the course of a conversation. However, without listening me, the Cardinal repeated, in the same hushed voice, his allegation: "He has said to me, to me personally, that you were the author of the work signed Herzog. And then I received a letter from an eminent religious who declared that he had heard you yourself admit that that you had written under the name of Denys Lenain." I replied, "I have never kept my authorship of the writings signed Denys Lenain a secret and I do not understand why these writings that are irreproachable from the dogmatic point of view, although somewhat daring, have been denounced to you." But the Cardinal, without paying attention to my reply, said: "It is an eminent religious who wrote that to me." After which, he announced to me that he was going to set up a commission to study the two Gallerand and Herzog affairs, ordering it to pause at the slightest doubt. I left after a converation of three quarters of an hour.

7. In the *Semaine religieuse* of December 7, 1929, Cardinal Charost published a note informing the public that very serious charges had been made against me by two professors and announcing the constitution of a tribunal of inquiry intended to verify these charges. With these two principal thoughts were associated various secondary observations, two of which should be noted here. The first dealt with the publicity given by "a widely circulated newspaper" to the charges issued by the *Bulletin* of Toulouse and it discreetly reprimanded this publicity. *La Croix* (for it was the one referred to) having justified its conduct in putting forward the honor of the Church and the duty incumbent upon it to inform its ecclesiastical readers, the Cardinal's reprimand let it be understood that these so-called justifications were a sham and that, under the pretext of informing ecclesiastics, *La Croix*'s articles had scandalized a hundred thousand laypeople.

The second observation was formulated in these terms: "In the interim M. Turmel has been questioned on several occasions by the Archdeacon of Rennes." The truth is that I had been questioned only once, at the beginning of May 1929, in an interview that lasted ten minutes and that, from that date until my conversation with Cardinal Charost, I had not seen either the archdeacon of Rennes or any other representative of ecclesiastical authority. Thus the assertion of the *Semaine religieuse* is inaccurate. I should add that the inaccuracy was intended. Not for a single instant did Cardinal Charost imagine giving one or another of his staff nonexistent missions. No. But he was anxious to exonerate himself from the reproach of negligence, of carelessness that *La Croix*'s fomentation had insinuated into minds, that *La Croix* was going to formulate shortly thereafter in the issue of December 12 (p. 149): his intention was to give proofs of his vigilance. And as these proofs did not exist, he fabricated them. In which he followed, no doubt without knowing it, Bellarmine's example. In effect that illustrious cardinal inserted a lie, a big lie into an item of greatest importance, namely in the preface printed at the head of the official Vulgate and that can be read still today on the first page of Latin Bibles published under the patronage of ecclesiastical authority (*Praefatio ad lectorem*, second half): the lie consists in saying that Sixtus V, in the final moments of his life, ordered the suppression of his edition of the Vulgate because of printing errors that had slipped into it. And this lie cannot be denied since the author himself in his Autobiography admits having committed it and ranks it among the fine actions of his life (De Récalde, *la cause du Vénérable Bellarmin*, p. 106 and 207[243]). Thus Bellarmine prides himself on having committed a falsehood in an official document of major importance. He prides himself because his goal in doing that was to save the honor of the papacy and to rescue the Church from a danger, possibly "the greatest ever." Far from reproving this lie the Church has approved it, since it has recently accorded its author the honors of canonization. In lying before the Catholic world in order to save his honor, that is the honor of the hierarchy, Cardinal Charost performed an act that from the theological point of view was beyond reproach.*

8. A few days later the tribunal announced by the *Semaine religieuse* of December 7 opened its sessions intended to investigate the Gallerand and Herzog affairs.

The investigation of the Gallerand affair brought me a surprise. One day Pouët informed me that Béon and Desbois, of whom I have spoken elsewhere (*Comment j'ai donné congé aux dogmes*, p. 56), when summoned,

---

* In 1885 the archbishop of Rennes, upon learning that a professor of Saint-Vincent was sought by the magistrature, quickly had conveyed to the unforunate a sum of money that enabled him to cross the border before the police had seized him in his hiding place, and he confided this delicate mission to Abbé Boulay, professor at the major seminary. Brought before the tribunal himself for this act, Abbé Boulay swore before God to have gone to see the guilty person as a friend without bringing him any monetary assistance and above all not to have received any instruction from ecclesiastical authority. Before taking this false oath he had been duly rehearsed by ecclesiastical authority itself. I was his confrere, I received this information from his own mouth.

The Condemnation

had given testimony under oath. Its result was that my methods, specifically those that had injured me, were linked with Gallerand's methods with regard to Rivière. I replied that all men more or less agree in giving the same expression to their indignation and their contempt. The deposition of these two individuals made a positive impression on Charost who inserted it into the judgment of January 23. Béon and Desbois, who had earlier dictated my course in theology, thus have the consolation and the honor of having effectively cooperated in my suspension and, indirectly, in my excommunication. I had informed them both in severe terms that they had grossly failed me. They took their revenge in centuple. As for Pouët, who, from beginning to end, executed his orders like a corporal, he thought to perform a duty in welcoming, even perhaps inciting the testimony of these two snitches.

9. While the tribunal investigated the Gallerand and Herzog affairs, Cardinal Charost traveled to Rome. No one could have known the conversations he had with the Pope and with the Holy Office unless he told them. On his return to Rennes the rumor arose and reached even me that he had been rebuked for the weakness that he had shown toward me. Perhaps it is under the influence of this reproof that he had the conversation with a bishop mentioned previously (n° 4). Probably it is also during his visit to the Holy Office that he received the following observation: "You said that you were absolutely ignorant of Turmel's writings. Here we have been aware of these writings for a long time." However, it is not impossible that the Cardinal's remark and the reply of the Holy Office had been the object of a correspondence exchanged before the trip to Rome.

10. In the *Semaine religieuse* of January 4, 1930, a new note from the Cardinal. a) He explains why he has not taken into consideration Rivière's denunciatory letter of July 27, 1928, a fragment of which he cites ("no analysis of resemblances was even sketched"). b) Alluding to the articles in *La Croix*, he noted the emotion that the "scandal of the simple faithful" caused him, and he "regrets not having been able, for want of being forewarned, to prevent it." c) In return, he holds as legitimate the articles of the *Bulletin* of Toulouse written for "readers who already have some knowledge of the subjects" (note numbers 3 and 5 where the Cardinal spoke of Saltet in very severe terms).

11. Judgment of January 23, 1930. Two principal parts, one of which treats the origin of the writings signed Gallerand and Herzog, the other their content or, if you will, their substance. The question of origins was

Part Two: How the Roman Church Freed Itself of Me

resolved by the members of the tribunal who unanimously affirmed that I was the author of the writings at issue. The question of content was reserved exclusively to the Cardinal. He declares that Herzog's book is contrary to the dogmas of the Church. As for Gallerand's writing, it is insulting to the Fathers and the tone is reprehensible (the Cardinal raises as very unseemly the place where, summarizing a sermon of Caesar of Arles, I said that Christ "descends into hell and turns it upside down." I noticed that he had not succeeded in finding the most important part of Gallerand's work that was devoted to Augustine and that appeared in the *Revue d'histoire et de littérature religieuses*). By way of conclusion, the Cardinal hits me with the penalty of interdiction, not without first having noted that the writings signed Gallerand and Herzog constituted a serious breach of my sacerdotal honor. A year later the newspapers revealed that this avenger of sacerdotal honor read lewd literature and did not go to confession.

12. On March 25, 1930, at the end of two months of suspension, I decided to own up to being the author of the Herzog-Gallerand writings. And I sent the following letter to Cardinal Charost:

> *Eminence. Warned that serious sanctions will be imposed if I reject the deductions that the tribunal has drawn from the private letters written in 1900, 1907, 1928, I declare that these deductions are fully justified. Consequently I reprove and regret all that in these incriminatory writings is contrary to the teaching of the Church to which I profess to adhere.*

Without this step of March 25, the canonical sanction which had been dealt me for two months would have been prolonged indefinitely. But also—I realize this now that experience has made it clear to me—as long as new writings signed with my name did not appear, the archdiocese would be powerless to carry on with its inquiry into my literary production: and the absolute silence that it observed over two months would, like my own position, also prolong itself indefinitely. In December of 1929 I resigned myself to appearing before a tribunal in the hope of freeing myself from the disciplinary sanctions. However, since the judgement of January 23, the cardinal no longer had any means of constraint against me; I could with impunity scorn his threats, refuse to appear before him or before his delegates. And a second canonical inquiry, should he have wished to institute one, could not function without my cooperation. It was the letter of March 25 that made possible a hidden process that I unsuspectingly fell in with. It was that which set me on the road that ended in excommunication. And, in writing it, I threw myself into the jaws of the wolf.

How was I led to write it? Clearly, I yielded to the desire to recover my faculties, my chapel, of renewing contact with the pious souls of the neighborhood, who—I knew indirectly—had nearly all preserved their attachment, their affection for me, and who urged me to make what they called my submission. However it is clear that I would have resisted the entreaties of pious souls and my personal desire, if I had had the slightest suspicion of the consequences of my action, if I had even foreseen that my chapel and the contact with souls would never be returned to me. I wrote my letter because I believed that it and it alone would suffice to restore me to the situation I was in on the morning of January 23. I wrote under the domination of pure illusion. It is this illusion that I must explain.

Five causes contributed to form and consolidate it.

The first was the care with which the canonical investigation instituted in December of 1929 had been rigorously circumscribed around the names of Gallerand and Herzog. Coulange, Delafosse, etc., whose writings had been widely talked about in the press and in the journals, had been completely eliminated. I concluded a little too quickly that Cardinal Charost wanted to leave them outside his investigations.

The second cause was the wording of the sentence of January 23. The penalty imposed on me was motivated by my refusal to bow before the conclusions of the judges. I deduced that the sanction would be lifted as soon as I declared my acceptance of these conclusions.

The third cause was the unanimity with which pious individuals gave me to understand that all would be terminated as soon as I submitted, that is, when I admitted my authorship of the writings signed Gallerand-Herzog. This idea which was on everyone's lips stemmed from ecclesiastics in contact with the archdiocese. Pious persons believed this was an exact expression of the cardinal's thought. And I shared their conviction.

The fourth cause was the state in which the chapel remained, by order of the cardinal, on March 25, that is, two whole months after my condemnation. With the exception of the pall and the candelabra that I had had removed because they belonged to me, everything remained intact; nothing had disappeared. This respect for the *status quo* annoyed the clergy of the parish, who for a long time had coveted the chapel in order to transform it into a room for the Church guild. Pious persons concluded that the day when I made what they called my submission, worship would again be held

Part Two: How the Roman Church Freed Itself of Me

there. And their conclusion appeared plausible to me. I shall return to this point shortly.

The fifth cause was my ignorance of my situation from the canonical point of view. If I had known that Rome had taken charge of the Herzog-Gallerand affair, I would not have been naive enough to believe that the cardinal was the master of events. I was informed of this detail for the first time by the cardinal during the conversation of March 28. Until then I was completely ignorant of it. Someone (not Pouët) had assured me that the proceeding would be managed locally and would not go to Rome.

13. My letter of March 25 reached the cardinal the next day, who upon its receipt sent Pouët to speak with me. The latter, after having shared with me the joy that my letter had given his master, added, "Unfortunately I must inform you that, beyond the Gallerand-Herzog affair, other things are imputed to you. First of all the *Revue d'apologétique* accuses you of being the author of the *Catéchisme pour adultes* signed Coulange[244] and, among other proofs, it notes the cartulary of Redon that is mentioned there." At these words I interrupted Pouët's speech and sharply exclaimed: "That is not serious. Redon's cartulary is no longer only in manuscript. It was published fifty years ago in the collection of *Documents inédits*. All those who work in the history of the Middle Ages use it." "That has a bearing" replied Pouët, who did not have any inkling of the manuscript's publication, but who wished to maintain his composure. "That has no bearing," I said to him, "since all the historians of the Middle Ages know and cite the said cartulary which is printed in a monumental collection." "There is another more serious item," added Pouët. "A priest has told me in a letter of having seen the manuscript of *La Messe* at M. Couchoud's and of having noticed the identity of the writing with that of your letters to Houtin that he saw at M. Sartiaux's and with the writing of your letters to M. Duchesne." "Is it X who wrote this to you?" I asked in a wrathful tone, naming a well-known religious. "No," he said, "it is a priest of the Orthodox Church who has frequented M. Couchoud, M. Sartiaux, M. Duchesne, the Renan lectures. All these writings that you have proliferated can only bring you a great deal of problems. If on the contrary you would cease troubling souls, your chapel, your faculties would be *returned immediately*. We should be happy and you as well."

I listened in silence to Pouët's monologue, spoken at length, but also with unction. While the vision of my chapel and my faculties *returned immediately* unfolded before my eyes I thought of the two or three hundred souls who, since the judgement of January 23, had been distraught and for whom my return was going to dry their tears. Overcome with emotion, I broke my silence and said: "All right, it is I who wrote *La Messe* and the *Catéchisme pour adultes*. Furthermore, I am the author of the books signed Delafosse and Perrin. However, henceforth I shall publish nothing further, and I am going, today even, to write to M. Couchoud in order that he may return to me the manuscripts he has in his keeping." My promise was sincere, because my confidence was unbounded and unsullied by any suspicion. From his side, Pouët, who was not expecting any such success, was effusive in his thanks. Before taking his leave, he vigorously advised me to let the cardinal know myself via letter of my current frame of mind. "However," he added, "it is not necessary to go into details: a general indication will suffice. And then, as His Eminence sometimes loses letters that are brought to him, perhaps it would be advisable to send me a duplicate so that I could, should the case arise, refresh his memory."

The next morning, March 27, I wrote the following letter that was brought immediately to the archbishop's residence with a duplicate for Pouët:

> *Eminence. M. the Vicar General Pouët has made some very wise observations to which I completely agree. I reprove and regret everything in my writings, even recent ones, that might be contrary to the teaching of the Church. And I promise in all sincerity not to publish anything further. I add that this solemn promise cannot be inspired by base motives since I am of independent means.*

The evening of the same day, at five o'clock, Pouët came back. He first said to me that the Cardinal was delighted with my letter and that I was expected by him the following Friday at five o'clock. Then he spoke to me of what he called the leaks, that is, the indiscretions that had been committed. However he brought no example other than that of the priest of the Orthodox Church of whom he had spoken the day before. On my part, I explained to him the passage in my letter relating to "even recent writings." I said that a new book appeared on March 19, that is, only eight days before my letter. And I let it be known that this new book was the second volume of the *Catéchisme*. He asked if it could not be withdrawn from sale, I replied that unfortunately that was impossible, since the book is the property of the publisher who had printed it at his expense. In taking his leave Pouët repeated several times that my chapel and my faculties would be returned to me immediately.

PART TWO: How the Roman Church Freed Itself of Me

14. Friday March 28, approaching five o'clock, I presented myself at the archbishop's residence in the absolute conviction that on my return I would have recovered my faculties and my chapel. The welcome that I received was jovial. In a strong voice the cardinal said to me while laughing:

"You would not believe what determination your enemies have displayed in searching out your writings. They were admirably informed. They had secret contacts everywhere. They saw the manuscript of *La Messe*. They were three whose declarations we have: a priest, a professor and someone in M. Couchoud's entourage." He added while lowering his tone: "Strictly speaking I have the right to lift the suspension. However the judgement having been taken to Rome, I could not lift it without being tactless. I am going to write to the Holy Office. In thirteen days I will have the response which, given the tenor of my report, will, I've no doubt, be favorable." Here I break in and serve as the spokesman for the ardent desire on the part of my faithful to have the chapel returned for worship. The cardinal replied with an air of embarrassment: "Very recently I was shown a letter in which my predecessor, Cardinal Dubourg, undertook to close the chapel as soon as the Church of the parish of Saint Joan of Arc was finished and set up for worship. So I do not have the right to reopen the chapel closed since January 23. Moreover, the pastor of Notre Dame has taken possession of it."

Struck dumb with amazement, I let pass the first part of this response without saying anything. However, scarcely were his last words out when I cried out the following contradiction: "Oh! No, the chapel is, I know, still just as it was on January 23."

The cardinal, as if he were mistaken, did not pick up on my observation: but he promised me again that in thirteen days he would receive a response from the Holy Office that he thought would be favorable. I left.

While I was at the archbishop's residence, the pastor of the parish entered my chapel, in the company of a workman who, under his direction, demolished the altar. This news that reached me when I had returned home, revealed a rather complicated plan. Pious persons, I have said, knowing that the parish clergy had been forbidden to touch the chapel, concluded that the cardinal was resolved to give it back to me after my submission. The cardinal had reckoned on this, counting on the influence that it would not fail to exercise on me. Maintaining the *status quo* was, in his mind, a means of leading me one day or another to yield to his verdict. After two months of waiting the means had proven satisfactory and obtained the desired result. From that time its purpose was lost. The same morning of the day when my letter reached the archbishop's residence (March 27) the pastor of the parish received the order to take possession of the chapel at the earliest possible moment. And this order he executed on the 28th, at the very moment when, with a lighthearted step, I went to the residence thinking, on the testimony of Pouët, to receive the immediate recompense for my belated docility.

15. Four days later, on Tuesday, April 1, Pouët one again presented himself at my home. His radiant face announced a favorable message. Scarcely seated, he hastened to tell me while smiling: "His Eminence the Cardinal sends me to ask where you would like to say Mass. He leaves you the choice between the Collège Saint-Vincent and the chapel of the sisters of Africa." I replied in substance: "If I have the choice only between Saint-Vincent which is four hundred meters from my home and the sisters of Africa which are nearly on my doorstep, I would opt without the least hesitation for the latter. But frankly I would prefer to return to my sisters who, in the absence of the chapel that is closed, would be happy to fix up an oratory for me with them. There I would be able to resume the ministry of confession that would be impossible for me at Saint-Vincent or at the sisters of Africa." "It shall be as you wish," replied Pouët. "Your choice will certainly be respected by His Eminence whose wish is to please you."

This point determined, a change of scenery. The joy that radiated from Pouët's face disappeared. His exhuberant demeanor vanished. He said to me in a low voice: "In the expectation of the polemic that your enemies may be going to bring up again and which could lead Rome to order a new inquiry, His Eminence requests that you send him in writing a more explicit retraction than the one before and in which all your books are specified." Surprised by this request and still more by the strange reason he gave for it, I replied that I would comply with the cardinal's order; but I added in a challenging tone and with a hard stare at Pouët: "I suppose all that will remain secret." Tilting his head back with the gesture of someone who repels a hurtful suspicion, Pouët pronounced in a hushed voice a muffled word that I thought was "Naturally" or "That's understood." "And besides," he added in a very conciliatory tone, "it is not necessary to go into details: general indications will be enough." I said to him then: "You told me the name of only one denouncer; the cardinal told me of three; why this divergence? Pouët replied, "I myself went through the file: the cardinal was briefed by me alone; there was only one letter written by a priest of the Eastern Orthodox Church." In my conscience I concluded that the Cardinal had a considerable capacity for misrepresentation. However without pausing to voice this observation, I imparted to Pouët the profound deception that I had suffered: "You had promised me," I said to him, "that my chapel and my faculties would be restored immediately. But, my chapel is definitively closed and I still await my faculties." In a casual, but worried tone Pouët reiterated the cardinal's explanations; however he assured me that my faculties would not be long in coming. "Yet," he added, "a certain delay would not be impossible because of the upheaval that the recent death of Cardinal Merry Del Val[245] has caused in the Holy Office." He went on at length regarding the said cardinal's death.

15b. Immediately after Pouët's departure, I wrote the following declaration that I carried myself to the archbishop's residence toward seven in the evening:

> *I admit to having written numerous articles and some fifteen books, two in English, under the pseudonyms that have been attributed to me, exception made for the name of Siouville for which I am not responsible. The book published under this pseudonym being irreproachable with respect to orthodoxy, I have no interest in rejecting its authorship. Moreover I have critiqued it under the name of Delafosse in the* Revue d'histoire des religions *in 1928 or 1929.*
>
> *I reject all that within these writings, of which one is very recent since it appeared on March 19, is contrary to the teaching of the Church to which I profess to adhere. And I make the solemn commitment to publish nothing, either with Rieder or in the* Revue d'histoire des religions *or anywhere else under any name whatsoever.*

Two words to avoid confusion. The letter that I had written on April 1st had been asked of me "in the expectation" of events that could lead Rome to stick its nose into the writings of Coulange, etc. "In the expectation," that is to say that Rome had not yet taken on this second affair. Only the Herzog-Gallerand proceeding had been brought to its tribunal. That is what the cardinal communicated to me, and that is what I believed. I did not have any idea that my letter could go farther than the archdiocese. Or rather I had this idea for an instant and it was that which caused me to stare at Pouët and provoked my question. But I did not pursue it. I was not able to after the inarticulate but vehement denials of my interlocutor: especially after the honeyed words: "His Eminence sends me to ask you where you would like to say Mass."

16. A dozen days later, Pouët, during a trip in the region of Saint-Malo, met the major superiors of my religious sisters who were on a tour

of inspection in one of their schools. He announced to them that, by Cardinal Charost's decision, I was going to recommence saying Mass, not in the former chapel closed definitively, but in an oratory specially set up for the purpose. A few days later the superiors in question profited from their passing through Rennes to bring this news to the attention of my sisters who came, full of joy, to share it with me. I had not seen them since the sentence of January 23; I never saw them again.

17. During Holy Week (in 1930 this feast fell on April 20) one of my religious sisters, on meeting Cardinal Charost, who was taking his daily walk, asked him when I would be starting to say Mass for them again. The cardinal said to her: "Do not be over hasty. The more time that it will take, the better it will be for M. Turmel and for us." She passed on these words through my servant as intermediary, to whom she spoke without crossing my threshold. Not having the least idea of what was going to happen, she saw nothing in the cardinal's response beyond the examination being a long one and that great patience was required. Some time thereafter, one day when Pouët was with me and continued to use the death of Cardinal Merry Del Val to explain the prolonged delay in the Holy Office's response, I presented him with the cardinal's words to the sister. For a moment he remained disconcerted: then he got out of it by saying that he did not understand their meaning. As for myself, as blind as my religious sisters, from early on I believed that Rome's tactic was never to respond and to leave me in the *status quo* in perpetuity.

18. I have just mentioned a visit by Pouët after April 1st. He made three. One of them, that preceded his departure for the round of confirmations, was on his own initiative and was simply an expression of sympathy designed to help me remain patient over Rome's delay. The other two were messages. One announced that proof of my identity with Siouville had been obtained. I replied that it sufficed to read *Philosophumena*[246] edited by this scholar in order to realize the accuracy of my declaration. My Pouët, whose master had set him to hunt down Siouville and who did not wish to return empty-handed, was bent on showing me that I was Siouville. In the end I lost patience and said several sharp words that obliged him to release his prey. I must say now that the Siouville affair had been preceded by the following message: "The Holy Office has asked for a precise list of your books with indication of the publisher." Thus the Holy Office was not concerned exclusively with the Herzog-Gallerand affair as they had caused me to believe up until this point. It was also judging the Coulange affair, etc. The

Part Two: How the Roman Church Freed Itself of Me

information was of major importance. However it was communicated in a tone so demure and moreover so many unexpected incidents had disconcerted me over the past seven months that I scarcely heeded it. I did point out to Pouët that, in my declaration of April 1st, I admitted to being the real owner of all the pseudonyms that the denouncers had imputed to me, Siouville excepted, and that this global declaration was tantamount to a detailed list of my books. He agreed with my observation and told that me that he himself was going to send Rome the requested list supported by my declaration of April. In reality what he spoke of as a future task was probably already done.

The third and last visit took place on June 3rd. It had a goal masked by a pretext. The goal was that of knowing which manuscript, according to my declaration of March 25, I had asked M. Couchoud to return. To which I replied that M. Couchoud had returned, on my request, a translation of the *Journal de Burchard*, master of ceremonies under Alexander VI and Julius II.[247] Pouët receved my reply without comment. The pretext that served as an introduction was amusing. I learned that the Holy Office, which had been sent precise details of my books, now demanded the books themselves. So Cardinal Charost bought the whole string of my works and had them sent to Rome. Already, in the past, he had submitted Gallerand's letter to expert examination. I was certainly costing him dearly.

18. In the *Bulletin* of Toulouse, 1931, Pouët wrote that Cardinal Charost had decided to wait at least two years before letting me say Mass. This admission exposed to the full the comedy of April 1st when I had received the message already cited: "His Eminence sends me to ask you where you would like to say Mass."

19. On November 6, 1930, Cardinal Charost communicated the following letter through his secretary:

> His Eminence the Cardinal requests me to inform you that he has just directed your allocation, pension included, be 500 fr. per quarter beginning October 1st, 1930. Thus henceforth you will receive every three months:
>
> Pension . . . . 225 fr.
> Archdiocese . . . . 275 fr.
> 500 fr.
>
> Please accept . . .
>
> LAMY, V.G.

The Condemnation

This token of generosity was the third the cardinal had given me since his promotion to the archdiocese of Rennes. Before him, I received from the Prefecture (since the Separation managing agent of the diocesan fund for older priests) an annual pension of 900 fr. in quarterly payments of 225 frs. In 1922 Mgr Charost, having succeeded Cardinal Dubourg, added the annual sum of 300 fr. in quarterly instalments of 75 fr. In April of 1930, he added a new sum of 400 fr. in quarterly amounts of 100 fr. Finally, the letter of November 6 promised me another increase of 400 fr. annually, which brought the quarterly payment to 500 fr.

This letter of November 6, 1930 preceded by one day the cardinal's death which occurred the morning of November 7. On the other hand, it coincided with the sentence of excommunication that was promulgated on the 8th but pronounced on Thursday the 6th. It thus conjures up two synchronicities. Since the cardinal surely was not expecting to die the next day, the first synchronicity is purely fortuitous, and there is no need to linger over it. It is on the second synchronicity alone, that we must fix our attention. We must ask ourselves whether in this case chance is at work, or whether the coincidence was intended. Certainly, the Cardinal, who had given me two allocations, could easily have granted me a third. Thus it is not when considered in itself that the gift of November 6 is strange. But let us move on to how it happened. On November 6, I was notified by letter that on the following January 1st my quarterly instalment would be increased by one hundred francs. It was the first time that I have been the object of this kind of attention. In the two preceding cases, the agent who, with my written authorization, went to the archdiocese to draw my pension brought me back a sum superior to my expectations. It was through him and not otherwise that I learned of the favor granted me. The letter of November 6 that informs me two months in advance of what will occur in January is an unusual attestation. Hence a new fact that it is necessary to explain. Why had the cardinal, desiring to show himself generous toward me for a third time, taken the trouble to inform me in advance, contrary to usual practice, of the generosity whose effect I would feel two months later? And why is it that this fine thought should have come to him on the very day when the pope was settling my fate in Rome? It is for these multiple reasons that the hypothesis of pure chance seems to me unsatisfactory as an explanation and that I consider it necessary to appeal to a conscious plan.

Here I may be interrupted. In the first place, the objection may be raised that the decisions of the Holy Office are made in the greatest secrecy

Part Two: How the Roman Church Freed Itself of Me

and remain so until the day of their official promulgation; in the second place that only the telegraph could have transmitted to Rennes on November 6 a decision taken in Rome the same day, and that the use of the telegraph for a sentence of excommunication is improbable. I reply. No doubt the Holy Office does not condescend to tell bishops or even archbishops unofficially of its decisions. However a cardinal is a prince of the Church: he has a right to special consideration, and there is no rule, however strict, that may not be bent for him. So much for the first objection. As for the second, it supposes that the assembly of November 6 presided over by the pope deliberated over a sentence not yet settled. Therein lies its error. All was decided upon before the 6th by members of the Holy Office, and the Pope had only to ratify a decision whose considerations were all drawn up and adopted. Thus Cardinal Charost could be informed on the 6th, by a letter sent from Rome on the 3rd or 4th, of the sentence on which the members of the Holy Office had agreed.

In sum, it appears certain to me that Cardinal Charost knew of the decree of excommunication on November 6 and that his letter of that date was intended to give me an expression of sympathy and also to facilitate the submission. Seven months earlier he had already given me an initial expression of sympathy in sending Pouët to ask me where I would like to say Mass, while he had decided to wait in all likelihood two years before letting me ascend the altar.

20. Tuesday, November 11, the day on which the decree appeared in the press, a lady of the neighborhood reported to me a conversation that she had just had with Pouët. Here it is in substance: "Reading the decree has dismayed all of us. We do not want to believe that the text given in the papers is authentic. We are waiting for the document from the Holy Office which will arrive tomorrow or the day after." Two days later, Thursday the 13th, toward 4:30, I made my daily pilgrimage to the University Library. Scarcely had I left my house when I was approached by a priest. Recognizing Pouët, without saying a word, I waved him aside with my hand. He said to me: "I have letters to give you" (these were the letters of congratulations whose influx had begun and two of which had been addressed to the archdiocese by mistake). In receiving his burden I said to him: "Your master is a total hypocrite: you as well." Then I went off to the library without listening to Pouët who poured out vehement protests (see below for some details).

21. On Saturday the 15th, the decree of the Holy Office having arrived at Rennes, the Vicar Apostolic, M. Gayet, called to me to appear before

him for the purpose of notification. Not having responded to this ludicrous convocation, I received on Monday morning by registered letter an authenticated copy of the pontifical document. I am going to cite the principal passages while adjoining to each the commentary that it calls for.

> a) *The priest Joseph Turmel... was, in 1892, removed from the chair he held at the major seminary of Rennes by his eminence Cardinal Place, his archbishop, because he had declared to some of his students that he did not believe in the real presence of Jesus Christ in the most holy eucharist.*

The superior of the Major Seminary, after receiving Bertrand's denunciation, limited himself to informing the episcopal council that I was no longer in a state to continue my functions as professor. Cardinal Place and his incumbent vicars general believed that I gave my resignation for health reasons. There was no trace in the episcopal archives of a removal that had been imposed upon me. Several years later, through some indiscretion it came to the ears of some priests who kept silent. In 1908 the Herzog affair loosened some tongues. It was probably then that Cardinal Charost collected the information reflected in the decree. Information that is inexact since my special courses had but a single auditor, they covered the entire range of Christian dogmatics and I had never been officially removed. On this last point, Abbé Charost, having become archbishop of Rennes and having the archives at his disposal, must have known the truth. So he gave the Holy Office information that he knew was inaccurate.

> b) *In 1901 his eminence Cardinal Richard, Archbishop of Paris, by special order of and in the name of the Sacred Congregation of the Index, gave a serious warning to the priest Turmel for the heretical articles published by him ... and forbade him in future to publish anything in the domain of sacred sciences without having first obtained ecclesiastical approval.*

Elsewhere will be found (*Congé aux dogmes*, p. 68) the exposition on this affair together with supporting texts. In 1901 Rome reproached me for the publication of articles that were not heretical but "bold" and "rash." And Cardinal Richard did not commit the impropriety of dealing with me directly since I was not under his jurisdiction. He contented himself with transmitting the pontifical document to my archbishop who communicated a copy to me for form's sake, but declared that he would not in any way hinder my freedom of writing at my own risk and peril. Thus in the decree of 1930 there is an inaccuracy for which the Holy Office is responsible and two others that reflect the inadequate manner in which Rome was informed.

> c) *In 1929 . . . his eminence Cardinal Charost, by order of the Supreme Sacred Congregation of the Holy Office, instituted official proceedings against the priest Turmel . . .*

At the time of the proceedings, I believed that Cardinal Charost was acting on his own initiative. Later, in the course of the year 1930, certain information of which I have spoken partly dispelled my illusion. Reading the decree gave me a clear vision of the real state of affairs. In the proceedings of December 1929–January 1930 the cardinal was but the executor of Rome's orders. When the judgement of January 23 appeared, the vehemence of the wording shocked, I know, priests among the elite of the clergy who openly condemned it. These priests, like me, labored under an illusion. They did not suspect the true state of affairs. The decree of excommunication sheds light on the proceedings of 1929 and the judgement that crowned them.

> d) *Seeing himself plainly discovered* (manifeste detectum) *the priest Turmel finally wrote two letters to Cardinal Charost on March 25 and April 1st of the present year [1930] in which he admitted having written numerous articles and fourteen books under the following fourteen pseudonyms: . . .*

I wrote the letter of March 25 (n° 12) because, under the influence of an illusion that the facts explain, I had the absolute conviction that this initiative would be enough to enable me to repossess my chapel and my priestly faculties. As for the letter of April 1st, it was the result of a shameful comedy that I have related and which the pontifical document carefully avoids mentioning. The decree of excommunication is thus a caricature of my actions and my letters, a caricature whose responsibility falls upon Cardinal Charost, if, as is highly likely, Rome used the terms of his report.

> e) *So many books and so many articles published under various names in order to propagate heresy and impiety gave rise to the suspicion, one can well believe, that there were, in France, precisely that many priests opposed to the Catholic faith. Which was for the French clergy a very serious and manifest insult.*

Here the decree does not mean that the number of priests capable of writing in complete independence on the history of dogma does not attain the number of fourteen. It says that there are not fourteen priests in France who are freed from dogmas (*qui fidei catholicae adversarentur*). This is a case of saying with John Hus: "O holy innocence!"

> f) *The priest Turmel... struck by ecclesiastical authority... has had the audacity to say Mass all this time.*

Simple souls, whom the episcopal censure had thrown into dismay, were reassured when they learned that the judgement of January 23 was, in my view, completely null and void and that I would continue to say Mass at least on Sundays. One of them, filled with joy, imparted this good news to one of the archdiocesan staff, who said to her that even under interdict I was able, in fact, to say Mass at my home (he later regretted this statement, I know, but he did say it). This junior official passed the remark on, either to to Pouët, or—what is more likely—to his colleague Lami, who, in turn, conveyed it to his master. It is this information, thus obtained, that the cardinal made use of and sent to Rome. Pouët never questioned me at all on this point. I add here that several pious individuals came, on the eve of feastdays, to ask me to hear their confession. Having learned from history that from the fourth century to the seventh, confessors generally were not priests and did not have any idea of what are called priestly faculties, I performed the service asked of me.

22. In the weeks that followed Cardinal Charost's death a local weekly taxed the deceased with the following charges:

a) Around 1905, during a trip to London, Abbé Charost entered a music hall and attended a spectacle little suited to the gravity of the ecclesiastical state. b) His library, given on his order to Saint-Vincent, contained a notable number of lewd novels that stunned the professors and the children responsible for transporting the books from the truck into the collège. c) He did not say the breviary. d) He did not go to confession. None of these allegations were denied; furthermore, the last two were the main topic of conversation among the clergy following the day of his death, November 7. The first two, less widely known, also rest on unimpeachable evidence. And the professor who brought this to my awareness, without being at Saint-Vincent at the time when the episcopal library was brought there, later learned from his colleagues the emotional reaction stirred up by the installation of the books.

It remains the case that, in the judgement of January 23, my heresies have been condemned by a prelate who did not go to confession.

Part Two: How the Roman Church Freed Itself of Me

23. Around the same time, several pious individuals whom the decree of excommunication had dismayed, sadly observed that the publicity given my heresies had not in any way increased the prestige of religion and could even have damaged it. In response to this complaint, rumor suddenly spread that Cardinal Charost had done everything possible to save me. And to this first rumor was added another relative to the Mass I had continued to say at home after the suspension. It was explained that this information had been supplied to the Holy Office, not by Cardinal Charost who, on the contrary, did not wish to divulge it, but by a bureau of denunciation organized at Rennes a few years before to combat the manoeuvres of *Action Française*[248] and directed against the cardinal.

There were not twenty persons, including the members of the chancery, who knew that I continued to say Mass at home after the judgement of January 23. And the "bureau of denunciation" was far from transmitting to Rome a secret that it never knew. The role attributed to it here is a fiction that does not even have the excuse of sincerity. As for the first allegation, it partly, but only partly conforms to the truth. At the outset Cardinal Charost had only contempt for the efforts of the denouncers. However he changed his attitude the day when Rome intervened in the affair. Then he believed himself authorized to employ any means, even deceit, to bring about my ruin. On several occasions he set traps and sometimes he enlisted Pouët to assist in this work, who managed it perfectly. Both of them, one as contriver, the other as executor, were complete hypocrites. I am stating facts, palpable, evident facts; but I do not condemn them. Far from that. Pouët was the corporal who received the orders and had no right to dispute them. The cardinal, Rome's lackey, wanted to repair the negligence he had been guilty of and to be in good repute. If Pouët was sincere when he said that the decree of November 6 had utterly dismayed them, himself and the other functionaries of the archdiocese (see n° 20), the success would have surpassed not only his expectations, but also his desires. He can only blame himself and his master for this slight accident. For, in their determination to pursue success, neither shrank from any means of obtaining it.

24. Under the bogus title of "Réponse au roman de M. Sartiaux," Pouët published in the *Bulletin* of Toulouse, March 1931, p. 97, a memorandum[249] written with great cunning and numerous inaccuracies. The objectives are the following: to justify the tenor of Rome's decree that says that I owned up when forced to do so by the obvious facts: to show that Charost set no traps for me (in conversations at Rennes he even added that his master

had done everything possible to save me from excommunication); finally to defend himself in declaring that he held strictly to his mandate (a rather useless apology given that no one had ever accused him of exceeding his instructions). He achieved these ends by complicating the questions, by shifting their emphasis and by giving the impression of saying things that he did not say.

All the rectifications that Pouët's memorandum calls for will be found in the preceding pages. Here I am content to make two observations. Here is the first: Pouët told M. Sartiaux (see the book M. Sartiaux devoted to me, p. 182, last line) that my attitude was inexplicable if things happened as he, Pouët, reports them. My attitude is explained, by contrast, in the version that I present. And here is the second: Pouët and his master welcomed right away the letter in which I was denounced as the author of the writings published under Coulange's signature. They passed judgement without making the least inquiry into the respectability of the document's author. They immediately believed they had "the overwhelming, unimpeachable, material proof" of my "identity with Coulange." However the proof has been given that the said letter came from a swindler (see M. Sartiaux's book, p. 178, supplemented by the newspapers of September 23 and November 26, 1931). I have already noted the comedy of April 1st, 1930 in which Charost, in all likelihood his mind made up to wait two years before letting me mount the altar, directed that I be asked in what chapel I would like to say Mass. Here I simply note that Pouët, who later admitted that he knew his master's intentions, several times used Merry Del Val's death to explain the prolongation of my suspension.

Conclusion

Two problems have dominated my life such as it has unfolded over forty years. The first has to do with the subject of my publications; the second with my relations with the hierarchy when the denouncers forced it to question me.

The first problem is complex, and the multiple elements that comprise it must be carefully separated in order to avoid regrettable confusion. It is clear that my labors would never have taken place if I had not renounced the beliefs of my youth beforehand. Which means that one must ask at the outset how and why I renounced them.

The beliefs of my youth disappeared the day I established that they did not in any come from God and that their origin was exclusively human. This observation occurred when the Bible, which is one of their sources, became for me a collection of allegations that were largely lies; when I knew that the book of Daniel was the work of a forger, that Deuteronomy was the work of another forger, that the legislation called Mosaic did not exist at the time of Isaiah, that the writings of the Pentateuch were legends bereft of any coherence (I pass over in silence a host of other examples). It was then that my beliefs vanished. Their disappearance happened automatically, mechanically. I was its grieving, shattered spectator: I took no part in it. No doubt this would not have happened if I had not opened the Bible or, if having opened it, I had immediately closed it after the first observations. In this sense I am responsible for what happened. However, my responsibility was limited to studying. To studying, first with the desire to defend the Church against unbelief, then with the hope of resolving, through deeper research, the difficulties encountered at the beginning. Through phenomenal sophistries I succeeded for a long time in closing my eyes to the progressively corrosive effects of study. However a day came when, faced with the clarity of the evidence, the veils of illusion fell. The sun dissipates the mists of autumn mornings. Study does the same thing with beliefs. Everyone can attempt the process. At the end of a few days results will appear. In France there are five or six hundred of us priests in this state. But we would be in the thousands if ecclesiastics desirous of instructing us were less rare. To congratulate the great mass of French clergy on its fidelity to orthodoxy is to render homage to indolence; and also to forget the first duty of an intelligent man, which is to work according to his means to know the truth.

2. After my liberation from dogma I remained in the Church in spite of the Church, which, if it had known my feelings, would have turned me out; but which, having conducted itself dishonestly toward me (*Congé aux dogmes*, p. 27 and 59) was not entitled to arrange my fate. I remained in the Church, resolved to respect the legitimate demands of the faithful, that is, to perform all the rites in conformity with the Church's instructions. Performed in accordance with these dispositions, my ritual observances had, from the theological point of view, the same value as the observances of ignorant priests, and I was thus in line with the requirements of justice. That was enough. And if the presumptions of the faithful required something else, I was never made aware of it. The six hundred priests who, enlightened by study, remain in the Church after having recognized the futility of dogmas, are inspired by the same principles of conduct. They as well have paid no heed to the recriminations of the Church that has shamefully deceived them. They also divide the faithful's requirements into two parts, respecting the claims founded on justice and taking no account of the prejudices of ignorance. They, like me, consider that the faithful must blame the Church when they come up against priests liberated from dogmas and that the Church alone is responsible for this misfortune.

3. All the products of the human mind have gone through multiple stages before arriving at the form they have today. Dogmas are products of the human mind: that I have known since 1886. So they have been subject to the general law. Their current form is the result of trial and error analogous to the trial and error of which the arts and sciences offer us the curious spectacle. There is a history of dogmas just as there is a history of philosophy, of the arts and the sciences. In 1886 I was nearly completely ignorant of this history. Yet, knowledge of it seemed to me to be the indispensable crowning of my previous studies that would otherwise have remained incomplete. I set about knowing it.

Part Two: How the Roman Church Freed Itself of Me

And also making it known. Especially from 1892 onward. The victim of a judicial error neither rests nor calls a truce until he has proclaimed his innocence and obtained his rehabilitation. In 1892 I had been the victim of a monstrous parody of justice carried out in the name of the Roman Church and under the authority of its legislation. However, since this Church never admits its errors, I could expect nothing from it or from its judges who were as blind as they were docile. Rehabilitation being an illusion, my only possible hope and my sole ambition was to enlighten souls of good will, to present them with proofs of the variability of the Christian dogmatic. The shipwrecked sailor clings to the plank that his clutching hands encounter with the energy born of despair. This program of life was my sole plank of salvation: I clung to it. In the absence of the justice that the hierarchy would never consent to render me, it satisfied the desire for revenge, for the *dies ultionis* (ibid. p. 47) that unceasingly seethed in me, and also the thirst for the apostolate embodied in the motto: Martyr to the truth, I will be its apostle. It consoled me, it sustained me. The Pharisees who would be scandalized by these sentiments would simply demonstrate that they know nothing of a life shattered in the service of truth and without hope of reparation.

4. One may object that in carrying out this program, I have undermined the foundation of the Church's beliefs and by this fact committed a betrayal. Is it my fault if the Church's claims are unwarranted, if the invariability that it attributes to its dogmas is a fiction and if one undermines its beliefs at their foundation simply by narrating their alteration? For all my work can be reduced to just that. Those who have not read me imagine that I heaped ridicule upon the Gospel accounts or on dogmas. They believe that I indulged in the kind of outcries over which preachers harry Freemasonry and the École laïque. I have never done any of that. My work consisted in searching through the writings of the Fathers, then reporting the results of my investigations; to serve up what my friend Paul Lejay called "strings of texts." I have never said to the reader: "Here is what you must believe." Always and throughout I have been content to modestly put forward what I have read and and to say: "Here is what was believed at such a time and here is what was believed at another such time." But if in the midst of an extensive output I happened to write a few lines that exceeded this program, surely the case is sufficiently rare that, for an impartial mind, it would not matter. I produced scholarly work; I did only that. Since when is scholarship a work of betrayal?

Conclusion

From my pen, it is said, it became a betrayal because I resurrected beliefs that had disappeared forever, buried under a thick layer of forgetfulness, because I was not unaware that this work of exhumation would irritate the Church and because, knowing that, it was in full awareness that I waged war upon the Church whose child I was.

Certainly, I foresaw that my "strings of texts" would irritate the Roman curia and its praetorian guard, I mean the body of theologians. In this sense I waged, I wanted to wage war on the Church. But how can it be said that exposing the variability of beliefs is to wage war upon the Church? The beliefs have evolved. What do you want me to do? It is reality. If this reality is harmful, blame the Church which had the duty of preventing this harm, and which has allowed it to happen. In any case, leave in peace the poor scholar who does not judge, does not condemn, who limits himself to declaring the facts.

No doubt the Roman Church wants the difficulty hidden. In order to obey its orders the apologists used to shamelessly interpolate the embarrassing texts. They did even better. They suppressed or mutilated the manuscripts. Since today these heroic means are more difficult to employ, they engage in exegetical tours de force; with consummate art they practice ridicule, caricature; they use all the tricks of bad theatre. I am repulsed by this deceitfulness and I take pride in that. I have shown that the Church's beliefs are no exception to the great law of evolution: in doing so I have fulfilled the first duty of the historian, which is to write with integrity.

5. "You were," they say to me, "a child of the Church; you did not have the right to make it grieve." And why not, if you please? Was not Abelard the child of the Church when he cast underfoot two or three dreadful dogmas invented by Saint Augustine that burdened the conscience of his time? Was not Burchard bishop and master of ceremonies at the Vatican when, with his clerk's pen, he denounced the pontifical corruption that he witnessed? Was not Luther a monk when he incited Germany against the abuses of the papacy? Was not Galileo the child of the Church when the Holy Office found him guilty of heresy in these terms: "You have taught something heretical in theology"? Was not Bossuet a bishop when, in his magisterial *Defensio Declarationis*,[250] he pulverized some of Rome's claims? Was it not by princely children of the Church that the infamous laws by which Rome struck at heresy were abrogated? We would still be in barbarism if the children of the Roman Church, at the risk of being crushed by it, had been unafraid to rise up against the errors dear to Rome. You do not wish the

Part Two: How the Roman Church Freed Itself of Me

Church to be disobeyed? Then, put the earth back to the center of universe and repel with horror Galileo's "heresy" that would have been suppressed if the papacy's verdict had not been contested. Restore to honor the Bull of Innocent VIII which, for several centuries, caused sorcerers to be burned by thousands upon thousands. And do not object that there are no longer today any so-called sorcerers. Here and there in the countryside they exist. And it will be enough for one sorcerer to be burned for the contagion of folly to do its work and by dozens at first, then by hundreds, then thousands, sorcerers will emerge on all fronts. Establish to Rome's benefit the universal monarchy that the popes have called for over several centuries. To assist this institution, propagate the Roman dogma according to which civil authority issues from the papacy. Then the pontifical state will encompass the entire world. Then we shall also have the good fortune to belong to this ideal kingdom that was a robbers' paradise contaminated neither by the "madness" of freedom of conscience nor "the execrable freedom of the press" (Encyclical *Mirari*[251]).

I address myself now, not to simple souls blinded by their prejudices, but to all those, ecclesiastics or laity, who have shaken the tutelage of dogmas, and I say: "You see what happens when it is made a matter of principle that the error supported by the Roman curia is sacred and must not be touched. If you reject this madness, then leave the sincere worker to expose, texts at the ready, the variability of Christian belief over the course of the centuries. Naturally, you will submit his assertions to the verification of other workers. Put them to the test of discussion, from which they will emerge either confirmed or amended or developed. But do not begin by shutting his mouth or breaking his pen under the pretext that he troubles consciences."

Or rather I am in complete agreement with you, if you mean to say that this problem of the variation of Christian beliefs ought not to be dealt with indifferently before all hearers. It would be shameful to explain the mysteries of life to a child. Just as with childhood, the ingenuousness of simple souls has the right to be respected and they must be spared certain revelations that would tarnish it. But who has been deficient in this elementary rule of decency? Who, if not the denouncers of Herzog's and Gallerand's writings? These works devoted to the Blessed Virgin and to redemption in the thought of Saint Augustine respectively were published in a journal numbered at two hundred copies. But they did not have two hundred readers. Both, in fact, were crammed with texts whose appearance

Conclusion

alone was enough to put off the majority of subscribers. The second had not been read by as many as three laypeople or twenty priests. It had gone completely unnoticed. The first, sensationally denounced in 1908, had the same fate up until the moment of its denunciation. The emotion that it had incited at that time was soon calmed and it had fallen into oblivion. In 1929 the clergy didn't know Gallerand's name, and no one, with the exception of priests in their fifties, had ever heard Herzog spoken of. It was the two articles from Toulouse and Strasbourg that, in 1929, fed the names of Gallerand and Herzog to the Catholic public at large: these two are the ones who have brought the writings of these unknown authors into the open and have troubled consciences.

6. What more do they reproach me with? Having assumed borrowed names? My reply is very simple: without this cover I would not have held for two days the position that I succeeded in occupying for more than twenty years. The danger is not the same for all branches of ecclesiastical science. In proceedng obliquely in his *Histoire ancienne de l'Église* in which, in Loisy's estimation (*Mémoires* 3, 239) "the official theology" is "tremendously undermined and shaken," in which "all the dogmas are disturbed," Duchesne was able to hold out for a long time before falling. In the same way, by being clever with Rome, Loisy was able to rummage about in exegesis for several years before being condemned. The historian of dogmas does not have the resource of equivocation that Duchesne and Loisy used as cover. His craft does not offer any escape. It is a swift passage to the abyss. That is so because the Roman Church, which has let variation work its way into its beliefs, obstinately claims an apostolic origin for its current beliefs; because under the authority of this claim it ranks the historian of dogmas among its worst enemies. The latter, if he is a priest, must take it for granted. In the Church's view, his purely scientific investigations will have an aggressive character; they will be treated as hostile acts. Relying on the value of his evidence would be complete naiveté on his part. The Church would wring his neck without leaving him time to justify himself. And the apologists would be in raptures over the Church's glorious victory. All reasoned arguments irremediably shatter against brutal force that does not know how to reason. What is there to be done?

6. [sic] In the fifth century Saint Vincent of Lerins, wanting to combat the triumphant Augustinianism in his *Commonitorium*, but seeing the danger of the undertaking, resolved the problem by issuing his book under the unknown name of Peregrinus. During the sixteenth century, Bellarmine,

canonized today, wrote a defense in favor of the Bible of Sixtus V under the name of François Romulus. He himself informs us of this in his Autobiography. In the seventeenth century, Pascal, considering himself to be engaged in a salutary work, but wary of exile, assigned the *Provinciales* to a certain De Montalte who was a complete unknown. Forty years later Fénelon wrote his anonymous letter to Louis XIV to place before him useful truths without incurring an inevitable disgrace. Mabillon, wanting to make known the thoughtlessness with which the Roman curia handled the distribution of relics, published his observations in the *Lettre d'Eusèbe á Théophile*. In October of 1901 the Jesuit Durand wrote in *Études* an article in which he hid behind a pseudonym. Everyone knows what Voltaire did to throw the royal police off the scent when they were watching him. One knows too that the most serious and most respected journals frequently publish anonymous or pseudonymous studies. Hunted down by the Roman Church which sought to strangle me, I have followed these examples. Saltet, who is himself more or less a clown, denounced my recourse to pseudonyms as "colossal imposture" and "a forgery in scientific writing." Rivière, in *La Croix*, has repeated this joke. Others, the Jesuit d'Alès among them, have spoken of mystification. I have also been accused (Saltet at the head) of cowardice. In reality I avoided being stupid and did not start by doing myself in. The Roman Church, in refusing to listen to reason, can only blame itself if reason fools its ferocious vigilance. Heaven itself, to speak of the gospel, gave the magi the means to fool Herod.

7. It remains the case, they say, that I undermined the foundation of the Church's dogmas at a time when I was celebrating its rites and that this duplicity offends the rectitude that must be the supreme rule of our conduct. What is there to say to that?

On the eve of his judgment, Socrates (*Gorgias*, 77) compares himself to a doctor whom a cook had brought before a tribunal of children to settle a grudge. And he does not hide his embarrassment at having to plead his cause before such judges. Here is exactly what Rome has done by its decree of November 1930 in which, motivated by vengeance, it has spread out the web of my life before the faithful of the whole world in setting them up as my judges. I would not think of defending a cause in front of simple souls incapable of understanding it. Their verdict, based upon an absolute lack of authority, leaves me unmoved. I suffer only because of their dismay which results from the strange mission with which the Holy Office has endowed them. I deplore the blindness of the Roman curia which, in its rage against

Conclusion

me and single-minded intention to harm me, has not hesitated to bring deep distress to souls. Incapable of putting to rights this damage for which Rome is solely responsible, I leave the faithful and move on to minds emancipated from dogmas.

There are layfolk among them. There are also priests, approximately five to six hundred in number. Among the latter several have shown me their greatest sympathy to the end. Others, by contrast, who had warmly applauded the *Angelologie*, *Péché originel*, the study on Daniel, my "chroniques" in the *Revue du clergé français*—all rather subversive—changed their attitude when more aggressive writings appeared, signed with borrowed names, whose true origin they were quick to sort out since I was the only one in France to be engaged seriously with the history of dogmas. They expressed regrets, reprobation even, echoes of which reached me bit by bit. After having read Coulange's *La Messe*, a learned prelate very far from orthodox, said to his friends: "This book is indeed M. Turmel's work, for no one else would be capable of writing it; but there is a lack of candour here." He was not the only one to speak in this way. Priests are not rare who, while remaining in the Church, have realized the vanity of dogma and discuss it discreetly among themselves, but refuse written propaganda on this point as long as there has been no break with the hierarchy. They point out to me the example of Loisy who, it is said, waited until he was thrown out before combating Roman dogma.

At the risk of grieving these ecclesiastics so worthy of interest, I am obliged to make two observations which they will not be able to get around. In the first place, their verdict is lacking in logic. They censure the writings in which, under borrowed names I have shaken the edifice of Roman theology. Why then did they approve so warmly those in which, under my own name, I devoted myself to the same work? To take but three examples, among a hundred, why did they applaud when I wrote *Péché originel*, when I showed that the book of Daniel was the work of a forger and that Saint John Chrysostom had no knowledge of confession? Any sensible man, after reflection on this matter, will be obliged to conclude that God could not have inspired the book of a forger and that a dogma unknown to one of the great doctors of the Church could not possibly be of divine origin. And all those who have read Albert Houtin's *Marcel Hébert*, p. 145, know Cardinal Richard's remark on my *Péché originel*: "When one reads these articles, M. Turmel's for example, it seems that nothing is left." Who could these enlightened priests possibly be trying to convince that they do not have

PART TWO: How the Roman Church Freed Itself of Me

Cardinal Richard's perceptiveness, and that they gave approval to my writings because they failed to see their consequences? They saw everything, understood everything. And, having given support to the signed works, they ought logically to support the works published under assumed names. But logic would be compromising: therein lies the secret of their about-face. The priests in question heartlessly but wisely censured me the day it became dangerous to approve of me. I do not condemn this tactic: I simply record it. I do not want anyone to be fooled.

No more do I want anyone to be fooled by the contrast made between Loisy's attitude and my own. Like me and before me, Loisy was excommunicated. Why did the Roman Church take this extreme measure against him if not in response to his attacks? This mother has observed that one of her sons, living under her roof, was attacking her: that is why she has shown him the door. Let no one say that the Church was mistaken. Of course, for a long time Loisy made himself out to be the victim of a horrendous misunderstanding. But, since the publication of *Choses passées* in 1913, it has no longer been possible to harbor any illusion over this expedient that, in any case, was seen through by connoisseurs for more than fifteen years. Loisy did not wait to be outside the Roman Church before he undermined the Church's theology. He did this work at the very time when he signed a magnificent profession of faith (*Mémoires* I, 312). I did nothing more.

My second observation deals with the canonical situation of priests who, having like the present author, discerned the truth, like him have remained at the service of the Church. I have said loudly enough that their conduct conforms to the strictest legality and that they have nothing over which to reproach themselves. But I must remind them that the faithful would be horrified by them if they knew the state of their soul. It may be granted that the aversion of the faithful for enlightened priests is not legitimate; that it rests on a prejudice unworthy of note. But in the end that is the reality. On the basis of this reality I feel entitled to stand up before these priests who remain in the Church after distancing themselves from its dogmas and to say to them: "Whether others have the right to cast a stone is a question I am going to examine in a moment; but in any case, you do not have this right, for if the faithful knew your minds, they would hurl back at you the lack of candour of which you accuse me; they would encompass you in the same condemnation that they have levelled at me."

Have others this right? I am now talking about the enlightened laity and I say to them: "That the faithful condemn me is for them an imperative

Conclusion

duty, since the Church, of which they are dupes, presents its dogmas to them as treasures that Heaven has entrusted to its care; since it holds heresy as the greatest of crimes and that even today it claims the right to put heretics to death. Not being able to help it exercise its right to put heretics to death, a right which these unfortunate times have rendered null, at least in France, the faithful must bless the bloodhounds who take up the scent and bring back the prey to the Church; those who formerly denounced the heresies of Loisy, Batiffol, Lagrange, Duchesne; those who recently, by special methods, have succeeded in discovering me. They must be joyful when the Church rewards these good servants. However, you do not have the mentality of the faithful. For you dogmas are products of the human mind; ephemeral products that yesterday were not and tomorrow will be no more. There was no confession at the time of Saint John Chrysostom; there was no real presence at the time of Saint Augustine. Saint Bernard, Saint Thomas, Saint Bonaventure forbade the faithful to believe in the Immaculate Conception; and, at the time of Bossuet, the supremacy of the pope over councils with the addition of pontifical infallibility was not accepted by the French clergy. Yesterday's heresy is today's orthodoxy, and today's heresy could be tomorrow's orthodoxy. Dogmas are nothing; only souls count for anything. And, since souls alone count, their education is the only true ministry of the priest.

A ministry in which the doctors of all ages, otherwise separated and divided, meet and unite in the same love, in the same zeal. A ministry in which the child, the young man, the young woman, the spouses, those favored by fortune, those unfortunate receive a supply of energy to respect parents, to hold passions in check, to resist the world's seductions, to cultivate the various forms of virtue, to respect those defeated by life, to receive with fortitude the blows of adversity.

A ministry that is not simply content to distribute strength to souls, but also tries to obtain for them a few rays of light. But here it runs up against the claims of the Roman Church which, with its books supposedly written by heaven, with its dogmas stemming from imaginative fancy, covers the faithful, enslaved to its law and bent under its yoke, with a thick layer of errors. Constrained by respect for souls to adjust and arrange the orthodoxy of the present day, the priest liberated from dogmas can scarcely prepare the orthodoxy of tomorrow, an orthodoxy no longer made up of deception and blind sentiment, but of truth and reason.

Part Two: How the Roman Church Freed Itself of Me

There is the work I have undertaken. I have labored for the future without knowing whether success would one day crown my efforts, with the certitude of not being present myself at their eventual success, without any joy other than that of duty accomplished. I have worked in secret, as the disciple whom the gospel of Saint John praises (19:38) served Jesus secretly "for fear of the Jews." I too hid myself away in order to serve the truth, because the lie incarnate in the Roman Church was on the watch to strangle me. In serving the truth, in the only manner possible for me, I have completed the apostolate of education that I have execised among souls confided to my care with an apostolate of light. That the Roman Church vents its rage against me who, for forty years, has given its police the slip, that it has heaped insults upon me, is its role because its interests were at stake. That the faithful blinded by the Roman Church incriminate me is also their role, since it is the marching order they have received. But you, enlightened laity, be attentive to the claims of logic. Do not treat as oracles fallen from heaven dogmas whose vanity does not escape you. Do not play the Roman Church's game, since you are not fooled by its impostures. Do not speak of duplicity where there is only a ministry of education that has tried to reach its end but whose exercise has been hampered by Rome. Or, if you persist in borrowing insults from the Roman Church and its champions, at least know that, from your mouth, this language is nonsense.

II. The second problem is one of knowing why I have hid the truth from my ecclesiastical superiors who required it from me under oath. This second accusation, like the first, rests on a complete lack of understanding of the situation. Yes, I hid the truth from Judges that required it of me. But you, paladins of the truth, do you tell it to the dying person who anxiously asks what you think of his condition? Do you tell it to the importunate person who attempts to extract from you the secrets of your family, those of your profession? And if, in a host of circumstances, you believe yourselves bound to keep the truth hidden, to deceive the questioners, then brush aside these grandiloquent maxims that you claim to stun me with. Renounce your indignation that aspires to be tragic and is only comic. Let us say that there are cases in which the truth must be declared to those who ask it, that there are others, on the contrary, in which one has the right and even the duty to conceal it; that one is bound to tell the truth to those who have the right to know, but only to them. Then, these principles put forward, let us examine my case.

Conclusion

I hid the truth from judges who asked it of me. But why? Because I found myself faced with men who obstinately refused to investigatge the proceedings they were supposed to become expert in and who by that very fact have trampled underfoot the fundamental rule of law operative in all civilized nations. It is said that I failed in my duty as accused. Say rather that my judges were first to fail and in the most important of their professional duties and that their immoral conduct deprived them of all right to the truth.

Misled by the feigned indignation of the apologists, who have sensationally denounced what they called my lying, the naive reader has come to forget that, if the accused has duties, the judges also have them, and that the first of those is to investigate the case, to acquire an exact knowledge of the substance of the offense. What was the substance of the offense in my affair? In 1892 it was a matter of knowing whether in the Bible there were multiple fabrications, if the book of Daniel was the work of a forger, if Deuteronomy was the work of another forger, etc., etc. (*Congé aux dogmes*, p. 16). What did my judges do? Their sole preoccupation was not to know, to close their eyes to avoid seeing anything, to stop up their ears in order not to hear. In 1908 it was a matter of knowing if the texts of the Fathers put forward by Herzog on the subject of the Blessed Virgin were authentic; if Saint Bernard had treated the feast of the Immaculate Conception as superstition; if Saint Anselm, Peter Lombard, nearly all of the doctors of the twelfth century had left the Blessed Virgin under the yoke of sin until the moment when she became the mother of God; if Tertullian had attributed to Mary conjugal relations with Saint Joseph after the birth of Jesus, etc. . . . What did my judge, Mgr Dubourg, do? It never occurred to him to look for more information. And in 1929, when the Herzog affair came back under discussion, intensified this time by the Gallerand affair which implied that the texts of Saint Augustine, Saint Leo, Saint Gregory disagreed with current orthodoxy on the redemption, Cardinal Charost thought of everything except checking Herzog's and Gallerand's allegations.

Note that, far from blaming my judges, I excuse their conduct completely. They could do only what they did. Behind them stood, in fact, the papacy, with its cruel law, of which they were but the instruments and that would have crushed them, had they not shown themselves docile. Fundamentally, it is the tribunal of the Holy Office that, through the intermediary of enslaved officials, summoned me in 1892, in 1908 and in 1929. It is this institution that judged me while disdainfully dismissing the evidence. It

PART TWO: How the Roman Church Freed Itself of Me

is this institution that has outraged morality and to which I gave the reply it deserved. Proverbs (26:5) teaches us that the truth is not owed to the questioner lacking in common sense: *responde stulto juxta stultitiam suam.* And the Gospel, taking this maxim a step further, adds (Matt 7:8) that one must not cast pearls before swine: *Neque mittatis margaritas vestras ante porcos.* It is really paying far too much honor to thieves to treat them as honest men. Since the Roman curia was lacking in integrity, I held myself freed from all obligation in its regard. In my playing with a tribunal that itself played with morality I escaped a shameful parody of justice for forty years: I congratulate myself on doing so.

It goes without saying that, for the apologists, Herzog's and Gallerand's books are the work of a mediocre pamphleteer. But if they are so lacking in scientific value, why did Rome not hasten to bring their content before the public, this great public to which it denounced me and whose approval it seeks? The emptiness of my arguments or even their bad faith would redound to my embarrassment and would crown orthodoxy's victory. However, far from pursuing this way to victory, the hierarchy was in terror of it. Rome forbade the faithful to read my books. And, in the spring of 1930, Cardinal Charost forbade, under pain of grave sin, the reading of Coulange's books, even to those who have received the permission of the Index (*Semaine religieuse* of Rennes 1930. p. 502). Singular pamphlets whose reading is dangerous even for studious priests.

This is my response. However, I perceive that my study on the denunciation of 1929 has completely neglected the juridical side. I am going summarily to repair this gap after first recalling that the denunciation of 1908 was energetically condemned by the elite of the clergy.

Civil law condemns defamation and considers all publication of secret documents susceptible of injuring their authors as defamatory. Now such was exactly the case with the denunciation of 1929. This act comprised an objective to be attained and means of obtaining it. The objective sought was that of attributing to me heresies published under borrowed names, and of bringing the vengeance of the Roman Church down upon me. In that regard the summons of 1929 renewed the summons of 1908 so vigorously condemned by the clergy's elite and it incurred the same condemnation. However, if the objective was the same from the one to the other, the means differed. In 1908 the denunciators had worked on writings published in journals or in books. In 1929 they used secret documents and published them. In so doing they committed the offense of defamation as provided in the code, and they became liable under the article of the code that punishes libellers without allowing them to prove their allegations.

I was in a position to bring the defamation before the court when it appeared for the first time in the *Bulletin* of Toulouse of April 1929. The affair would have been settled to my advantage by the month of June, that is, before the Court's recess. The thought of placing myself under the protection of French law did occur to me; and in spite of my horror of wrangling, I would not have hesitated to defend myself, if I had the slightest suspicion of the defamers' plan. But who could then imagine that Rome was behind these men and that *La Croix*, on Rome's order, was going to place itself at their disposal in order to serve as loudspeaker? I believed that, confined to the *Bulletin* of Toulouse which was unknown to the mass of the clergy, the denunciation would dwindle of its own accord, unless it were taken up again by Cardinal Charost; and as I thought I had nothing to fear from this quarter, I gave up all pursuit.

The blindfold fell from my eyes and the slanderers' campaign was revealed in all its scope when, two months later, the first of the *La Croix* articles appeared. The Court was then in recess and would not resume for many months. A legal prosecution would not achieve its purpose before November. Would that not be too late? And, given the scandal that the slanderers had succeeded in creating, would not my archbishop think himself obliged to act? Without pausing over these questions I decided to make a complaint. I had a choice between Rennes and Toulouse. I ruled out Rennes in order not to create agitation in my entourage and I wrote successively to two lawyers in Toulouse whose names a friend had obtained for me. I sent them, one and the other, the documents in the case, confiding my case to them, but adding that, given my age and state of health it was impossible for me to make the trip to Toulouse. I did not know that the complainant must present himself before the tribunal to which he appeals. The lawyers did not take me for a serious client and they each in turn sent back my documents while refusing to involve themselves in my affair. Moreover, one of the two was I believe a clerical and would never have litigated against a journal protected by ecclesiastical authority.

I did not succeed in bringing the defamation before the tribunals that certainly would have condemned it. And this condemnation that could not have been unforeseen by the libellers would have put them off their enterprise, if they had been acting alone as I believed at the time. But later I came to know the illusion I harbored in imagining them acting on

Part Two: How the Roman Church Freed Itself of Me

their own. Behind them stood Rome, which they had consulted from the outset, and to which they had pointed out the risks of publishing secret documents, and which had put their minds at ease regarding any eventual danger. Immediately after the condemnation, Cardinal Charost, on Rome's order, would have carried the conflict into the ecclesiastical arena, where any new proceedings against my enemies would henceforth be impossible, and where censures awaited me.

A word yet before closing this book. When the Roman curia denounced my transgressions to the universe and banished me from the Catholic world, a cry of triumph arose among the clergy and in a sector of the press. Without doubt I would be constrained to flee, to hide myself in an obscure hole, to die there of hunger. They thought me crushed, annihilated forever. And they admired the Roman Church that avenged itself so magisterially on its enemies. A pack of publicists lashed out against me. Not being able to devour me, these cannibals inundated me with insults whose violence has perhaps never been surpassed.

All celebrations have their morning after. Rome's great victory has had its own. Here it is. Several religious communities immediately began novenas for my conversion that they repeated and no doubt go on repeating today. A Little Sister of the Poor living in Peking refused to undergo an operation that would have wrested her from death, and announced she was making the sacrifice of her life for the salvation of my soul. These facts have been officially brought to the attention of the clergy of Ille-et-Vilaine by the capitular vicar, M. Gayet, in the course of the ecclesiastical retreats of 1931. They are in the public domain. How many others as painfaul, as lamentable have been known only to restricted circles! How many souls deeply distressed, distraught, have shed tears, moaned, sobbed!

There is what the Roman Church obtained by its theatrical gesture of November 1930. This is what its resounding victory over me cost.

Let us speak now of this victory. Rome has fulminated a sentence of degradation against me that in olden times would have led me directly to the stake: I have not changed my residence; I continue to wear the ecclesiastical habit, I remain a priest in spite of it, and in that I only follow the Christian dogma that recognizes in me the permanence of an indelible character, that says to me: *tu es sacerdos in aeternum*. Rome has doomed me to the reprobation of the entire world: from all corners of Europe and even from America have come stacks of letters of congratulations. Even today, Rome teaches that the first comer has the right to kill me: the law of my country protects me, I have nothing to fear. Rome forbids the faithful to approach me: my solitude is, indeed, complete; but, for many long years it has been nearly what it is today. Rome's decree has made it impossible for me to exercise ecclesiastical functions; I have been in that state ever since Cardinal Charost suspended me ten months ago. Rome has proscribed all my books: these books, for which it has given free publicity, sell better than before its edict of proscription; a dozen new books that I had before kept carefully hidden have, since then, appeared under my name; others will follow. Rome, which has forgotten nothing and learned nothing, has drawn from its arsenal its most redoubtable weapons and launched them at me, without suspecting that these weapons, formerly so powerful, are today hollow scarecrows. The target toward which its blows were directed has escaped it to the point of altering nothing in his life. But it has succeeded in grievously wounding thousands of pious souls.

It has made men who had faith read my books, and they have it no longer. What fury was ever more blind?

But the troubling of souls, their confusion, are, I know, negligible contingencies in Rome's view, whose sole preoccupation is to display its force. It has succeeded in separating the faithful from me, in grossly insulting me via the mob of its hirelings. It is proud of its victory, it congratulates itself upon it.

AND THAT IS THE DECISIVE PROOF THAT NO BOOK OF THE BIBLE IS THE WORK OF AN IMPOSTER; THE PEREMPTORY PROOF THAT THE CHRISTIAN DOGMAS COME FROM HEAVEN AND ARE NOT THE PRODUCTS OF HUMAN IMAGINATION.

Appendix I

The *Nouvelles Rennaises* of January 29, 1931

> The Death of Cardinal Charost
> Worse and Worse
> Not only did the late archbishop
> die intestate,
> but he did not go to confession . . .

WE HAVE RECEIVED FROM an eminent religious person, whose name we are obliged not to divulge, at least until we have an archbishop of Rennes who completely shares our ideas, something which will come about not long hence, the following letter that our readers will find of interest:

"For several weeks the clergy of Rennes and of the region have been in turmoil. The priests have learned little by little that no one has been able to find Cardinal Charost's confessor. At this news some have looked away and appeared dismayed. Others have poured out a torrent of indignation. According to a rumor that we do not want to believe well founded, some would intend to bring the affair to Rome.

"My dear sirs, please calm down; confession is no doubt an excellent and highly commended practice, but it is, after all, of late origin. Over long centuries, the Church believed that the power to bind and loose was only to be used to expel notorious sinners from its gatherings, for example murderers and thieves, and to receive them back when they were repentant. Confession made its first appearance among the monks; and it was Irish monks who, toward the end of the Merovingian period, introduced it into France. At Rome, it was unknown before the 11th century. The apologists admit that Saint Augustine never went to confession. Cardinal Charost has followed Saint Augustine's example.

Appendix I

"Bring the affair to Rome! Have you carefully considered the terrible consequences such an initiative could entail? Rome has principles of which several among you have no notion. They were revealed the day when Pope Stephen VI summoned his predecessor, Formosus, nine months deceased, for judgment over an infraction of an ecclesiastical regulation. The cadaver of the unfortunate pontiff was disinterred and seated in a chair opposite a council of bishops presided over by the Pope. He was given a lawyer who undertook his defense. Futile endeavor! The unfortunate Formosus was condemned, then thrown into the water. And all the ordinations that he had celebrated were declared nul.

"Do you want to see Cardinal Charost disinterred by Rome's order, condemned and thrown into the water? Do you want to see all the priests ordained by him relegated to civil life? It is enough to make one tremble! For goodness sake do not bring his case to Rome."

Thus the Cardinal Charost affair—which has caused an enormous uproar in ecclesiastical circles—has not ceased to grow and be embellished . . . "I will not go to Rome if I am called," the Cardinal said two years ago, a statement that we reported in the *Nouvelles Rennaises* at the time: "if I went I would not return."

Then these facts follow in succession . . . Condemnation of Cardinal Charost through the person of Abbé Turmel.

Sudden death, after vomiting, of Cardinal Charost, the day of the condemnation.

Contradictory accounts of the prelate's final moments and certain odd details.

The cardinal did not leave a will. Either he did not execute one or they did not want to find the one that he had made.

And to put the finishing touches on it all, we learn that Cardinal Charost did not have a confessor.

He did not practice! He was no longer going to confession! A mighty mystery looms over the life as well as the death of this strange man and, sooner or later, the conspiracy of silence that has formed around him will be broken. It will be necessary to speak.

For ourselves, we do not ask that Cardinal Charost's cadaver be called before an ecclesiastical tribunal, as happened, according to our learned correspondent, to Pope Formosus.

However we would very much like to see an exhumation of the said cadaver in the presence of a forensic surgeon and for the purpose of an autopsy.

Yves Le Coz

Appendix II

Letter of Salomon Reinach[252] to the *Mercure de France*

November 30, 1930

Monsieur Director,

In the insulting lines that your collaborator has written on M. Turmel (Dec. 1, p. 428), he has forgotten only one thing: namely that M. Turmel is a great scholar, author of books of undisputed value, of veritable discoveries in the history of dogmas and of Christian origins. Also, the great dictionary of theology and religious philosophy published in 1913 in Tübingen (by Schiele and numerous scholars)[253] devotes no less than 24 lines to him, citing 10 books of his: some under his name, others under the pseudonym of Dupin and of Herzog. So his polyonymy thus was recognized seventeen years ago!

I know neither when nor how, or even if, under oath he denied being the author of these bold, but profoundly learned books, published under names other than his own. However I believe I recall that Pascal did not sign his name to the Provinciales, or what is called that for short.

Yours faithfully.

S. Reinach

Appendix III

Note on My Theological Tracts

From 1882 to 1887 I taught fundamental theology, comprising the tracts on Revelation, the Church and General Ethics. From 1887 to 1892 I taught dogma. Throughout this period the seminarians had for their manual a work in six volumes of which three were given over to moral theology.

Over the years 1882–1887, observing that the portion of the manual reserved to fundamental theology left a great deal to be desired, I set about composing tracts on Revelation, the Church and General Moral Theology. Beginning in 1887, I extended this work to the dogmatic tracts whose exposition in the manual was worthless.

In 1887 I was replaced in the chair of fundamental theology by M. Desbois. At the end of several weeks, I learned that M. Desbois was dictating my tracts to his students. But this information came to me only indirectly, for authorization had never been asked of me. However, I am inclined to believe that the superior, M. Guillois, who made no secret of his esteem for my writings, himself ordered my successor to use it.

After my dismissal in 1892, M. Desbois succeeded me in the chair of dogma as he had in the chair of fundamental theology. Once again, he did me the honor of dictating my tracts, and the news came to me indirectly: as regards my tracts on Revelation and the Church, on M. Cellier's request, in 1893 I made a second edition that was dictated to students from October 1893.

Things went along thus until the year 1897 (or 1896): at that time, my tracts, by order of the superior, Michel, gave way to the manual by the Sulpician Tanquerey.[254] And, since Tanquerey's manual treated dogma only, Marc's manual[255] was added to it to over moral theology.

Note on My Theological Tracts

    The moral professor, M. Sourdin, judged that the tract on conscience in Marc's manual was too confusing to serve as a useful guide for seminarians. Finding in old student notebooks the modest pages I had earlier devoted to this area of theology, he considered himself in possession of goods without an owner. He laid hold of it and dictated it in class. This operation came so naturally to him that it did not occur to him to inform me of it.

    His successor, M. Jourdan, also felt the desire to use my pages. However, reckoning that they had not ceased to belong to me, he came to me to present his request that was granted immediately. I do not know when M. Jourdan left the seminary. No more do I know who became his successor. What is certain is that my tract on conscience was dictated until around 1905 and perhaps beyond.

Editor's Notes

1. Félix Sartiaux, *Joseph Turmel: prêtre, historien des dogmes* (Paris: Rieder, 1931).

2. Garry Wills, *Saint Augustine's Childhood*. Confessions *Book One* (New York: Viking Penguin, 2001), 7.

3. Dupin's articles appeared in the *Revue d'histoire et de littérature religieuses* 11 (1906): 219–31; 353–65; 515–32; and Herzog's in vol. 12 (1907): 118–33; 320–40; 483–607. Both series were also published separately in book form.

4. Joseph Turmel, *Comment j'ai donné congé aux dogmes* (Herblay: Éditions de l'idée libre, 1935) and *Comment l'Église romaine m'a donné congé* (Herblay: Éditions de l'idée libre, [1939]). Republished as Joseph Turmel, *Autobiographie* (Rennes: La libre pensée Rennaise, 2003).

5 Roman Catholic Modernism emerged more as a loosely coordinated series of initiatives by reform-minded Catholics than as the coherent movement portrayed in the Vatican condemnation. What may be termed intellectual Modernism bore in one of its aspects upon problems in the area of what is now called fundamental theology—those engaging the credibility of revelation and the foundations of Christian faith. At the core of Modernism lie attempts to come to terms with modern historical consciousness—the awareness of the historical distance between past and present, and the necessity to bridge that gap with historical-critical methods in order to interpret properly documents from the past. For partisans of the dominant neo-Scholastic theology, such efforts relativized divine truth and reduced dogma and its historical development to a series of human initiatives. Although Turmel began with attempts to master historical-critical exegesis of Scripture in order to defend Catholicism against its excesses, his own contributions were made primarily in the history of dogma. He came to adopt a rationalist position which set him in the company of Marcel Hébert, Albert Houtin, and Félix Sartiaux. There was also a social and political side to Modernism. In some areas of the Church this aspect overshadowed the intellectual issues.

The historiography of Roman Catholic Modernism begins with those who were involved with the movement. Among early contributions may be found Paul Sabatier, *Modernism* (New York: Charles Scribner, 1908): Albert Houtin, *Histoire du modernisme catholique* (Paris: chez l'auteur, 1913); Maude D. Petre, *Modernism: Its Failure and Its Fruits* (London: T. C. & E. C. Jack, 1918); Jean Rivière, *Le modernisme dans l'Église* (Paris: Letouzey, 1929). More recent studies include Thomas Loome, *Liberal Catholicism,*

Editor's Notes

Reform Catholicism, Modernism (Mainz: Matthias-Grünewald-Verlag, 1979); Gabriel Daly, *Transcendence and Immanence. A Study in Roman Catholic Modernism and Integralism* (Oxford: Clarendon Press, 1980); Marvin O'Connell, *Critics on Trial: An Introduction to the Catholic Modernist Crisis* (Washington, D. C.: The Catholic University of America Press, 1998); *Catholicism Contending with Modernity. Roman Catholic Modernism and Anti-Modernism in Historical Context*, edited by Darrell Jodock. (Cambridge: Cambridge University Press, 2000). Maurilio Guasco, *Il modernismo. I fatti, le idee, i personaggi* (Rome: San Paulo Edizioni, 1995). French translation *Le modernisme. Les faits, les idées, les hommes* (Paris: Desclée de Brouwer, 2007); Claus Arnold, *Kleine Geschichte des Modernismus* (Freiburg: Herder, 2007). There are several good regional studies of the movement which include Lawrence Barmann, *Baron Friedrich von Hügel and the Modernist Crisis in England* (Cambridge: Cambridge University Press, 1972); R. Scott Appleby, *"Church and Age Unite": The Modernist Impulse in American Catholicism* (Notre Dame, In.: University of Notre Dame Press, 1992); Pierre Colin, *L'audace et le soupçon. La crise du modernisme dans le catholicisme français 1893-1914* (Paris: Desclée de Brouwer, 1997); Pietro Scoppola, *Crisi modernista e rinnovamento cattolico in Italia* (Bologna: Il Mulino, 1969); Lorenzo Bedeschi, *Il modernismo italiano. Voci e volti* (Cinisello Balsamo, 1995); Otto Weiss, *Der Modernismus in Deutschland, Ein Beitragzur Theologie-geschichte* (Regensburg: Pustet, 1995).

6. C. J. T. Talar, "Multiple Identities: Joseph Turmel, *Moderniste Démasqué*." In *Personal Faith and Institutional Commitments*, edited by Lawrence Barmann and Harvey Hill. (Scranton, Pa.: University of Scranton Press, 2002), 67–89.

7. Albert Houtin, *Une vie de prêtre. Mon expérience 1867-1912* (Paris: F. Rieder, 1926), 317. *The Life of a Priest. My Own Experience 1867-1912*. Translated by Winifred S. Whale. (London: Watts & Co., 1927), 188.

8. For analysis of Turmel's autobiography see Talar, "Multiple Identities. Joseph Turmel: *Moderniste Démasqué*."

9. Sartiaux, 218. On Hébert see Albert Houtin, *Un prêtre symboliste. Marcel Hébert (1851-1916)* (Paris: Rieder, 1925). In addition to Loisy's extensive autobiographical writings see the concise biography by Émile Goichot, *Alfred Loisy et ses amis* (Paris: Cerf, 2002).

10. In July of 1907 the Vatican moved against Modernism in issuing a syllabus of propositions extracted from Modernist works and condemned. The following September the encyclical *Pascendi dominici gregis* presented a synthesis of the Modernist positions and specified a series of social controls designed to suppress such initiatives. See the issue of *U. S. Catholic Historian* 25/1 (2007) devoted to "Centennial Essays on Responses to the Encyclical on Modernism."

11. *Pascendi* explicitly notes this double duplicity, first, in asserting "the fact, which indeed is well calculated to deceive souls, that they lead a life of the greatest activity, of assiduous and ardent application to every branch of learning, and that they possess, as a rule, a reputation for irreproachable morality" (§3). Second, in the observation that, "Under their own names and under pseudonyms they publish numbers of books, newspapers, reviews, and sometimes one and the same writer adopts a variety of pseudonyms to trap the incautious reader into believing in a multitude of Modernist writers" (§43). The text of *Pascendi* may be found in Vincent A. Yzermans, *All Things in Christ*.

Encyclicals and Selected Documents of Saint Pius X (Westminster, Md.: The Newman Press, 1954), 89–132. While Turmel was not the only one to use pseudonyms, the articles by Antoine Dupin and Guillaume Herzog attained a great deal of notoriety as pseudonymous productions.

12. See, for example, Turmel's perceptions of Loisy as those surface in the course of his narrative, especially the "Note" on Alfred Loisy that he published at the end of *Comment j'ai donné congé aux dogmes*.

13. For an example of this approach, applied to the doctrine of purgatory, see Constantin Chauvin, *Le purgatoire. S'il existe et ce qu'il est* (Paris: Librairie Bloud et Barral, 1901).

14. See Daly, 7–25.

15. For an example of Turmel's mode of proceeding, see C. J. T. Talar, "The Author of Evil: The Devil in the Patristic Scholarship of Joseph Turmel," *Downside Review* 127 (2009): 279–91.

16. For an analysis of Modernist views on these multiple levels, configured as a clash of rival paradigms, see C. J. T. Talar, *Metaphor and Modernist: The Polarization of Alfred Loisy and his Neo-Thomist Critics* (Lanham, Md.: University Press of America, 1987).

17. See Christophe Théobald, "L'entrée de l'histoire dans l'univers théologique au moment de la 'crise moderniste.'" In Jean Greisch et al. *La crise contemporaine. Du modernisme à la crise des herméneutiques* (Paris: Beauchesne, 1973), 5–85.

18. Justin Oakley, *Morality and the Emotions* (New York: Routledge, 1993), 186.

19. John Corrigan, "Introduction: Emotions Research and the Academic Study of Religion." In *Religion and Emotion: Approaches and Interpretations*, edited by John Corrigan (Oxford: Oxford University Press, 2004), 6.

20. Oakley attributes the relative neglect of the moral importance of emotions by contemporary moral philosophy to a predominance of Kantianism and a preoccupation with moral action. See Oakley, 1. Part of the impetus for interest in the moral significance of emotions comes from a confluence of psychology and ethics on the subject of virtue and traits of character, in which the emotions assume an important role. Thus "ethics has taken a psychological turn, and philosophers now regularly engage in a discipline they call 'moral psychology,' which is reflection about ethical traits, ethical motivation, ethical emotions, and ethical understanding and judgment." Robert C. Roberts, *Spiritual Emotions: a psychology of Christian virtues* (Grand Rapids, Mich.: Wm. B. Eerdmans, 2007), 6.

21. Solomon has developed his views in a series of articles collected in *Not Passion's Slave: Emotions and Choice* (Oxford: Oxford University Press, 2003), in his *In Defense of Sentimentality* (Oxford: Oxford University Press, 2004), and in *True to Our Feelings: What Our Emotions Are Really Telling Us* (Oxford: Oxford University Press, 2007). See also Ronald de Sousa, *The Rationality of Emotion* (Cambridge: The MIT Press, 1987).

22. Robert Solomon, "Sympathy and Vengeance: The Role of Feelings in Justice," *In Defense of Sentimentality*, 24.

23. Linda Trinhaus Zagzebski, *Divine Motivation Theory* (Cambridge: Cambridge University Press, 2004), 87.

24. Martha C. Nussbaum, *Upheavals of Thought: The Intelligence of Emotions*

Editor's Notes

(Cambridge: Cambridge University Press, 2001), 33. Cf. Roberts, 11–13.

25. Solomon, *True to Our Feelings*, 218–19.

26. Théobald, "L'entrée de l'histoire dans l'univers théologique au moment de la 'crise moderniste,'" 10–11.

27. Houtin, *Vie de prêtre*, 197; *Life of a Priest*, 116.

28. Louis Coulange [Joseph Turmel], *Catéchisme pour adultes* 2 vols. (Paris: Rieder, 1929 and 1930). English translation *Religious Inventions and Frauds* (Melbourne: Thomas C. Lothian Proprietary Limited, 1936).

29. Ibid., 11–13. Cf. Daly, 7–25.

30. Maude Petre knew a number of prominent Modernist figures first hand and closely followed controversies of the period. As she retrospectively observed, "We must remember, in fairness to those who were not always fair, that the impact of historical criticism on the traditional teaching of the Church was terrifying; that it seemed a case of saving the very essence of the Christian faith from destruction. Not, perhaps, since the startling revelation of Copernicanism, had the shock been greater." M. D. Petre, *Alfred Loisy: His Religious Significance* (Cambridge: Cambridge University Press, 1944), 112.

31. Joseph Turmel, *Comment j'ai donné congé aux dogmes*, 47 (see page 28 of the translation).

32. Ibid., 80 (page 47 of the translation).

33. Joseph Turmel, *Comment l'Église romaine m'a donné congé*, 40–41 (page 120 of the translation).

34. Ibid., 140 (page 185 of the translation).

35. Ibid., 126 (page 176 of the translation),

36. Although Turmel adopts a virtually eremetical lifestyle, emerging from his academic solitude only to say Mass and hear confessions at a chapel near his residence, this appears to be in response to an ostracization on the part of the majority of the clergy. For the effects of such marginalization, especially its effects upon self-esteem, see Kipling D. Williams, *Ostracism: The Power of Silence* (New York: Guilford Press, 2001).

37. See Philip Fisher, *The Vehement Passions* (Princeton: Princeton University Press, 2002), 66, 171–98. Also Robert M. Gordon, *The Structure of Emotions* (Cambridge: Cambridge University Press, 1987), 56–57, 62.

38. Nussbaum, 70–75.

39. Solomon, *Not Passion's Slave*, 154–55.

40. Turmel, *Comment j'ai donné congé aux dogmes*, 110–11 (pages 65–66 of the translation). In his comments on vengeance, Peter French reinforces the sense that revenge is designed to send a message: "Revenge is a very personal matter, and when it is inflicted, it is important that the target grasp the reason why. If the target does not know that he or she is paying the penalty because of his or her specific prior harming or injuring of someone or of the avenger himself or herself, the act of revenge has misfired. Revenge . . . is, in very large measure, an act of communication." Peter A. French, *The Virtues of Vengeance* (Lawrence: University Press of Kansas, 2001), 12.

41. Solomon, *Not Passion's Slave*, 37.

42. Ibid., 101.

43. French, 87.

44. Thomas J. Scheff, *Microsociology: Discourse, Emotion and Social Structure* (Chicago: University of Chicago Press, 1990), 75–76.

45. Noted in a letter from Turmel to Alfred Loisy, 16 November 1930. Quoted in Alec Vidler, *A Variety of Catholic Modernists* (Cambridge: Cambridge University Press, 1970), 62.

46. The period of Turmel's life that follows his excommunication and eventual association with Libre Pensée is rather vague. It is likely that Turmel was introduced to the association through the intermediary of André Lorulot (1885–1963), one of the leaders of Libre Pensée during the interwar years and its great leader under the Fourth Republic. See Jacqueline Lalouette, *La libre pensée en France 1848–1940* (Paris: Albin Michel, 1997), 505. In addition to the autobiography's two volumes, Lorulot's L'Idée Libre published Turmel's *Jésus* (three booklets 1936), *La Bible expliquée* (1936), *La Réfutation du catéchisme* (1937), *Le Suaire de Turin* (1939) and finally *Les Religions* (1939). See Jean-Sébastien Pierre, "Joseph Turmel et l'enseignement du 'fait religieux'" in *Actualité de l'oeuvre anticlericale et antireligieuse de l'abbé Joseph Turmel*, edited by Michel Le Normand and Marc Le Bris. (Rennes: La libre pensée Rennaise, 2004).

47. "Bearing witness, in other words, can express character and conviction, and its relationship to character and conviction is an important part of the explanation of its moral value." Jeffrey Blustein, *The Moral Demands of Memory* (Cambridge: Cambridge University Press, 2008), 329.

48. Ibid., 337.

49. Constant-Ludovic-Marie Guillois (1833–1910). Ordained priest in 1857, he became superior of the major seminary in 1873. Appointed bishop of Le-Puy-en-Valey in 1894, he retired in 1907.

50. François Duine gives a portrait of Abbé Gendron in *Souvenirs et observations de l'abbé François Duine*, edited by Bernard Heudré. (Rennes: Presses Universitaires de Rennes, 2009), 242.

51. Hugo von Hurter (1825–1895). Jesuit theologian who taught on the theological faculty of the University of Innsbruck. His *Theologiae dogmaticae compendium* (3 vols.) was published over 1876–1878.

52. Louis Billot (1846–1931). Jesuit theologian, an important figure in the Thomistic revival under Leo XIII. When the Faculté de Théologie d'Angers was founded, Billot was named professor of theology in 1879. For two years he taught successively *De Verbo incarno* and *De Ecclesia*. Later called to the Gregorian Univesity in Rome, his teaching formed generations of students. In 1911 he was created a cardinal by Pius X.

53. Eugène Paultier (1834–1917) entered the Jesuits in 1853. In 1896 he became superior of the region of Champagne. He was the co-author of a text, *Concordantiarum universae Scripturae Sacrae thesaurus* (Paris: Lethielleux, 1897).

54. Francisco de Suarez (1548–1617). Spanish Jesuit philosopher and theologian. Part of the late Scholasticism of the sixteenth century, Suarez reaffirmed the Scholastic

tradition, especially the work of Thomas Aquinas, over Renaissance scholarship. The nineteenth-century Thomistic revival was significantly influenced by Suarez.

55. Denis Pétau (1583–1652). French Jesuit and patrologist. Noted for his contributions to positive theology, Pétau's work became significant for those interested in the development of doctrine. His work on the Trinity and on the early history of penance would have been of particular interest to Turmel.

56. Charles René Billuart (1685–1757). Dominican preacher, theologian and controversialist. His major work, published in 19 volumes over 1746–1751, was entitled *Summa S. Thomae hodiernis Academiarum moribus accommodate*. Turmel is likely referring to the compendium *Summa S. Thomae sive compendium theologiae* (1754).

57. Charles Émile Freppel (1827–1891). French theologian, apologist and writer; appointed bishop of Angers in 1869. His *Études sur les Pères des trois premiers siècles* (1859–1893) ran to 11 volumes. His critical rejoinder to Renan, *Examen critique de la Vie de Jésus par E. Renan* (1863) was widely read. On Freppel see Bernard Plongeron, Isabelle Émerian and Jean Riaud, *Catholiques entre monarchie et république. Monseigneur Freppel et son temps* (Letouzey et ané, 1995).

58. Dionysius the Pseudo-Areopagite. Acts 17:34 relates the conversion of the judge of the Areopagus by the preaching of St. Paul. In Eusebius's Church History Dionysius appears as the bishop of Athens. Several writings showing the strong influence of neo-Platonic philosophy were ascribed to the Areopagite, conferring upon them great authority. This identification came into question during the Renaissance and by the nineteenth century there was growing opposition to it among Catholic scholars, although the traditional ascription still found staunch defenders. From internal evidence it appears that these writings date from the fifth century and that their author was likely a native of Syria.

59. Tommaso Zigliara (1833–1893). Dominican philosopher and theologian. Zigliara was one of the chief figures in the Thomistic revival under Pope Leo XIII, both through his teaching and his writing.

60. Jacques-Bénigne Bossuet (1627–1704). Noted French preacher, writer and controversialist. Appointed bishop of Condom in 1670 and of Meaux in 1681. His *Traité de la connaissance de Dieu et de soi-même* reflects the ideas of Descartes, which he later repudiated.

61. François de Salignac de la Mothe Fénelon (1651–1715). Archbishop of Cambrai (1696–1715). Fénelon achieved a certain notoriety over his controversy with Bossuet on the nature and scope of mysticism. The primary work for the expression of Fénelon's philosophical ideas remains his *Traité de l'existence de Dieu*.

62. Ontologism refers to the teaching that the idea of being, which is immediately and intuitively present to the human intellect, is Being, God himself. From a theological perspective ontologism threatened the distinction between Creator and creature, and that between nature and grace. It was condemned in 1861.

63. Innéism or Innatism refers to the teaching that humans are born with ideas. Herbert Spencer (1820–1903). English sociologist and philosopher, an early proponent of the theory of evolution who advocated the preeminence of science over religion. René Descartes (1596–1650). French mathematician and philosopher. In his *Méditations*

touchant la première philosophie Descartes argued that the mind is innately possessed of ideas such as God.

64. Jean-Baptiste Glaire (1798–1879). French Hebraist and biblical scholar noted for his publications in oriental languages and scripture. The reference is to Glaire's *Principes de grammaire hébraïque et chaldaïque, accompagnés d'une chrestomathie hébraïque et chaldaïque avec une traduction française et une analyse grammaticale* (multiple editions).

65. Heinrich F. W. Gesenius (1786–1842). Orientalist and exegete. He made important and lasting contributions to the study of Hebrew grammar and lexicography. His *Lexicon Hebraicum* (1810–1812) was translated into English as *A Hebrew Lexicon of the Books of the Old Testament* (Cambridge: Cambridge University Press, 1825–1828). See Edward Friedrich Miller, *The Influence of Gesenius on Hebrew Lexicography* [1927] (Piscataway: Gorgias Press, 2009).

66. Count Friedrich Leopold Stolberg (1750–1819). After his conversion to Roman Catholicism in 1800, he published *Geschichte der Religion Jesu Christi* (15 vols. 1806–1818), a work that was—as Turmel remarks—more edifying than critical.

67. Charles Litter (1853–1923) was professor of Sacred Scripture at Angers from 1879 until 1894.

68. Jacques-Bénigne Bossuet, *Explication de la prophétie d'Isaïe sur l'enfantement de la sainte Vierge*, Oeuvres complètes de Bossuet vol. 1, 256–263.

69. Johann Lorenz Isenbiehl (1774–1818). German exegete. He ran into difficulties over his interpretation of Isa 7:14 in which he concluded that the "young woman" was a contemporary of Isaiah himself and, consequently, neither a literal nor a typical Christological sense could be sustained for the passage. Its use in Matt 1:22–23 must therefore be viewed as a loose application. He published this thesis and, not only was the book condemned by papal Brief in 1779, but already in 1777 Isenbiehl had been suspended from his priestly functions and incarcerated in the Prince-Episcopal jail in Mainz. Upon signing a document of self-condemnation in 1779 he obtained his release and published nothing further in biblical studies.

70. Victor Auguste Dechamps (1810–1883). Bishop of Namur (1865–1867), named bishop of Malines in 1867 and created a cardinal in 1875. He developed his apologetic method, called the "method of Providence," in *Entretiens sur la Démonstration de la Foi* (1856); *Lettres théologiques* (1861) and in *La Question religieuse* (1861).

71. Henri Lesêtre (1848–1914). Although involved in parish ministry, Lesêtre wrote numerous books and articles bearing on biblical scholarship. He contributed several commentaries to the Lethielleux Bible and wrote multiple articles for the *Dictionnaire de la Bible*. In 1903 he became a consultor of the Pontifical Biblical Commission.

72. The Lethielleux Bible was a new edition of the bible accompanied by learned commentaries. The collection received the approbation of Pope Leo XIII in 1880.

73. In Roman legend the Horatii and the Curatii refer to two sets of triplet brothers who engaged in mortal combat to settle a war between Rome and Alba Longa. Turmel refers to the part of the legend which has it that, two of the Horatii being immediately vanquished, the third took to flight, stringing out his pursuers and enabling him to engage and overcome them one by one.

Editor's Notes

74. Edouard Reuss (1804-1891). Protestant biblical scholar. A strong advocate of the historical-critical approach to the scriptures, Reuss's facility with both German and French made him a conduit for German critical scholarship into France.

75. Henry Ceillier (1854-1911). Ordained priest in 1876, he was named professor of philosophy at the major seminary. In 1892 he published his *Leçons de philosophie scholastiques*. See *Souvenirs et observations de l'abbé François Duine*, 247-49.

76. Jean de la Fontaine (1621-1695) is remembered particularly for his fables, successive volumes of which appeared in 1668, 1678-1679 and 1693.

77. Eudoxe Irenée Mignot (1842-1918). Bishop of Fréjus (1890-1899) and archbishop of Albi (1899-1918). Mignot's interest in renewal of Catholicism is expressed in his *Lettres sur les études ecclésiastiques* (1908) and *L'Église et la critique* (1910). He followed biblical scholarship attentively and was supportive of Loisy's efforts. On Mignot see Louis-Pierre Sardella, *Mgr Eudoxe Irénée Mignot (1842-1918). Un évêque français au temps du modernisme* (Paris: Cerf, 2004).

78. Louis Sébastian Le Nain de Tillemont (1637-1698). French historian. He is remembered primarily for his *Mémoires pour servir à l'histoire ecclésiastique des six premiers siècles* (16 vols. 1693-1712), which reflects his thorough and exacting scholarship.

79. Jean Morin (1591-1659). Oratortian theologian and orientalist. His major works focused on the Samaritan Pentateuch, but he also published rare texts on the sacraments and studies on the ancient discipline of the Church.

80. Jean de Launoy (1603-1678). French theologian and critic. His historical studies, critical of pious legends, earned him the title of "dénicheur de saints"—an epithet also applied to some critics by their opponents during the Modernist period.

81. Thomas Henri Martin (1813-1884), *La vie future suivant la foi et suivant la raison* (Paris: Dezobry, E. Magdeleine et Cie, 1858).

82. The *Manuel biblique* of Fulcran Vigouroux (1837-1915) and Louis Bacuez (1820-1892) went through multiple editions. Its second volume was placed on the Index of Forbidden Books in 1923.

83. Ernest Renan (1823-1892). Orientalist, historian and exegete. His *Vie de Jésus* (1863) evoked controversy and spawned a cottage industry of refutations from Catholic authors. Turmel makes reference to Renan's *Histoire du people d'Israël* (5 vols. Calman Levy, 1887).

84. Albert Réville (1826-1906). First holder of the Chair of the History of Religions, created especially for him, at the Collège de France in 1880. Director of the *Revue d'Histoire des religions*, also founded in 1880. Turmel refers to *Les religions des peuples non civilisés* (Paris: Fischbacher, 1883) and to *Histoire du dogme de la divinité de Jésus-Christ* (Paris: Germer Baillière, 1869) English translation *History of the Dogma of the Deity of Jesus Christ* [1878] (Kessinger Publishing, 2008). See Jacques Marty, *Albert Réville. Sa vie, son oeuvre* (Cahors & Alençon: Imprimieries typographiques A. Coueslant, 1913).

85. Maurice Vernes (1845-1923). Founder of the *Revue d'Histoire des religions* (1880), director of the section of the École pratique des Hautes Études on sciences religieuses, he advanced the scientific study of religions, beginning with Judaism and Christianity.

86. Abraham Kuenen (1828-1891). Dutch theologian and biblical scholar, a leader

of the modern school who contributed to the debate over the origin and composition of the Hexateuch, as well as publishing works on the Hebrew prophets and the history of Israel. See *Abraham Kuenen (1828-1891). His Major Contributions to the Study of the Old Testament*, ed. P. B. Dirksen & A. van der Kooij (Leiden: E. J. Brill, 1993).

87. Michel Nicolas (1810-1886). French Protestant writer whose publications included critical studies on the Old and New Testaments (1861 and 1863) as well as the apocryphal gospels (1865).

88. Timothée Colani (1824-1888). French liberal Protestant, co-founder of the controversial *Revue de théologie et de philosophie chrétienne* in 1850. The positions taken by Colani and his collaborators, highly critical of orthodox Protestantism, led to the founding of the *Revue Chrétienne* in 1854 as a counter. On Colani see Jacques Marty, *Timothée Colani, théologian protestant, 1824-1888. Essai biographique* (Paris: Fischbacher, 1947).

89. Hippolyte Taine (1828-1893). French critic and historian. Taine was one of the noted exponents of French Positivism with its cult of science. Turmel refers to *De l'intelligence* 2 vols. (Paris: Librairie Hachette, 1870) English translation *On Intelligence*. Translated by T. D. Haye (New York: Holt & Williams, 1872).

90. Alfred Jules Émile Fouillée (1838-1912). French philosopher noted for his work on Plato and Socrates. In elaborating his own position, he attempted to reconcile metaphysical idealism with the naturalistic perspective of science.

91. Jean-Marie Guyau (1854-1888). French philosopher and poet. His philosophical work centered on ethics.

92. Théodule Ribot (1839-1916). Together with Hippolyte Taine, Ribot founded the *Revue philosophique*. His major work centered on psychology which he sought to establish on a scientific basis that depended on facts and took into account physiological and biological data.

93. Athanase Coquerel (1820-1875), *Premières transformations historiques du christianisme* (Paris: Gemer-Ballière et Cie, 1880). English translation *First Historical Transformations of Christianity* (Boston: W. V. Spencer, 1867).

94. Eugène Auguste Ernest Havet (1813-1889). French scholar. One of his major works was entitled *Le Christianisme et ses origines* (4 vols. 1871-1884) which would explain Turmel's interest in him.

95. Étienne Vacherot (1809-1897). French philosophical writer who succeeded Victor Cousin at the Sorbonne. His first and best-known work, *Histoire critique de l'école d'Alexandrie* (3 vols. 1846-1851) elicited attacks from the clerical party, which led to his suspension in 1851.

96. Jean Réville (1855-1908), *La doctrine du logos dans la quatrième Évangile et les oeuvres de Philon* (Paris: Fischbacher, 1881).

97. Benjamin Aubé (1826-1887), *De l'apologétique chrétienne au IIème siècle: Saint Justin, philosophe et martyr, Essai de critique religieuse* (Paris-Orléans: Firmin Didot-Auguste Durand-H. Herlusion, 1861).

98. Jacques François Denis (1821-1897), *De la philosophie de l'Origène* (Paris: Thorin, 1884).

99. Jacques-Bénigne Bossuet, *Defensio Declarationis cleri gallicani* in *Oeuvres*

complètes de Bossuet 2nd ed., edited by Abbé Guillaume, vol. 10 (Paris: Berche et Tralin, 1885), 5-340.

100. Philippe Labbe (1607-1667). Jesuit writer on historical, geographical and philological questions. Turmel is referring to Labbe's chief work, a collection of councils entitled *Sacrosancta concilia ad regiam editonem exacta* (18 vols. 1671-1672).

101. Karl Joseph Héfélé (1809-1893). Professor of ecclesiastical history at Tübingen, then appointed bishop of Rottenburg in 1869. On the strength of his study of the councils he opposed the definition of papal infallibility at Vatican I, but gave his adhesion once it was defined. His publications on the Apostolic Fathers would have attracted Turmel's attention.

102. Franz Xaver von Funk (1821-1907). Church historian, Héfélé's successor at the University of Tübingen.

103. Jacques-Bénigne Bossuet, *La tradition défendue sur la matière de la communion sous une espèce contre les réponses des deux auteurs protestants*, Oeuvres complètes de Bossuet vol. 4: 288-396. Jean Mabillon (1632-1701). French Benedictine scholar. Turmel is referring to the second volume of Mabillon's *Museum Italicum* (1689) which included the ancient *Ordines Romani*, comprising fifteen ritual books of the Roman Rite used in the early period of the Church, together with his commentary on it.

104. Louis Ménard (1706-1767). French historian. He collected and published original documents of importance for French history.

105. Jacques- Bénigne Bossuet, "Mémoire de ce qui est à corriger dans la Nouvelle Bibliothèque des auteurs ecclésiastiques, de M. Dupin," *Oeuvres complètes* vol. 3: 1-11. Nicolas Rigault (Rigaltius) (1577-1654). French classical scholar. Turmel refers to his annotated edition of Saint Cyprian (1666).

106. Johann Karl von Otto (1816-1897). German Protestant scholar. His prize essay, *De Justini Martyris scriptis et doctrine* (1841) prepared the way for his life-work, the *Corpus apologetarum Christianorum saeculi secundi* (9 vols. 1847-1872) which included a critical and exegetical edition of Justin Martyr.

107. Peter Lombard (c. 1095-1160). Theologian, consecrated bishop of Paris in 1159. His *Liber Sententiarum* presents the whole of Christian doctrine in one volume which gained wide usage throughout the schools of western Christendom until well into the seventeenth century.

108. When the feast of the Immaculate Conception was introduced into France, St. Bernard of Clairvaux objected, writing Epist. 174 in support of his objections. At the time it was feared that the Immaculate Conception of Mary would compromise the universality of redemption through Christ.

109. The problem of theodicy was a factor in the loss of faith of more than one Modernist. Marcel Hébert identifies it as a significant cause of his own rejection of theism. See *The Philosopher as Modernist: Selected Writings of Marcel Hébert*, edited by C. J. T. Talar. (Washington, D. C.: The Catholic University of America Press, 2011).

110. Further details of this incident are given in *Souvenirs et observations de l'abbé François Duine*, 245-46. The student to whom Turmel revealed his inmost thoughts is identified as Constant Delehaye (1867-1941), recently ordained to the priesthood in

1891 and appointed professor at the Collège Saint-Vincent.

111. Paul de Broglie (1834–1895). Professor of apologetics at the Paris Institut catholique who achieved renown for his many writings on apologetic subjects. See Clodius Piat, *L'apologétique de l'abbé de Broglie* (Paris: Victor Lecoffre, 1896).

112. According to the *Catholic Encyclopedia* vol. 5: 686, excommunications specially reserved to the pope include "All apostates from the Christian faith." "Strictly speaking, an apostate is one who goes over to a non-Christian religion, e.g., Islam; to such apostates are assimilated those who publicly renounce all religion; this apostasy is not to be presumed; it is evident that both kinds of apostates exclude themselves from the Church."

113. Under the editorship of Louis Veuillot (1813–1883) *L'Univers*, originally founded in 1833 by Abbé Migne, became an influential organ of ultramontane Catholicism among the French clergy. At the time of the modernist crisis it continued to be a champion of Catholic orthodoxy.

114. Charles-Philippe Cardinal Place (1814–1893). Ordained priest in 1850, consecrated bishop of Marseille in 1866, he was appointed archbishop of Rennes in 1878 and elevated to the cardinalate in 1886. *Pieux souvenir de son éminence le Cardinal Place* (Lyon: E. Vitte, 1895) contains a Notice biographique (xi–lxv).

115. Adolphe Tanquerey (1854–1932). Sulpician theologian. While teaching at St. Mary's Seminary in Baltimore, he published his *Synopsis theologiae dogmaticae* (2 vols. 1894) and in 1896 his *Synopsis theologiae dogmaticae fundamentalis*. The former was published as *A Manual of Dogmatic Theology* 2 vols., translated by John J. Byrnes (New York: Desclée, 1959).

116. Jacques Paul Migne (1800–1875). Patrologist and ecclesiastical publisher. His Patrologia Latina (221 vols. 1844–1864) covered Latin authors from Tertullian to Inocent III; the Patrologia Graeca included Greek and Latin texts of authors from the pseudo-Barnabas to the Council of Florence (161 vols. 1857–1866) and the Latin text only of the Greek Fathers (8 vols. 1856–1867). On Migne see R. Howard Bloch, *God's Plagairist: Being an Account of the Fabulous Industry and Irregular Commerce of the Abbé Migne* (Chicago: University of Chicago Press, 1995).

117. Adrian Pautonnier (1853–1943). Professor at the Collège Stanislaus, then director from 1903.

118. Albert Houtin (1867–1926). Historian. Houtin raised controversy with his *La controverse de l'apostolocité des Églises de France* (1901, 3rd ed. 1903) which chronicled the challenges posed by criticism to the legends surrounding the apostolic foundation of French dioceses, and still more by his two books on Catholic biblical scholarship, *La Question biblique chez les catholiques de France au XIXe siècle* (1902) and *La Question biblique au XXe siècle* (1906). Several of his works found their way onto the Index and Houtin left the Church in 1912. The reference in the text is to Albert Houtin, *Courte histoire du célibat ecclésiastique* (Paris: Rieder, 1929). Allegations of sexual improprieties in one of the novitiates occurring over several decades, beginning in the 1860s, are cited.

119. Joseph Turmel, *Histoire de la théologie positive* (Paris: Beauchesne, 1904). A second volume appeared in 1906.

120. Pierre Gayet (1873–1952). Ordained in 1895, Gayet eventually became superior of the major seminary of Pondichéry, India.

Editor's Notes

121. François Durusselle (1843–1916). Ordained in 1868, he held a succession of diocesan posts in the chancery.

122. Perrault. There are several priests of the Rennes archdiocese for which the archdiocesan archives has no information. Thus no identification is possible beyond that which Turmel provides in his text.

123. Duine refers to the formidable superior as "le torquémadaire Michel."

124. Julien Fontaine (1839–1917). Jesuit apologist who judged Kant ultimately responsable for much of the ills afflicting the Catholic Church in France. See as representative his *Les infiltrations kantiennes et protestantes et le clergé français* (Paris: Victor Retaux, 1902).

125. Léon Béon (1865–1948). Ordained in 1890 he was appointed professor of dogma at the major seminary in 1892. In 1896 he became the seminary's Econome. Named honorary canon in 1907.

126. In the course of describing his seminary years Duine mentions a Charles Desbois as one of his professors. *Souvenirs et observations de l'abbé Duine*, 47–48.

127. Guillaume-Marie-Joseph Cardinal Laboré (1841–1906). Ordained priest for the diocese of Arras in 1865, he was consecrated bishop of Le Mans in 1885 and appointed archbishop of Rennes in 1893. He was created cardinal in 1897.

128. Abbé Gendron, *Oeuvres oratoires I. Retraites de séminaires* (Paris: Gabriel Beauchesne et Cie, 1906).

129. Jules Croulbois (1855–1929). Ordained in 1878, he was for a time pastor at Cossé-le-Vivien before resigning for reasons of health and retiring to Paris. He published in the *Revue d'histoire et de littérature religieuses* (articles in 1901 and 1904).

130. Adolf von Harnack (1851–1930). Church historian and patrologist. In addition to his own writings Harnack was instrumental in the foundation of several series that served as standard sources for a critical approach to the Fathers. Turmel makes reference to Harnack's *Lehrbuch der Dogmengeschichte* (3 vols. 1885–1889).

131. Heinrich Holtzmann (1832–1910) through his teaching and writing was the leading New Testament scholar of the liberal school in his day.

132. Alfred Loisy (1857–1940). Loisy is identified as one of the principal exponents of what became known as Roman Catholic Modernism. His *L'Évangile et l'Église* (1902) may be said to have catalyzed the "modernist crisis." He set forth his own perspective on events in his autobiographical *Choses passées* (Paris: Émile Nourry, 1913) (English translation *My Duel with the Vatican*. Translated by Richard Wilson Boynton. [New York: Greenwood Press, 1968]) and in *Mémoires pour servir à l'histoire religieuse de notre temps* (3 vols. 1930–1931).

133. Karl Heinrich von Weizsaecker (1822–1899). German theologian, author of influential works on early Christianity who taught at Tübingen.

134. Rudolf Sohm (1841–1917). German Protestant jurist who wrote a number of works of theological interest, including *Kirchengeschichte im Grundiss* (1888).

135. Otto Pfleiderer (1839–1908). German Protestant theologian. A prolific writer, his contributions included work on the history of early Christianity. He was a vigorous

defender of the non-miraculous origin of Christianity.

136. Emil Schürer (1844-1917). German Protestant theologian, a representative of the moderate historical and critical school. His work contributed to an understanding of the Jewish context of early Christianity.

137. François Duine notes that the *Revue* began with a modest number of about 90 subscribers. When it ceased publication in 1907 that had grown to nearly 250, mostly ecclesiastics. *Souvenirs et observations*, 251.

138. Paul Lejay (1861-1920). Classical and patristic scholar. Lejay held the position of professor of Latin philology at the Institut catholique in Paris. In addition to his involvement with the *Revue d'histoire et de littérature religieuses*, he became associate editor of the *Revue de philologie de littérature et d'histoire ancienne* in 1911. He also collaborated in editing *Textes et documents pour l'étude historique du christianisme* (20 vols. 1904-1916).

139. Joseph Turmel, "Histoire de l'angélologie des temps apostoliques à la fin du Ve siècle," *Revue d'histoire et de littérature religieuses* 3 (1898): 289-308; 407-34; 533-52; "L'angélologie depuis le faux Denys l'Aréopagite," Ibid. 4 (1899): 217-38; 289-309; 414-34; 537-62.

140. Armand Turpin (1829-1910). Ordained in 1853, in 1872 he became director of the major seminary at Rennes. He receives brief mention in *Souvenirs et observations de l'abbé Duine*, 48.

141. François Cardinal Richard (1819-1908). Ordained priest in 1884, named bishop of Bellay in 1871, then in 1875 became coadjutor of Mgr Guibert, Archbishop of Paris, succeeding him in 1886. See Maurice Clément, *Vie du Cardinal Richard* (Paris: De Gigord, éditeurs, 1924).

142. In his "L'Erreur capitale du Clergé français au XIXe siècle," *Revue du monde catholique* 137 (1899): 193-225. Fontaine criticized Turmel's interpretation of patristic texts bearing on salvation and eternal damnation. Turmel replied with a note published in the same review 138 (1899): 209-11, to which was appended further observations by Fontaine (pp. 212-18). Turmel continued the exchange with "L'éternité des peines et les miséricordieux" in *Revue du monde catholique* 139 (1899): 226-34, which elicited a reply by Fontaine (pp. 234-44). Turmel responded (140 [1899]: 144-57) and Fontaine wrote "Dernière réplique à M. l'abbé Turmel. Les fantasies d'un érudite et l'orthodoxie catholique sur l'éternité des peines de l'enfer" (pp. 157-80). The review carried a letter by Turmel (140 [1899]: 610-15, prefaced by a short note from Fontaine essentially challenging him with the obligation to subscribe to the faith as defined by the Church and considering the controversy closed from his side. See C. J. T. Talar, "The Author of Evil: The Devil in the Patristic Scholarship of Joseph Turmel," *The Downside Review* 127 (2009): 279-91.

143. Joseph Turmel, "L'eschatologie à la fin du IVe siècle": 1. "L'eschatologie origéniste": 97-127; 2. "La doctrine du salut de tous les chrétiens": 200-32; 3. "Problèmes et solutions": 289-321.

144. Joseph Turmel, *L'eschatologie à la fin du IVe siècle* (Macon: Protat frères, imprimeurs, 1900).

145. Mgr Mignot. See note 77 *supra*.

Editor's Notes

146. Louis Duchesne (1843-1922). French historian whose critical work evoked controversy while he taught at the Paris Institut catholique. In 1895 he was appointed director of the École française de Rome. His 3 volume *Histoire ancienne de l'Église* (1906, 1907, 1910) was placed on the Index. On Duchesne see Brigitte Waché, *Monseigneur Louis Duchesne (1843-1922)* (Rome: École française de Rome, 1992) and *Monseigneur Duchesne et son temps* (Rome: École française de Rome, 1975).

147. Guillaume-René Meignan (1817-1896). Named bishop of Châlons-sur-Marne in 1864, in 1882 he was transferred to the see of Arras, then to the archdiocese of Toulouse in 1884. He was created a cardinal by Leo XIII in 1893. Adopting a posture of "orthodox liberalism," he wrote on contemporary problems, especially those bearing upon the bible.

148. Marcel Hébert (1851-1916). A representative of philosophical Modernism, Hébert advocated a religious symbolism that denied personality in God. Suspended for the ideas he put forth in *Souvenirs d'Assise* (1899), he eventually left the Church in 1903. See Albert Houtin, *Un prêtre symboliste. Marcel Hébert (1851-1916)* (Paris: F. Rieder, 1925) and *The Philosopher as Modernist: Selected Writings of Marcel Hébert*.

149. Alexis Armand Charost (1860-1930). Ordained priest in 1883, he served as Episcopal secretary, then vicar general at Rennes before being appointed auxiliary bishop of Cambrai in May of 1913 and then bishop of Lille in November of that year. In 1920 he became co-adjutor of Mgr Dubourg at Rennes, succeeding him in 1921. He was named cardinal in 1922. A royalist at heart, the condemnation of Action Française placed him in a delicate position.

150. Under Denys Lenain, Turmel published "Notes d'histoire de la théologie" I. Problème littéraire in *Revue d'histoire et de littérature religieuses* 5 (1900): 552-62 and II. Problème doctrinal in the same journal 6 (1900): 530-36. As Goulvan Lezurec he published "A propos de la Rédemption. Les origines et la doctrine," *La Justice sociale. Journal des Intérêts démocratiques* 9 (1901): 1-2.

151. Joseph Bricout (1867-1930). Director of the *Revue du clergé français* as successor to Lucien Lacoix, to which he contributed numerous articles.

152. Louis D'Eynac Thomassin (1619-1695). Theologian, historian and canonist. He stands with Denis Pétau as one of the masters of positive theology.

153. Joseph Turmel, "Quelques 'hommes éminents de l'Église de France" I. Pétau, *Revue du clergé français* 29 (1902): 161-80. Its sequel appeared the following January, pp. 372-88.

154. Articles on Mabillon appeared in the *Revue du clergé français* 30 (1902): 468-92 and 617-33 under the title "Quelques 'hommes illustres de l'Église.'" On Thomassin: "Quelques 'hommes éminents de l'Église de France,'" *Revue du clergé français* 31 (1902): 561-85. Lastly, Joseph Turmel, "Bossuet," *Revue du clergé français* 37 (1904): 359-89; "Bossuet: Ses luttes pour defender la pureté de la foi" Ibid. 38 (1904): 337-83; "Bossuet: Son administration épiscopale, sa mort, publications de ses oeuves," Ibid., 39 (1904): 449-71.

155. Jean-Vincent Bainvel (1858-1937). Jesuit, ordained in 1889; in 1900 he became professor of fundamental theology at the Institut catholique de Paris and Dean of its theological faculty.

156. Henri Louis Odelin (1846–1939). Ordained to the priesthood in 1875, he became vicar general in 1892.

157. Paul Pisani (1852–1933). Professor of ecclesiastical history at the Paris Institut catholique (1889–1898) and member of the archdiocesan doctrinal council of vigilance.

158. Auguste Boudinhon (1858–1941). Professor of canon law at the Paris Institut catholique (1884–1916), he directed the *Canoniste contemporain* for twenty-five years.

159. Hippolyte Hemmer (1864–1945). With Paul Lejay, he directed the *Textes et documents pour l'étude historique du christianisme*. Pastor of la Trinité at Paris.

160. In 1906, in the midst of the controversy over the separation law in France, a member of the nunciature staff, Montagnini, was expelled from the country. His papers were confiscated and some were published, providing damaging evidence of the Holy See's interference in French internal politics.

161. Councils of Vigilance were mandated by the encyclical *Pascendi dominici gregis*, issued by Pope Pius X in 1907, as part of the measures designed to combat Modernism.

162. E. Vacandard, "La confession dans l'Église latine du Ve au XIIIe siècle," *Revue du clergé français* (15 October 1905): 339–72 and "Confession (Du concile de Latran au concile de Trente)," *Dictionnaire de théologie catholique* 3: col. 838–94. Elphèse Vacandard (1849–1927). A priest of the diocese of Rodez, Vacandard as a critical historian was a regular contributor to the *Revue du clergé français* and the *Revue apologétique*.

163. Constantin Patrizi (1798–1876). He was created cardinal *in pectore* in 1834 and named publicly in 1836. An Ultramontane, and a champion of the temporal power of the papacy and of the Syllabus of 1864, he held several curial positions over the course of his career.

164. Giovanni Genocchi (1860–1926). Consultor of the Biblical Commission in 1903, he played a moderating role in the controversies raised by critical biblical scholarship. He drew criticism from anti-Modernists and lost his position as professor of biblical exegesis at the Apollinaire in Rome, subsequently holding several diplomatic posts. See Francesco Turvasi, *Giovanni Genocchi e la controversia modernista* (Rome: Edizioni di Storia e Letteratura, 1974).

165. Sylvan Leblanc. Pseudonym of Henri Bremond (1865–1933) under which he published *Un clerc qui n'a pas trahi. Alfred Loisy d'après ses Mémoires* (1931). Reprinted as *Une oeuvre clandestine d'Henri Bremond*, edited by Émile Poulat. (Rome: Edizioni di Storia e Letteratura, 1972). Loisy's loss of dogmatic faith is acknowledged, but it is argued that he retained a mystical faith. See Harvey Hill, "In Defense of Loisy's Mysticism: Bremond's Modernist Confession" in Harvey Hill, Louis-Pierre Sardella and C. J. T. Talar, *By Those Who Knew Them: Modernists Left, Right and Center* (Washington, D.C.: Catholic University of America Press, 2008), 122–49.

166. More familiarly, *Providentissimus Deus*, dated November 18, 1893.

167. Pierre Batiffol (1861–1929). Theologian, Church historian. In 1898 he was named rector of the Institut catholique at Toulouse. Though opposed to Modernism, his book on the Eucharist was placed on the Index and he resigned his rectorship in 1907. On Batiffol see Jean Rivière, *Mgr Pierre Batiffol* (Paris: Librairie Lecoffre, 1929) and Pierre Fernessole, *Témoins de la pensée catholique en France sous le IIIe république*. (Paris:

Editor's Notes

Beauchesne et ses fils, 1940), 187–280.

168. Marie-Joseph Lagrange (1855–1938). Dominican biblical scholar. He founded the École Biblique at Jerusalem in 1890 and in 1892 launched the *Revue biblique*. Although Lagrange was more moderate in his use of historical-critical method than Loisy, he experienced difficulties with ecclesiastical authorities over his work. On Lagrange, see Bernard Montagnes, *Le père Lagrange (1855–1938). L'exégèse catholique dans la crise moderniste* (Paris: Cerf, 1995). English Translation *The Story of Father Marie-Joseph Lagrange. Founder of Modern Biblical Study*. Translated by Benedict Viviano. (New York: Paulist Press, 2006). An expanded version of the French biography was published as *Marie-Joseph Lagrange. Une biographie critique* (Paris: Cerf, 2004).

169. François Désiré Mathieu (1839–1908). Consecrated bishop of Angers in 1893, he was later transferred to the Archdiocese of Toulouse in 1896. He was created a cardinal in 1899.

170. Paul-Louis Couchoud (1879–1959). Trained as a medical doctor, he developed an interest in exegesis, becoming an advocate of the non-historicity of Jesus. He founded with Éditions Rieder the collection "Christianisme" to which Houtin, Loisy, Turmel (under pseudonyms and later under his his own name) and Sartiaux contributed.

171. Félix Sartiaux (1876–1944). Former student of Marcel Hébert at the École Fénelon who did not find the latter's symbolist position persuasive and lost faith in Christianity. Sartiaux was Houtin's literary executor and Turmel's biographer, publishing *Joseph Turmel prêtre, historien des dogmes* (1931).

172. Jean Rivière (1878–1946). A student of Pierre Batiffol and Eugène Portalié at Toulouse, Rivière became a professor in the Catholic Faculty of Theology at Strasbourg. His numerous publications contributed to historical theology.

173. Louis Saltet (1878–1952). Priest of the diocese of Rodez, he was from 1898 to 1946 professor of ecclesiastical history at the Faculté de théologie of the Toulouse Institut catholique. An implacable critic, he unmasked literary and historical frauds. In the second volume of the autobiography Turmel will mention the controversy raised by Saltet over the scapular of Mount Carmel and will dwell at length on Saltet's pursuit of two of Turmel's pseudonymous identities, Dupin and Herzog.

174. Ordained in 1925, Verdin eventually left the priesthood and resided in Paris where he gained a reputation as a swindler and profiteer.

175. English Translation *Recollections of My Youth*. Translated by C. B. Pitman (London: Chapman and Hall, 1892).

176. Joseph Turmel, *Histoire des dogmes* 6 vols. (Paris: Rieder, 1931–1936).

177. Alfred Loisy, *La naissance de christianisme* (Paris: Émile Nourry, 1933). English Translation *The Birth of the Christian Religion & The Origins of the New Testament*, translated by L. P. Jacks. (New Hyde Park, New York: University Books, 1962).

178. Jules Lebreton (1873–1956). Jesuit theologian and Church historian. For many years he was professor in the Faculty of Theology at the Paris Institut catholique. In 1910, with his fellow Jesuit Léonce de Grandmaison, he founded the *Recherches de Science religieuse*. A frequent contributor to *Études*, he wrote extensively on the subject of Christian origins. The article referenced by Turmel is Lebreton's "La Naissance du christianisme

d'après M. Loisy," *Études* 218 (January–March 1934): 622–31. In *La Naissance du christianisme* (1933) Loisy made reference to H. Delafosse (at this point known to be one of Turmel's pseudonyms and identified as such), "Nouvel examen des Lettres d'Ignace d'Antioche," *Revue d'histoire et de littérature religieuses* n.s. 8 (1922): 303–37, 477–533 and *Lettres d'Ignace d'Antioche* (Paris: Rieder, 1927) which Turmel published under the same pseudonym.

179. Paul Doncoeur (1880–1961), "L' 'Augustin' de M. J. Malègue," *Études* 218 (January–March 1934): 95–102. Doncoeur entered the Society of Jesus in 1898. After service as a chaplain in the Great War he was assigned to the Jesuit review.

180. Ferdinand Cavallera (1875–1954) Jesuit theologian, Eugène Portalié's successor at the Institut catholique de Toulouse. The entry Turmel refers to is "Eugène Portalié" in vol. 12 of the *Dictionnaire de théologie catholique*, col. 2590–93. On Cavallera see E. Boularand, "In Memoriam, Le Père Ferdinand Cavallera," *Bulletin de littérature ecclésiastique* 55 (1954): 3–20.

181. Eugène Portalié (1852–1909) held the chair of positive theology at the Toulouse Institut catholique where he was a close collaborator of Mgr Batiffol. In addition to his opposition to Turmel's pseudonymous work, he critiqued Loisy, Edouard Le Roy and George Tyrrell. On Portalié see "Notice sur M. Eugène Portalié," *Bulletin de littérature ecclésiastique* 10 (1909): ix–xix.

182. Auguste-René-Marie Dubourg (1842–1921). Ordained priest in 1866, he became bishop of Moulins in 1893 and archbishop of Rennes in 1906. In 1916 he was elevated to the cardinalate by Benedict XV. At Rennes his administration of the archdiocese dealt with the organizational challenges posed by the Law of Separation of 1905.

183. Louis Saltet, "Le service scientifique de la doctrine d'après S.S. Pie XI et à l'Institut Catholique," *Bulletin de littérature ecclésiastique* 32 (1931): 228–46.

184. Antoine Dupin, "Les origines des controverses trinitaires," "La Trinité et la théologie des hypostes dans les trois premiers siècles," and "La Trinité dans l'école modaliste jusqu'à la fin du troisième siècle," *Revue d'histoire et de littérature religieuses* 11 (1906): 219–31, 353–65, and 515–32 respectively. Guillaume Herzog, "La conception virginale du Christ," "La virginité de Marie après l'enfantement," and "La sainte Vierge dans l'histoire," *Revue d'histoire et de littérature religieuses* 12 (1907): 118–33; 320–40; 483–607. Published separately as *La sainte Vierge dans l'histoire* (Paris: Émile Nourry, 1908).

185. Pierre-Louis Péchenard (1842–1920). Priest of the diocese of Reims, he was d'Hulst's successor as rector of the Institut catholique de Paris (1896–1907) before becoming bishop of Soissons in 1907.

186. Alfred Baudrillart (1859–1942). Professor (1894–1907), then rector of the Paris Institut catholique. In addition to his scholarly work he served as diplomatic representative of the Holy See.

187. Léonce de Grandmaison (1868–1927). Jesuit theologian, apologist who opposed Modernism. In 1904 he became editor of *Études*. His biography, *Le Père Léonce de Grandmaison* (1932) was written by Jules Lebreton.

188. Alfred Loisy, *Quelques lettres sur des questions actuelles et sur des événements récents* (Ceffonds: chez l'auteur, 1908).

Editor's Notes

189. Turmel may be referring to Joachim Troncy's *Réfutation de la christologie de M. Albert Réville*, published a decade earlier (1875) than he recalls here.

190. Jacques Ginoulhiac (1806–1875). French bishop and theologian. He became bishop of Grenoble (1852–1870) then archbishop of Lyons in 1870. His reputation as a theologian rests primarily on his *Histoire du dogme catholique pendant les trois premiers siècles* (2 vols. 1852).

191. Henri Leclercq (1869–1945). Leclercq entered Solesmes in 1893 and was ordained to the priesthood in 1898. With Dom Fernand Cabrol (1855–1937) he inaugurated the collection *Monumenta Ecclesiae Liturgica* and collaborated with Cabrol in the *Dictionnaire d'Archéologie chrétienne et Liturgie*. He translated the first eight volumes of Héfélé's *Histoire des conciles* 15 vols. (1907–1921).

192. Pierre-Julien Hamard (1847–1914). Priest of the Oratory of Rennes, he contributed to the literature on the antiquity of humans within the limits of biblical chronology. Hamard is mentioned at several points in *Souvenirs et observations de l'abbé François Duine*.

193. Liberius was pope from 352 to 366. Caught up in the controversies following upon the Council of Nicea, he experienced political pressure to condemn Athanasius. Whether or not Liberius himself subscribed to a formula inadequate to the faith is dependent in part on the testimony of four letters attributed to Liberius. Among modern historians Saltet and Batiffol argued that they were forgeries; others however accept them as genuine compositions of Liberius.

194. Lord I believe, help my unbelief.

195. Louis Duchesne, "Libère et Fortunatien," *Mélanges de l'École Française de Rome* 28 (1908): 31–78. Published separately (Rome: Impr. de P. Cuggiani, 1908).

196. Louis-Eugène Venard (1874–1945). As a chronicler of developments in biblical scholarship in the *Revue du clergé français* (1901–1922) Venard adopted a moderate position, pointing to weaknesses in conservative exegesis, acknowledging the value of historical critical studies without wishing to follow its more liberal tendencies.

197. The reference is to a review of Philippe-Hector Dunand's *Histoire complète de Jeanne d'Arc* which appeared in *L'Université catholique* of February 15, 1908 and is summarized and commented on in the Chronique.

198. Adhémar d'Alès (1861–1938). Jesuit theologian, patrologist, an active collaborator of *Études* and later in *Recherches de science religeuse*. He taught at the Paris Institut catholique from 1907–1934.

199. Joseph Turmel, "La sainte Vierge dans l'histoire," *Revue du clergé français* 53 (1908): 661–70.

200. *Bulletin de littérature ecclésiastique* 9 (1908): 73–89. Reprinted in Louis Saltet, *La Question Herzog-Dupin* (Paris: P. Lethielleux, 1908), 17–44.

201. "Guillaume Herzog et Antoine Dupin. Deux pseudonymes d'un plagiaire," *Bulletin de littérature ecclésiastique* 9 (1908): 109–30. Reprinted in Saltet, *La Question Herzog-Dupin*, 51–87.

202. Louis Saltet, "Notes et critiques," *Bulletin de littérature ecclésiastique* 9 (1908): 169–72.

203. As a result of a book that treated the development of the eucharist that was delated to the Index, Batiffol had lost his position as rector of the Toulouse Institut catholique.

204. Jean Guibert (1857–1914). Sulpician, historian and theologian. He served as rector from 1897 until his retirement for reasons of health in 1912.

205. Louis Saltet, "Monseigneur Batiffol," *Bulletin de littérature ecclésiastique* 30 (1929): 126–41. This is the third in a series of articles. The previous two appeared in the *Bulletin de littérature ecclésiastique* 30 (1929): 7–18 and 49–62.

206. Louis Saltet, "Un roman inexcusable: Monseigneur Batiffol et l'abbé Turmel par M. Félix Sartiaux," *Bulletin de littérature ecclésiastique* 32 (1931): 19–36. Saltet is critiquing Sartiaux's "Une grande figure d'excommunié," *Europe* (Jan. 15, 1931): 129–31.

207. "Casserole" is argot for "snitch."

208. The reference is to articles entitled "Que penser du Sillon?" which appeared initially in *La Croix*, then were reprinted in *Les Questions actuelles*.

209. "Notes et critiques," *Bulletin de littérature ecclésiastique* 9 (1908): 169–72.

210. Ibid.

211. "Solution de l'incident Turmel," *Revue pratique d'apologétique* 6 (1908): 371 and "Doctrine—VI," *L'Ami du clergé*: 583–86.

212. Louis Saltet, "Le suite des pseudonymes de M. J. Turmel," *Bulletin de littérature ecclésiastique* 30 (1929): 104–25. This follows a previous article of the same title on pp. 83–90.

213. Alfred Baudrillart, "La question Herzog-Dupin," *Revue pratique d'apologétique* 6 (1908): 801–2. Saltet's book was the occasion for the piece.

214. "Sommation et observations de M. l'abbé Turmel," *Études* 118 (January–March 1909): 438–46.

215. Fernand Portal (1855–1926) worked for the rapprochement of the Roman and Anglican Churches, launching the *Revue anglo-romaine* in 1895, which ceased publication after Leo XIII's declaration of the invalidity of Anglican orders in 1896. In 1925–1926 he participated in the "Malines Conversations" with Cardinal Mercier and Lord Halifax.

216. Roman doctor, German ass.

217. "Un roman inexcusable."

218. Louis Saltet, "Monseigneur Batiffol" II, *Bulletin de littérature ecclésiastique* 30 (1929): 49–62. The extract referred to reads: "It was the time at which the publication of L'Évangile et l'Église ignited the Modernist controversies. Had we already foreseen this hour as early as in 1900! Père Portalié and I threw ourselves into the controversy, in which we very deliberately involved the authority of our Institut, when so many others still hesitated to follow us, and others did not hesitate to criticize us. M. Franon quickly allied himself with us and took on the task of unmasking Tyrrell. M. Saltet subsequently set about unmasking Turmel. Père Lagrange and Père de Grandmaison, along with others lent us their support. These were four years of alert and combat for which I retain an unforgettable feeling." (p. 61)

219. Joseph Turmel, *Histoire du dogme de la papauté des origines à la fin du quatrième*

Editor's Notes

siècle (Paris: Alphonse Picard et fils, 1908).

220. Louis Duchesne, *Histoire ancienne de l'Église* 3 vols. (Paris: A. Fontenmoing, 1906-1910). Eng. trans. *The Early History of the Church* 3 vols. (London: John Murray, 1909-1924).

221. André Lagarde, "La doctrine pénitentielle de saint Augustin," *Revue d'histoire et de littérature religieuses* n.s. 7 (1921): 251-57.

222. "'La Question Herzog-Dupin' et la critique catholique," *Études* 116 (July-September 1908): 335-59 (August 5); 506-38 (August 20); 605-38 (September 5); 763-94 (September 20).

223. Yves de la Brière (1877-1941) entered the Society of Jesus in 1894 and was assigned to the staff of Études in 1909.

224. Yves de la Brière, "Saint Cyprien et la papauté d'après un ouvrage récent," *Études* 117 (1908): 339-56. The "recent work" is Turmel's *Histoire de la papauté: des origines à la fin du quatrième siècle* (1908).

225. Joseph Tixeront (1851-1925). French theologian, patrologist. A student of Louis Duchesne, he spent his teaching career at the University of Lyons. His *Histoire des dogmes dans l'antiquité chrétienne* (3 vols.) was published over 1906-1912.

226. Turmel is referring here to an interpretive issue that relates to Rom 5:12, specifically the translation of the Greek *eph'hō*. Augustine understood this to mean "in whom" (*in quo*), that is, in Adam. An alternative way of understanding the Greek would be "because, inasmuch as"—with different implications for a theology of original sin. See Henri Blocher, *Original Sin: Illuminating the Riddle* (Grand Rapids, Mich.: William B. Eerdmans Publishing Company, 1997), 65-76.

227. Joseph Turmel, *Saint Jérôme* (Paris: Librairie Bloud, 1906).

228. Joseph Turmel, *Tertullien* (Paris: Librairie Bloud, 1904).

229. J. Turmel, *La descente du Christ aux enfers* (Paris: Librairie Bloud, 1905).

230. François Pouët (1873-1923). Ordained in 1896, he held various positions in the archdiocese of Rennes, including professor of Sacred Scripture at the major seminary.

231. Louis Saltet, "La suite des pseudonymes de M. J. Turmel" II.

232. Louis Saltert, "L'oeuvre théologique pseudonyme de M. l'abbé Turmel," *Bulletin de littérature ecclésiastique* 30 (1929): 165-82.

233. The novelist Theophile Gautier published *Capitaine Fracasse* in 1863. Its protagonist is a member of a theatrical troupe which journeys to Paris.

234. One was sentenced to two years in prison, another to eight and the third to fifteen years of hard labor.

235. Jules Croulbois, "La religion de Chateaubriand," *Revue d'histoire et de littérature religieuses* 6 (1901): 1-12 and "L'intrigue romaine de la Compagnie de Saint-Sacrement," Ibid., 9 (1904): 519-64.

236. The letter is dated December 10, 1928. Reproduced in "Un roman inexcusable de M. Félix Sartiaux," pp. 33-35.

237. Louis Coulange, *La messe* (Paris: Rieder, 1927). English translation *The Evolution of the Mass*. Trans. C.B. Bonner (London: Watts & Co., 1930).

238. Robert Lawson, "L'Eucharistie dans saint Augustin," *Revue d'histoire et de littérature religieuses* n.s. 6 (1920): 99–152, 472–525.

239. Jean Rivière, "La rédemption chez saint Augustin," *Revue des sciences religieuses* 7 (1927): 429–51. At the outset of the article Rivière associates Hippolyte Gallerand's "La rédemption dans saint Augustin," *Revue d'histoire et de littérature religieuses* n.s. 8 (1922): 38–77 with the work of "G. Herzog and A. Dupin whom all of our readers no doubt have forgotten" and in a note points out coincidences with several works published under Turmel's name.

240. "Le dogme de la rédemption au début du moyen-age," *Revue des sciences religieuses* 11 (1931): 566–77.

241. As Gallerand. Jean Rivière, "Le dogme de la rédemption après saint Augustin: I. La rédemption chez Léon le grand," *Revue des sciences religieuses* 9 (1929): 11–42. Its sequel, on pp. 153–87, also mentions Gallerand.

242. Jean Rivière, *Le dogme de la rédemption. Essai d'étude historique* (Paris: Librairie Victor Lecoffre, 1905).

243. I. de Récalde, *La cause du Vénérable Bellarmin. L'autobiographie—Votum de Passionei—Lettre à Clément VIII* (Paris: Librairie moderne, 1923).

244. Louis Coulange, *Catéchisme pour adultes* I. *Les dogmes* (Paris: Rieder, 1929); *Catéchisme pour adultes* II. *Les institutions* (Paris: Rieder, 1930). English translation Louis Coulange, *Religious Inventions and Frauds* (Melbourne: Thomas C. Lothian Proprietary Limited, 1936).

245. Rafael Merry Del Val (1865–1930). Cardinal, papal Secretary of State (1903–1914) during the pontificate of Pius X.

246. Hippolyte de Rome, *Philosophumena, ou, Réfutation de toutes des hérésies*, traduction par André Siouville (Paris: Rieder, 1928). Émile Poulat identifies Siouville as Abbé Auguste Lelong (1855–1933) who had earlier in 1910 published two volumes on the Apostolic Fathers in the Hemmer-Lejay collection. Émile Poulat, *Histoire, dogme et critique dans la crise moderniste*, 660, 657.

247. Subsequently published as Joseph Turmel, *Le journal de Jean Burchard, évêque et cérémoniaire au Vatican* (Paris: Rieder, 1932). Johann Burchard (1450–1506). Appointed Master of Ceremonies in 1483, he held that post under successive popes until his death. In his *Liber Notarum* he left an official record of the more significant papal ceremonies in which he was involved.

248. Action Française, a league established to combat every republican regime and re-establish the monarchy, exercised considerable intellectual influence among Catholics. See Eugen J. Weber, *Action Française* (Stanford: Stanford University Press, 1962).

249. Actually entitled "Suite du roman de M. F. Sartiaux sur M. l'abbé Turmel," *Bulletin de littérature ecclésiastique* 32 (1931): 97–100.

250. *Defensio Declarationis Cleri Gallicani de Ecclesiae potestate anni MDCLXXXII*, *Oeuvres complètes de Bossuet* vol. 10: 3–340.

Editor's Notes

251. *Mirari Vos*, Encyclical of Pope Gregory XVI on Liberalism and Religious Indifferentism, August 15, 1832.

252. Salomon Reinach (1858–1932). French classical scholar, archaeologist and historian. His *Orpheus, histoire générale des religions* (1909) evoked controversy. Its hostility to Christianity brought replies from Catholic scholars, Pierre Batiffol and Marie-Joseph Lagrange among them.

253. *Die Religion in Geschichte und Gegenwart.*

254. See note 115 *supra*.

255. Clément Marc (1831-1887), *Institutiones Morales Alphonsianae seu Doctoris Ecclesiae S. AlphonsiMariae de Ligornio, Doctrina Morales, ad usum scholarum accomodata* (Roma: Ph. Cuggiani, 1896).

Bibliography of Works Published Under Pseudonym

For a comprehensive list of Turmel's publications see Karl-Peter Gertz, Joseph Turmel (1859–1943). *Ein theogiegeschichtlicher Beitrag zum Problem der Geschichtlichkeit der Dogmen* (Frankfurt: Peter Lang, 1975), 310–339

ARTICLES

In *La Justice sociale*

"A propos de la Rédemption," 13 July 1901 (Goulven Lézuec)

In *Revue d'histoire et de littérature religieuses* 1st series (1898–1907)

"Notes d'histoire de la théologie," 1900: 552–62 (Denys Lenain)
"Esssais et notices: Mélanges du Professeur Funk," 1901: 454–65 (Denys Lenain)
"Histoire de la théologie," 1901: 531–36 (Denys Lenain)
"Les origines des controverses trinitaires," 1906: 219–31 (Antoine Dupin)
"La Trinité et la théologie des hypostases dans les trois premiers siècles," 1906: 353–65 (Antoine Dupin)
"La Trinité dans l'école modaliste jusqu'à la fin du IIIe siècle," 1906: 515–32 (Antoine Dupin)
"La conception virginale du Christ," 1907: 118–33 (Guillaume Herzog)

In *Revue d'histoire et de littérature religieuses* 2e series (1910–1914, 1920–1922)

"L'idée messianique," 1910: 131–43 (Louis Coulange)

Bibliography of Works Published Under Pseudonym

"La discipline pénitentielle dans les écrits de saint Paul," 1910: 241–51 (Alexis Vanbeck)
"Jésus prédicateur du royaume," 1910: 313–42 (Louis Coulange)
"La pénitence dans les écrits des premières générations chrétiennes," 1910: 436–65 (Alexis Vanbeck)
"Le manuel du confesseur au XIe siècle," 1910: 542–50 (André Lagarde)
"Chroniques bibliographiques," 1910: 586–96 (Robert Lawson)
"La résurrection de Jésus," 1911: 145–59 (Louis Coulange)
"La pénitence dans le Pasteur d'Hermas, 1911: 389–403 (Alexis Vanbeck)
"Bernold de Constance," 1911: 464–74 (Armand Dulac)
"Le retour du Christ," 1911: 544–56 (Louis Coulange)
"Le pape saint Grégoire a-t-il connu la confession?" 1912: 160–83 (André Lagarde)
"Bonizo: le *Libellus de Sacramentis* et le *Decretum*," 1912: 230–39 (Armand Dulac)
"La pénitence dans Tertullien," 1912: 350–69 (Alexis Vanbeck)
"La légende de Jésus," 1912: 455–82 (Louis Coulange)
"La pénitence dans Origène," 1912: 544–57; 1913: 115–29 (Alexis Vanbeck)
"Le Christ de Paul," 1913: 20–44 (Louis Coulange)
"Saint Augustin a-t-il connu la confession?" 1913: 226–60 (André Lagarde)
"Le Christ alexandrin," 1913: 327–51 (Louis Coulange)
"La pénitence dans saint Cyprien," 1913: 422–42 (Alexis Vanbeck)
"Saint Jean Chrysostome a-t-il connu la confession?" 1913: 540–59; 1914: 26–62 (André Lagarde)
"L'homélie dite de Léon IV," 1914: 117–37 (Robert Lawson)
"Le Christ Dieu," 1914: 227–51 (Louis Coulange)
"Les origines de la confession," 1914: 332–51 (André Lagarde)
"L'Eucharistie dans saint Augustin," 1920: 99–152; 472–525 (Robert Lawson)
"La discipline pénitentielle en Orient de Denys de Corinthe à Athanase," 1920: 181–229 (Alexis Vanbeck)
"Le symbole de Nicée," 1920: 350–72 (Louis Coulange)
"Notes sur l'origine de l'homélie clémentine, 1920: 276–79 (Henri Delafosse)
"Note sur deux textes d'Amalaire relatifs à la consécration de l'Eucharistie," 1920: 415–18 (Armand Dulac)
"Confessions et absolutions données par écrit," 1921: 58–75 (André Michel)
"Quelques textes de Walafrid Strabon relatifs à l'Eucharistie," 1921: 126–28 (Armand Dulac)
"Le cardinal Billot et le dogme du péché originel," 1921: 181–212 (Edmond Perrin)
"La discipline pénitentielle de saint Augustin," 1921: 251–57 (André Lagarde)
"Le cardinal Billot et le sort des infidèles défunts," 1921: 349–417 (Edmond Perrin)
"Réaction contre le consubstantiel," 1921: 481–512 (Louis Coulange)
"La rédemption dans saint Augustin," 1922: 38–77 (Hippolyte Gallerand)
"La doctrine pénitentielle du pape Grégoire," 1922: 118–26 (André Lagarde)
"Métamorphose du le consubstantiel," 1922: 169–214 (Louis Coulange)
"Nouvel examen des lettres d'Ignace d'Antioche," 1922: 303–37; 477–533 (Henri Delafosse)
"Le cardinal Billot et la prophétie de la parousie," 1922: 370–93 (Edmond Perrin)

In *Revue d'histoire des religions*

"Rapports de Matthieu et de Luc," 1924: 1–38 (Henri Delafosse)

Bibliography of Works Published Under Pseudonym

"Nouvel examen des épîtres pauliniennes," 1924: 193–224 (Henri Delafosse)
"La rédemption dans l'Église latine d'Augustin à Anselme," 1925: 35–76 (Hippolyte Gallerand)
"La rédemption dans les écrits d'Anselme et d'Abélard," 1925: 212–41 (Hippolyte Gallerand)
"La pénitence dans les Églises d'Italie au cours des IVe et Ve siècles," 1925: 108–47 (André Lagarde)
Compte-rendu de: A. von Harnack, *Marcion*, 1925: 169–79 (Henri Delafosse)
Compte-rendu de: V. Normand, *La Confession*, 1926: 322–24 (André Lgarde)
"Les élections épiscopales dans l'Église latine au moyen âge, 1926: 76–113 (Armand Dulac)
Compte-rendu de: M. Goguel, *Introduction au Nouveau Testament*, 1927: 87–88 (Henri Delafosse)
Compte-rendu de: Van den Bergh, *La littérature chrétienne primitive*, 1927: 88–89 (Henri Delafosse)
"La lettre de Clément Romain aux Corinthiens." 1928: 53–89 (Henri Delafosse)
Compte-rendu de: A. Siouville, *Philosophumena d'Hippolyte*, 1928: 144–48 (Henri Delafosse)

In *Impartial français*

"Catéchisme pour adultes," 50 articles in 234 (February 22, 1927) to 283 (January 31, 1928) (Paul Letourneur)
"Saint Bernard," 263 (September 13, 1927) (Edmond Perrin)
"Noël," 278 (December 27, 1927) (Armand Dulac)

WORKS

Le dogme de la Trinité dans les trois premiers siècles (Paris: Émile Nourry, 1907) (Antoine Dupin)
La Sainte Vierge dans l'histoire (Paris: Èmile Nourry, 1908) (Guillaime Herzog)
The Latin Church in the Middle Ages (New York: Scribner, 1915) (André Lagarde)
Le Quatrième Évangile (Paris: Rieder, 1915) (Henri Delafosse)
La Vierge Marie (Paris: Rieder, 1925) (Louis Coulange)
Les écrits de saint Paul. I. L'épître aux Romains (Paris: Rieder, 1926) (Henri Delafosse)
Les écrits de saint Paul. II. La première épître aux Corinthiens (Paris: Rieder, 1926) (Henri Delafosse)
Les écrits de saint Paul. III. La seconde épître aux Corinthiens, les épîtres aux Galates, aux Colossiens, aux Éphésiens, à Philémon (Paris: Rieder, 1927) (Henri Delafosse) [English translation, *The Second Epistle to the Corinthians, the Epistles to the Galatians, to the Colossians, to the Ephesians, and the Epistle to Philemon*, translated by C. Bradleigh Bonner, (London Watts & Co., 1937). Under Henri Delafosse appears (Joseph Turmel)]
Les écrits de saint Paul. IV. L'épître aux Philippiens, les épîtres aux Thessaloniciens, les épîtres pastorales, l'épître aux Hébreux (Paris: Rieder, 1928) (Henri Delafosse)

Bibliography of Works Published Under Pseudonym

La Messe (Paris: Rieder, 1927) (Louis Coulange) [English translation, *The Evolution of the Mass*, translated by C. Bradlaugh Bonner, (London: Watts & Co., 1930)]

Les lettres d'Ignace d'Antioche New translation with an introduction and notes (Paris: Rieder, 1927) (Henri Delafosse)

Saint Thomas d'Aquin, Somme théologique New translation with an introduction and notes *I. Dieu, II. Dieu en trois personnes, la création, les anges, les six jours* (Paris: Rieder, 1927, 1929) (Edmond Perrin)

With Albert Houtin, *Courte histoire du célibat ecclésiastique* (Paris: Rieder, 1929) (Armand Dulac)

Catéchisme pour adultes 2 vols. *I. Les dogmes, II., Les institutions* (Paris: Rieder, 1929, 1930) (Louis Coulange) [English translation, *Religious Inventions and Frauds* (Melbourne: Thomas C. Lothian, 1936)]

The Life of the Devil Translated by Stephen Haden Guest. (New York: Alfred A. Knopf, 1930) (Louis Coulange) [Later published under Turmel's own name as *Histoire du diable* (Paris: Rieder, 1931)]

Afterword*

Émile Poulat

IN THE UNITED STATES there has long existed a double tradition, little known in France, of French professors making a career—from Michel de Certeau to René Girard, for example—and of French studies being done in American universities, by scholars such as John Baldwin, the great specialist of Phillipe-Auguste, and Robert Paxton on Vichy France. Still, what distance from one culture to the next! The American translation of the autobiography of Joseph Turmel—a Breton priest having lost all Christian and even religious faith—will no doubt surprise an American society founded on the motto "In God We Trust" inscribed on its currency.

An extensive examination of the interest shown by North American university culture in the religious history of western Europe and most particularly for France would make a good research project, as would Liberal Protestantism and Catholic Modernism, the chapters of this history most of interest for it.

Along these lines, very different approaches have been utilized. The first has been the constitution, within the American Academy of Religion, of a working group, itself entitled Working Group on Roman Catholic Modernism, which did excellent work in the course of its annual sessions. A radical and politically engaged faction developed simultaneously, presenting itself as a "new theology," based on the paradoxical foundational theme of the "death of God" (Death of God Group).

Joseph Turmel had been dead for many years when they became aware of him and they did not seem to have been interested in him. It does not seem likely Turmel would have sympathized with them either,

---

* Translated by C. J. T. Talar and Elizabeth Emery.

Afterword

for a fundamental reason inviting reflection: they were and remained theologians; Turmel never deviated from his pure and simple desire to be an historian of Christian thought.

A century ago the "Modernist crisis" rudely shook the Roman Catholic Church in western Europe, particularly in France and Italy; 1907, the encyclical *Pascendi* of Pope Pius X; 1908, solemn excommunication of Alfred Loisy.

Strictly speaking, this crisis stemmed from the advent of a new biblical exegesis—characterized by its "historical-critical" method, by a considerable expansion in the field of religious studies, and by the resulting conflict with traditional theology, which was wedded to its scholastic form. In the broadest possible terms, it challenged everything conveyed by a Church confronted by modernity and its social agenda for a new post-Revolutionary society founded on the ruins of the Ancien Régime. We move here, if I may put it thus, from a restricted (or intellectual) modernism to a generalized (or social) modernism.

The United States, and more broadly the Americas, seem to have been little affected by such turmoil and controversy. American Catholics knew how to diffuse the proceedings against Americanism occurring under Leo XIII: the doctrinal proceedings brought against them were cut short, but without arresting the underlying historical process and which, if I am not mistaken, has not yet received the study it deserves. This is an example of a case of successful *acculturation*, seemingly without apparent drama and without great interest for what was happening in Europe.

My Sorbonne thesis, *Histoire, dogme et critique dans la crise moderniste* in 1962 ushered in a renewal of modernist studies, particularly in France and Italy. Unless I am mistaken, it did not attract the attention of American scholars, with the exception of several thoughtful and favorable reviews. A new wave began with the American Group on Roman Catholic Modernism in 1976. Its work has only confirmed the quasi absence of interest in and initiative toward these questions in the United States.

The autobiography of Joseph Turmel presented to the American public by Charles Talar falls within this intellectual orientation. It should interest the French and even the European public for everything it adds to this autobiography, including an exhaustive bibliography of Turmel's pseudonymous writings.

In Catholic Modernism, Turmel was an extreme and exceptional case, more consistent perhaps with a general study of *faith lived personally*, of its

Afterword

anxieties and its doubts until its loss, than with that of the Roman Catholic institution subjected to the historical turbulence of its time.

Loisy wanted to modernize the Church and, in particular, modify its intellectual regime. Turmel was at opposite ends: his sole idea was to fight against it and destroy it. He has explained himself: it remains for us to understand him.

Joseph Turmel, "priest, historian of dogma," according to the epitaph he drew up himself and which may be read on the crossless standing stone erected on his tomb by the Rennes Libre Pensée. And yet, he had been solemnly excommunicated by Rome in 1930. Moreover, since he lost his faith in 1886, at the age of 26, he had never stopped fighting the Church of his baptism. Today it is impossible to conceive of such an unusual case. It is often described as incomprehensible. "A monster," wrote one of his former students, contradicted by others who remained very connected to him. "My life as hircocerf," he confided in 1940 to his friend and biographer Félix Sartiaux.

A homebody, he never went far from Rennes where he was born on December 13, 1859 and where he died on February 5, 1943. There were only two exceptions: a period of studies—eighteen months—at Angers (1881 – 1882), a short stretch in Paris (1901) to deal with some difficulties. A tireless reader, only stopping to read in order to write, he composed "at one go" following his excommunication in 1931—a uniquely vengeful autobiography. It was published, with a few suppressions and improvements, by Éditions de l'Idée libre, in two volumes carrying the eloquent titles: *Comment j'ai donné congé aux dogmes* (1935) and *Comment l'Église romaine m'a donné congé* (1937).

Why with so radical an unbelief did he remain in the clergy and wear the soutane until his final day? He provides three reasons whose sincerity cannot be doubted: the sorrow and scandal his departure would have caused those around him. He thought of his mother and brother, of Abbé Gendron, his quasi father who had underwritten his education, and lastly of pious souls, people of modest condition who placed their confidence in him. He always sides with the little people whose religion managed to resist the grip of learned theology. But these reasons do not explain everything: he would not have remained if his ecclesiastical milieu had not resolved to protect him, little suspecting the trap would close around him. Turmel's story is something quite different from that of an undeceived priest who deems himself authorized to continue his ministry.

Afterword

He was born into a humble and poor family, the second of five surviving children. His parents, illiterate farmworkers, had become woodsellers. As a child he suffered from malnutrition. The parochial vicar, Abbé Gendron—who would end as dean of the cathedral chapter—became attached to him and took on his education. Turmel's intelligence and piety destined him for priesthood. At the major seminary, his love of books very quickly led to his appointment as librarian. At age 21, he received sub-diaconate and was sent to the Catholic Faculties at Angers where he had the future Cardinal Billot as a professor. The first shock to his faith came not from the teaching received, but because his professor of sacred Scripture lent him Gesenius's German commentary on Isaiah. Under the latter's pen, "the heavenly origin of the Bible was not denied, but ignored," while study of the text showed the composite character of the inspired book. Scholarly exegesis pulverized theological commentary.

Ordained a priest on June 3, 1882, with a dispensation for age, he was quickly named professor at the major seminary. He continued to work and accumulate notes, some thirty notebooks, until the day—March 18, 1886—the veil was torn: he no longer had faith, could no longer believe in everything the daily reading of his breviary imposed on him. He decided to keep his secret to himself, only later letting a half confidence escape to one of his students, who repeated it. This resulted in catastrophe and lack of understanding for something never before encountered: "a case of excommunication specially reserved to the pope," they said to him. It was a moment of trial for everyone and each person hoped to settle it as well as possible. In the end he gave up his teaching and lent his services to the House of late vocations founded by Abbé Gendron, while waiting to be named chaplain of the old folks home run by the Little Sisters of the Poor. His situation was attributed to a "nervous disorder" due to excessive work.

He gave up exegesis and turned his efforts toward patrology. Very quickly, he made a reputation for himself as the most knowledgeable in France regarding the history of dogma and theology, at the moment of a renewed interest in the Fathers—Greek, Latin, but also Syriac—shared by specialists. He was well-versed with Migne's work, whose quarto volumes adorned his library.

Social history, history of mentalités as we now say, was not his preoccupation. His interest was confined to the history of ideas and their progressive formulation, the transformations of Christian belief introduced into theology by successive centuries. This was a patient work of deconstruction, beyond all polemics. His method: to let the texts speak, believing that their internal evidence would convince those who read in good faith: to show *by the texts* how dogmas appeared at times that precluded their attribution to a gospel origin; accessorily, to hide behind these texts in order to escape condemnation.

He had to reconsider: on the one hand, in establishing that this internal evidence varied according to readers; on the other hand, in resorting to German science, Gesenius and Harnack in particular. "Until then I placed unlimited confidence in direct study of patristic texts. I believed it possible to limit myself to them .... It was a mistake ...." In combination with his interior dispositions toward the Roman Church—this "school of lies"—this science explains the unending troubles that would plague him. The latter stem from the neglected story of the period's clerical mores. It suffices to evoke them briefly.

Solicited, Turmel became an encyclopedic and tireless collaborator for three periodicals which began to raise concern: the scholarly *Revue d'histoire et de littérature religieuses*, managed by Lejay and Loisy; then the *Revue du clergé français*, directed by Abbé Bricout, at the same time as the *Annales de philosophie chrétienne* until the death of Abbé Denis. The initial difficulty came from Cardinal Richard, archbishop of Paris, who, following a study by Turmel on "eschatology at the end of the fourth century," was tasked by Rome in 1901 with intervening with the archbishop of Rennes, Cardinal Labouré. The latter hardly appreciated this intervention and thus did nothing to reign in the suspect.

The second difficulty was more serious. In order to publish more freely, Turmel resorted to two pseudonyms: Herzog and Dupin. A professor at the Institut catholique de Toulouse, Abbé Louis Saltet (1878 - 1952), showed, through internal criticism, the true identity of these two unknowns (*La Question Herzog-Dupin. Contribution à l'histoire de la théologie française pendant ces dernières années, 1908*). He was seconded in the Jesuit review Études by his colleague, Père Eugène Portalié (1852–1909), who attacked Turmel himself. The latter solemnly swore, in a letter drawn up by his archbishop, that he had nothing in common with Herzog and Dupin. Before them, others had already plagiarized him and had even admitted to having done so, but these were known authors. At Rome, the Congregation of the Index got involved. After Herzog and Dupin, it first entered into its catalog two of Turmel's articles and his *Histoire du dogme de la papauté des origins jusqu'à la fin du IVe siècle* (July 5, 1909); then *Histoire de la théologie positive*, vol. 1, *Tertullien* and *Saint Jérôme* (March 9, 1910); finally, vol. 2 of the *Histoire de la théologie positive* (January 2, 1911). The author submitted.

The third offensive was decisive: it was orchestrated in 1929 by Abbés Louis Saltet and Jean Rivière, a former student of the Institut catholique de Toulouse who had become professor at the Faculty of Catholic Theology at Strasbourg. It forced the Archbishop of Rennes, Cardinal Charost, a native of the diocese, to conduct the canonical proceedings against Turmel, toward whom he had always shown great kindness. On January 23, 1930, he declared him suspended *a divinis*. The sentence was relatively light. Turmel changed nothing in his life, continued to say Mass for his regulars and attempted to repeal the sanction. At seventy years of age, he wanted to end his days in peace, in familiar conditions. The affair, far from being settled, continued in Rome. Two new facts intervened: Turmel's acknowledgement of his fourteen pseudonyms, at the archbishop's request, in two private letters that would be published in *La Civiltà cattolica* of December 6, 1930; the sudden death of Cardinal Charost the preceding November 7th.

Three days later, a decree of the Holy Office dated November 6 appeared in *L'Osservatore romano* and in *La Croix*, declaring the major excommunication—*vitandus*—of Turmel, his canonical degradation and the Indexing of his entire oeuvre. Had the cardinal been informed? The decision was submitted to the pope only on November 8. It did not deal with the dissimulation, but the heresy, impiety and obstinacy.

This ultimate attack had an identifiable cause. Over thirty years Turmel had a restricted number of pseudonyms. In 1925, Doctor Paul-Louis Couchoud had begun the collection *Christianisme* published by Rieder and intended for a broad public. Over five years it published a dozen scholarly works whose authors were as unknown as Herzog and Dupin. Henri Delafosse (six titles), Louis Coulange, Edmond Perrin, Armand Dulac . . . . Saltet and Rivière took up internal criticism again. The latter was effective without being infallible: these two adversaries wrongly accused him of publishing as A. Siouville, which was the pseudonym of a Parisian vicar, Abbé Auguste Lelong, a literary scholar.

In losing a faith that was no more than fable, he had found *the truth*. Once excommunicated, he could make himself "the apostle of truth after having been its martyr." Under his own name, with the financial aid of Félix Sartiaux (an engineer smitten with the history of religions who had been a student of Marcel Hébert), he began to publish his life's work, his great *Histoire des dogmes* in six volumes and a fascicle (Rieder, 1931 – 1936). Then

Afterword

he placed his pen in service of militant rationalism and of Idée libre (André Lorulot). He died on February 5, 1943 in his house on the rue Waldeck-Rousseau. His friends of the Rennes Libre Pensée accompanied him to the cemetery and attended to his tomb.

Beyond his resentment for "a broken life without hope of reparation" and for having been a priest bereft of all religious belief who had to remain faithful to the obligations of a priestly existence, beyond his adversaries' relentless tracking of his "hypostases," there was indeed a "Turmel case," which went beyond his person. It was less the long separation—nearly forty years—between his life and his thoughts, than the obscure relationship among his state of mind, the quality of his work and the behavior of people around him. The man could remain silent regarding his intimate dispositions: his published works remain.

In his domain Turmel was a great autodidact scholar and pioneer who identified real problems, even when his positions and his method were debatable. At the time of the modernist crisis, he was an author sought after by reputable houses: his *Tertullien* (1905) and his *Saint Jérôme* (1906) appeared with Bloud; his *Historie de la théologie positive* (2 vols., 1904 and 1906) were commissioned by the Jesuits of the Catholic theological faculty of Paris to inaugurate their "Bibliothèque de théologie historique" series, published with Beauchesne. He was the first to raise the question that the founders of *Sources chrétiennes* would ask once again. It is freely acknowledged, he explained, that dogmas have a history, a life, a development analogous to that of the seed, but what does that metaphor conceal? "Theologians generally believe that the Fathers thought exactly what we think, but that, furnished with an imperfect and imprecise vocabulary, they sometimes said the contrary of what they wanted to say . . . ."

In his time, Joseph Turmel was not the only one in such circumstances. The case that seems closest to his is undoubtedly that of Paul Lejay, eminent Latinist, professor at the Institut catholique at Paris and member of the Institut de France. Ernest Renan, professor at the Collège de France studied by Jean Pommier, is the prototype of a former generation. In public opinion, the incontestable paradigm is Alfred Loisy, also professor at the Collège de France, whose name symbolizes the "modernist crisis" with which I am associated. He also had drawn up an epitath: "Priest, retired from ministry and from teaching." Alongside them, Marcel Hébert and Albert Houtin, dear to Félix Sartiaux.

Afterword

The list could easily go on and on, but what we still lack, beyond all these individual cases, is their comparative study and, in this "religious crisis," the role and the division of what brought about the occurrence and the development of what we call the "human sciences" of religions and, in their midst, biblical exegesis. "We shall not teach dogmas, we shall study texts," the Minister of Public Instruction replied to Mgr Freppel in 1885 during the creation of a "section des sciences religieuses" at the École pratique des Hautes Études, which would replace the State Faculties of Catholic Theology.

A concluding, but not final, question: once this double—American and French—reading completed, what gap can be measured between them? What is the import and significance? A Canadian friend prematurely deceased, a professor at the University of Laval, then in Toronto, said to me forty years ago: "Do not forget that between France and Quebec there is an ocean and three hundred winters."

Index

Abelard, 62, 177
Alès. Adhémar d', 104, 214n, 139n, 154, 180
Ambrose, Saint, 80, 127, 129, 151
Action Française, 172, 217n
Annales de philosophie chrétienne, 102, 124, 133
Anselm, Saint, 62, 74n, 185
anti-Modernists, xiii
apostasy, xv
Aquinas, Thomas, 6, 62, 183
Aristotle, 6
Aubé, Benjamin, 30, 205n
Augustine, Saint, xi, 62, 71, 140, 151, 158, 177, 178, 185, 192
  and eucharist, 31, 40, 58, 80, 146; and original sin, 125-29; and penance, 122

Bainvel, Jean-Vincent, 78, 210n
Basil, Saint, 80. 129
Batiffol, Pierre, 83, 107, 108, 109, 120, 121, 124, 150, 183, 210-11n
Baudrillart, Alfred, 99, 106, 108-9, 116, 117, 144
Bellarmine, Robert, 156, 179-80
Béon, Léon, 55-56, 156-57, 208n
Bernard, Saint, 31, 34, 183, 185
Bible, xv, 7, 8-14, 16, 18, 19-20, 23-24, 39, 40, 46, 59, 82, 95, 124, 174, 191
  inspiration of, 20, 59
biblical scholarship, xvii, xviii
Billot, Louis, 5, 123n, 201n
Billuart, Charles, 5, 202n

Blustein, Jeffrey, xxiii
Bonaventure, Saint, 183
Bossuet, Jacques-Bénigne, 6, 8-10, 30, 31, 75, 177, 202n
Boucard, Père, 139, 143, 145, 146
Boudinhon, Auguste, 79, 211n
Bremond, Henri, 82, 211n
Bricout, Joseph, 75-81, 103-4, 106, 109, 110, 120, 154, 210n
Brière, Yves de la, 124, 127
Broglie, Paul de, 36, 207n
Bulletin de littérature ecclésiastique, 91, 105-9, 115, 116, 120, 139-40, 145-47, 149, 152, 155, 157, 166, 172

Cavallera, Ferdinand, 91, 213n
Ceillier, Henri, 19, 35-40, 42-43, 45-47, 49-53, 194, 204n
Charost, Alexis, 72-73, 76, 79n, 101, 113, 119, 122-23, 132-33, 136, 138, 139, 145, 147, 148, 152-73, 191-92, 210n
Chrysostom, John, 80, 123
Church Fathers, xiv, 18, 20 31, 62, 69n, 124, 126, 151, 176
Colani, Timothée, 29, 205n
Coquerel, Athanase, 30, 205n
Couchoud, Paul-Louis, 87-88, 89, 140, 160-62, 166, 212n
Council of Trent, 8
Coulange, Louis (pseudonym), See Turmel, Joseph

Index

Croulbois, Jules, 61, 139, 143–44, 146, 208n
Cyprian, Saint, 31, 126, 127

Dechamps, Victor, 11, 12n, 13–14, 32, 203n
deconversion, xi
Delafosse, Henri (pseudonym), See Turmel, Joseph
Denis, Jacques, 30
Desbois, Charles, 56, 156–57, 194
Descartes, René, 6
Dictionnaire de théologie catholique, 81, 91, 97n, 150
Dionysius the Areopagite, 6, 21–22, 202n
doctrine, xix
dogma, xii–xiv, xvii–xix, 9, 10, 18–20, 26, 29–31, 32, 34, 45–47, 63, 65, 70–71, 80, 95, 97–98, 102, 122, 124, 174, 177, 181, 183, 191
  development of, xiv
  history of, 29, 31, 39, 62, 63, 87, 125, 170, 174
dogmatism, xvii–xviii
Doncoeur, Paul, 91, 213n
Dubourg, Auguste, 91, 109–15, 120, 131–132, 135, 153, 162, 167, 185213n
Duchesne, Louis, 68, 82, 83, 85, 100, 101, 103, 106, 107, 120–123, 154–55, 160, 179, 183, 210n
Duine, François, 100
Dulac, Armand (pseudonym), See Turmel, Joseph
Dupin, Antoine (pseudonym), See Turmel, Joseph
Durand, Philippe-Hector, 104, 180, 214n
Durusselle, François, 53, 68, 69, 72, 77, 79, 133, 208n

emotions
  and moral evaluations, xv, xvi
  and rationality, xvi
  cognitive dimension of, xv, xvi
  moral indignation, xvi, xix, xx, xxi, xxii
  moral righteousness, xvi
  strong emotions, xx, xxii
ethics, xv, xvi
Études, 107, 108, 116, 123, 124, 125, 131, 133, 147, 154
eucharist, 31, 40, 58
evil, problem of, 32, 37
excommunication, 42, 57, 82, 87, 138, 159, 167–68
exegesis, 7, 14–19, 22, 24, 33–34, 39, 83, 129
  theological exegesis, 10

faith, 8, 12, 23, 26, 42, 44–45, 84
Fathers of the Church, See Church Fathers
Fénelon, François, 6, 180, 202n
Fontaine, Julien, 54, 66, 67, 71, 208n, 208n, 209n
Formosus, Pope, 192
Fouillée, Alfred, 29, 205n
Freethinkers, xx
Freppel, Charles, 6, 21–22, 202n
Funk, Franz Xavier, 30, 206n

Galileo, 15, 177–78
Gallerand, Hippolyte (pseudonym), See Turmel, Joseph
Gayet, Pierre, 53, 112, 113, 132, 134, 136–37, 152, 168, 188, 207–8n
Gendron, Abbé, 3n, 5, 19, 22, 27, 35–38, 41, 45, 49–52, 66, 68, 102
  break with Turmel, 56–61
Genocchi, Giovanni, 81, 211n
Gesenius, Heinrich, 7–10, 203n
Ginhoulac, Jacques, 101, 214n
Glaire, Jean-Baptiste, 6, 203n
Grandmaison, Léonce, 99, 213n
Gregory Nazienzen, 129
Gregory of Nyssa, 129, 130
Guibert, Jean, 107, 108, 215n
Guillois, Abbé, 5, 41, 44, 47, 49, 65, 194, 201n
Guyau, Jean-Marie, 29, 205n

Hamard, Pierre-Julien, 101, 133, 214n
Harnack, Adolf, 63–64, 83–84, 208n
Havet, Eugène, 30, 205n
Hébert, Marcel, xiii, 70, 210n

Index

Héfélé, Karl, 30, 103, 206n
Hemmer, Hippolyte, 79, 211n
heresy, xiii, 9, 67, 127, 131, 141, 183
Herzog, Guillaume (pseudonym), See Turmel, Joseph
historical consciousness, xv
Holtzmann, Heinrich, 63, 208n
Holy Office, xx, 15, 118, 120, 123, 132, 136, 139, 141, 142, 143, 153, 157, 162, 164, 165, 167-74, 177, 180, 184, 185, 201n
Houtin, Albert, xii, xiii, xvii, 53, 70, 88, 89, 113, 118, 160, 181, 207n
Hurter, Hugo, 5, 18, 201n

Index (of Forbidden Books), xx, 13, 69, 70, 71, 132, 133, 134, 135-37, 169, 185
innéism, 6, 202-3n
Innocent VIII, Pope, 178
Isenbiehl, Johann, 10, 203n

Jérôme, Saint, 127, 129-31
Justice sociale, 73

Kantianism, xv
Kuenen, Abraham, 29, 205n

Labbe, Philippe, 30, 206n
Labouré, Guillaume, 60, 70, 71, 77, 102, 133, 208n
La Croix, 109, 112, 115, 116, 117, 145, 148, 149, 152, 155, 156, 157, 180, 187
Lagarde, André (pseudonym), See Turmel, Joseph
Lagrange, Marie-Joseph, 83, 88, 150, 183, 212n
Launoy, Jean, 21, 204n
Lawson, Robert (pseudonym), See Turmel, Joseph
legend, xvii, xviii, 20
Leblanc, Sylvan (pseudonym), See Bremond, Henri
Lebreton, Jules, 91, 212-13n
Leclercq, Henri, 97n, 101, 110, 214n

Lejay, Paul, 65, 71, 95, 98-100, 117, 118-19, 140, 143-45, 148, 154, 176, 209n
Leo, Saint, 63, 82
Lenain, Denys (pseudonym), See Turmel, Joseph
Lesêtre, Henri, 12, 14-15, 76, 79, 203n
Lézurec, Goulven (pseudonym), See Turmel, Joseph
Liberius, Pope, 103, 107, 214n
Libre Pensée, xxii
Litter, Charles, 7, 203n
Loisy, Alfred, xiii, xiv, 63, 64, 65, 82-90, 100, 123, 140, 179, 181, 183, 208n
  and dogma, 82, 83, 84, 87
  and the Church, 83-87
  L'Évangile et l'Église, 83, 85
Lombard, Peter, 31, 185, 206n

Mabillon, Jean, 30, 75, 77, 180
Marc, Clément, 194
Martin, Thomas, 22
Mathieu, François, 83, 212n
Meignan, Guillaume-René, 70, 82, 85, 210n
Ménard, Louis, 31, 206n
Merry del Val, Raphael, 164, 165, 173
Michel, Abbé (superior of major seminary), 54-55, 113, 115-16, 119, 208n
Michel, André (pseudonym), See Turmel, Joseph
Migne, Jacques, 50, 207n
Mignot, Eudoxe Irenée, 21, 68, 82, 204n
miracles, xvii, 12, 14
Modernism, xi-xv, 147, 150, 197-198n
Montaigne, xxii
moral decisions, xvi
moral justifications, xiii, xvi
Morin, Jean, 21, 204n
myth, 18, 20, 27

Neo-Thomism, xiv
Newman, John Henry, xi
New York Review, 124, 133
Nicolas, Michel, 29, 205n

Oakley, Justin, xv

Index

Odelin, Henri, 78, 211n
ontologism, 6, 202n
Origen, 30, 129, 130
original sin, 34, 62, 64, 126–29
orthodoxy, xiii, xiv, 12, 71, 119, 131, 144, 183
Otto, Rudolf, 31, 206n

Pascal, Blaise, 180
Pascendi dominici gregis, xiii
Patrizi, Constantin, 81, 211n
Paultier, Eugène, 5, 201n
papacy, 31, 132, 178
Pautonnier, Adrian, 53, 63–65, 66, 207n
Péchenard, Pierre-Louis, 98–99, 213n
Perrin, Edmond (pseudonym), See Turmel, Joseph
Pétau, Denis, 5, 66, 75, 77, 78, 202n
Petre, Maude, 200n
Pfleiderer, Otto, 64, 208–9n
philosophy, 29
Pisani, Paul, 79, 211n
Pius X, Pope, 150
Place, Charles-Philippe, 43–44, , 169, 207n
Portal, Fernand, 118, 215n
Portalié, Eugène, 91, 213n
  denunciation of Turmel (1908), 105, 107, 123–37
Pouët, François, 139, 156–57, 160–161, 163–68, 171–73, 216n
prophecy, 7–10, 12, 14, 15

rationalism, xviii
reason, 8, 12, 23
Reinach, Salomon, 193, 218n
Renan, Ernest, 66, 89, 204n
René, Saint, xvii–xviii
Reuss, Edouard, 14–19, 22, 24, 204n
revelation, 11–14, 20, 24, 32, 124
Réville, Albert, 29, 30, 204n
Réville, Jean, 30
Revue des sciences religieuses, 145, 147
Revue d'histoire des religions, 87
Revue d'histoire et de littérature religieuses, xix, xxi, 64, 67, 70, 71, 73, 75, 80, 87, 95, 97, 99–100, 103, 106, 107, 117, 122, 140, 151, 158

Revue du clergé français, 75–81, 97n, 101, 109, 124, 133–34, 181
Revue du monde catholique, 66
Revue pratique d'apologétique, 108, 115, 116
Ribot, Théodule, 29, 205n
Richard, François, 66, 67–71, 73, 76–77, 80, 99–102, 169, 181–82, 209n
Rigault, Nicolas, 31, 206n
Rivière, Jean, 88, 138n, 139, 140, 153, 157, 180, 212n
  denunciation of Herzog and Dupin (1908), 145–51

sacrilege, xxiii, 27, 42, 58
Saltet, Louis, 88, 146–51, 212n
  denunciation of Herzog and Dupin (1908), 105–23
  denunciation of Herzog and Gallerand (1929), 139–45
Sartiaux, Félix, xi, 87–88, 89, , 139, 160, 172–73, 212n
Schürer, Emile, 64, 209n
Scripture, See Bible
Scholasticism, 6, 83–84, 102
seminary education, xvii, 24–25, 28–29
Siouxville, André (pseudonym of Auguste Lelong), 164, 165, 217n
Sixtus V, Pope, 156, 180
Sohm, Rudolf, 64, 208n
Solomon, Robert, xv, xxi
Spencer, Herbert, 6, 202n
Stolberg, Frederich, 7, 9, 203n
Suarez, Francisco, 5, 104, 201–2n

Taine, Hippolyte, 29, 205n
Tanquerey, Adolphe, 47, 194, 207n
Tertullian, 185
Théobald, Christoph, xvii
theology, xv, xviii, 83, 97
Thomassin, Louis, 75, 77, 210n
Tillemont, Louis, 21, 30, 52, 204n
Tixeront, Joseph, 127–31, 216n
tradition, xv, xvii–xviii, 8
Tronly, Abbé, 101, 214n
truth, xii, xviii–xx, xxiii, 9, 15, 26, 28, 33, 44, 88, 95, 174, 184, 185

Index

Turmel, Joseph
  canonical suspension, 158, 162, 172
  chaplain at the former Carmelite convent, 53–54
  chaplain at the Little Sisters of the Poor, 49–54
  condemnation in 1908, 67–74; in 1929, 152–73
  deception, xii–xiii, xix–xx, xxiii, 110–13, 120, 184–86
  excommunication, 167, 169–72
  higher studies at Angers, 5–10
  loss of faith, 23 –24, 32
  profession of faith, 44–45, 62
  professor at major seminary, 11–40
  pseudonyms: Louis Coulange, 87, 122, 139, 140, 142, 146, 147, 152, 159, 160, 164, 165, 173, 181, 185, 186; Henri Delafosse, 87, 140, 152, 159, 161, 164; Armand Dulac, 87, 89, 122, 140; Antoine Dupin, xi, xix, xx, 98–100, 105–7, 110–13, 116–17, 193; Hippolyte Gallerand, 87, 88, 140, 145, 147, 151, 152–60, 164–66, 178–79, 184–86; Guillaume Herzog, xi, xix, xx, 98–100, 105–17, 120–23, 133, 140, 143–44, 147, 149, 152–60, 169, 178–79, 184–86, 193; André Lagarde, 87, 122, 140; Robert Lawson, 87, 122, 146, 147; Denys Lenain, 73, 75, 155, 210n; Goulven Lézurec, 74, 210n; André Michel, 87; Edmond Perrin, 87, 123n, 140; Alexis Vanbeck, 87, 122, 140
  works: articles on angelology, 64–66, 181, 209n; articles on the Blessed Virgin, 98–104; articles on eschatology, 67, 125, 133, 181, 209n; articles on Mabillon, Pétau, Thomassin, and Bossuet, 75–78, 97n, 210n; articles on original sin, 71, 133, 181; articles on the Trinity, 98–100; *Catéchisme pour adultes*, xviii, 160–61; *Comment j'ai donné congé aux dogmes*, xii; *Comment l'Église m'a donné congé*, xii; *Descente du Christ aux enfers*, 133, 134; *Histoire du dogme de la papauté*, 97n, 103, 121–22, 125, 126, 131–33, 135; *Histoire des dogmes*, 98n; *Journal de Jean Burchard*, 166; *La Messe*, 161–62, 181; *Saint Jérôme*, 133; *Tertullian*, 133; *Théologie positive*, 53, 55, 81, 101, 105, 133, 154
Turpin, Armand, 66, 209n

Univers, 42

Vacandard, Elphèse, 81, 101, 110, 111, 211n
Vacherot, Étienne, 30, 205n
Vanbeck, Alexis (pseudonym), See Turmel, Joseph
Vénard, Louis-Eugène, 104, 214n
Verdin, Abbé, 88, 139, 212n
Vernes, Maurice, 29, 204n
Vigouroux, Fulcran, 33, 34
Vincent of Lerins, 179
Voltaire, 29, 114, 118
  Discours du vicaire Savoyard, 13
Vulgate, 8, 156

Weizsaecker, Karl von, 64, 208n

Zigliara, Tommaso, 6, 202n

www.ingramcontent.com/pod-product-compliance
Lightning Source LLC
Chambersburg PA
CBHW050438240426
43661CB00055B/2433